To George

With great Thanks of
all your help & my
most enjoyed the meal &
having a chance to know you.

Paul

October 1st, 1981

The Road From Here

The Road From Here

Liberalism and Realities in the 1980s

Paul Tsongas

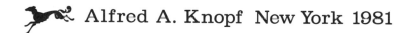 Alfred A. Knopf New York 1981

THIS IS A BORZOI BOOK
PUBLISHED BY ALFRED A. KNOPF, INC.

Copyright © 1981 by Paul Tsongas
All rights reserved under International and Pan-American
Copyright Conventions. Published in the United States by
Alfred A. Knopf, Inc., New York, and simultaneously in
Canada by Random House of Canada Limited, Toronto.
Distributed by Random House, Inc., New York.

Library of Congress Cataloging in Publication Data

Tsongas, Paul. (Date)
    The road from here, liberalism and realities in the 1980s

    1. United States—Economic policy—1971–
    2. United States—Politics and government—1961–
    3. Liberalism—United States.   I. Title.
    HC106.7.T75   1981   338.973   81–47511
    ISBN 0–394–52035–1   AACR2

Manufactured in the United States of America
FIRST EDITION

This book is dedicated to my father, Efthemios George Tsongas,
who died while it was being written. We all miss him,
and hope this dedication will help us to keep his memory bright.

Oh that one would hear me!
behold, my desire is, that the Almighty
would answer me, and that mine adversary
had written a book.

JOB 31:35

Contents

Acknowledgments

Being a United States Senator has one distinct disadvantage for a would-be author: there is never enough time. The world doesn't pause to allow you to give your full attention to writing. From El Salvador to the Reagan budget to trying to build a new Boston arena, there were always matters competing for the time set aside to write. As a result, much of this book was composed on airplanes, in airports, during congressional recesses, and at various odd times at home.

It has all been compensated for by the access I have to minds of great talent. Although the book is mine, and I accept full responsibility for it, the fact is that I was able to run my ideas and first drafts past some very knowledgeable people. They were all willing reviewers, and their suggestions were either accepted with gratitude or rejected with gratitude. This final version of the book has been amply enriched by their comments, and it is a pleasure to acknowledge their help. The list that follows is incomplete, but includes those whose efforts were most time-consuming: Richard Arenberg, Alan J. Auerbach, Robert J. Barbera, Jim Blanchard, Al Carnesale, Christopher Chamberlin, Deb Cline, Chuck Clusen, Glenn Cooper, John Deutch, Brock Evans, Frank Ferrari, Bill Griffith, Jerome Grossman, Bob Hayden, Alfred Kahn, Dennis Kanin, George Kistiakowsky, Ernest May, Randall Naiman, Douglas A. Pike, Harold Rosenbaum, Bob Russell, Karl Ryaver, John Sewell, Leonard Sugarman, Mary Helen Thompson, Lester Thurow, Kostas Tsipis, George Tsitos, Theodora Tsongas, Mitchell G. Tyson, Frank von Hippel, Robert Williams, Keith Willoughby, and Daniel Yergin.

Most helpful of all was Nicola Sauvage Tsongas, without whose assistance, advice, support, and constructive criticism this book would still be just a wistful intent. Thanks, Niki. You, too, Ashley, and Katina and Molly.

I wish to acknowledge the steadfastness of my staff, who typed the various drafts and endless revisions. Marsha McMullin, Margie Conte, Carmen Schmelebeck, and Avis Beckler were loyal and hard-working, and oh so patient.

Finally, I would like to thank my editor, Ashbel Green, who makes me sound more coherent than I am, and my literary agent, Esther Newberg, who guided me through the maze of the publishing world, one that makes national politics seem rational by comparison. They have become friends.

PAUL E. TSONGAS

Preface

When I started writing this book in the late summer of 1980, I thought of it as a warning of political upheaval if liberals did not apply their philosophy to today's realities in a more effective way. The warning was overtaken by events, because the 1980 election changed the political face of America.

The conservative wing of the Republican Party gained the White House and stormed into the United States Senate. The fifty-year legacy of Franklin Delano Roosevelt came to an end, and for Democrats it was a time of despair. For liberals of both parties, it seemed to border on the catastrophic.

I do not intend in this book to yearn for the past or sorrow for the present. Rather, I hope to define a direction for the future, a direction that has been termed the "New Liberalism." While resigned to that label, I feel it is inadequate.

I can offer no nice, neat, snappy phrases that are adaptable for easy bumper-sticker reading. I view my approach as compassionate realism. Can you imagine a bumper sticker with those words on it?

The core of this book is realism—non-ideological, clear-eyed realism. My interest is in what works, not what should work, and then within the boundaries of what works my interest is in the application of liberal democratic values. I believe that the demise of Democratic Party rule was due to one basic fact: reality does not bend to fit political theory. Much of the thrust of the 1980 Democratic platform reflected the realities of the 1930s and 1960s, not those of the decade ahead. The same observation, of course, applies to the current Republican takeover: their policies must be congruent with existent reality, or they too will come a cropper.

I also believe that there must be an overlay of compassion—the embrace of those values that have given texture to the liberal tradition. The message of this book is the blending of realism and compassion in a manner that does not disrupt society. This combination requires judgment devoid of the dogmatic blinders of both ideological extremes. Some people argue that realism and compassion are by definition incompatible. That may be true in a totalitarian country, but not in a democratic society based upon the consent of the governed.

This book is no call to arms, nor an attempt to artificially stir the soul or tug at the heart. It is an effort to convince and to persuade. It seeks to identify clearly the forces that make up our world and to demonstrate that a liberal program consistent with those forces has a legitimate—indeed necessary—place in our society.

As I have watched the current political trends in both parties, I have sadly concluded that they are taking America on a collision course with reality. It is no revelation to say that there exist on our planet certain phenomena whose inevitability cannot be avoided. Some reside in a simple law of physics—oil, for example, is a finite resource. Some are not necessarily visible—hazardous wastes dumped into the biosphere will remain a threat to the globe's future inhabitants. Others have their base in the complex laws of human nature. Blacks in South Africa and Namibia, for example, who see self-determination coming to their brothers and sisters in Africa, cannot be at peace with themselves while they have less. And people enduring the hardships of a shrinking economy will not be generous to other, less fortunate citizens seeking advancement.

These phenomena have a force that knows no denial. And America, which became man's greatest nation by harnessing its own inevitabilities—revolution, expansion, industrialization, world leadership—finds itself trying to ward off realities in the vain hope that they will disappear.

They won't. Victor Hugo was correct: nothing *is* more powerful than an idea whose time has come.

This book deals with eight realities, the handling of which will determine our future, our children's future, and conceivably the future of life on this earth. I don't think I am overstating their importance.

These eight realities—finite energy resources, Soviet aggressiveness, economic productivity, resource allocation, Third World nationalism, international trade competition, environmental overload, and inflation—are too often discounted or neglected by many Americans, in and out of government. So we are faced with a series of self-fulfilling prophecies. To the extent that these realities are brushed aside, the critical mass of thought and effort required to deal with them becomes magnified. They are like toothaches or cancers that are left untreated.

Worse still, we are addressing these realities with dogma—a dogma that provides the illusion of response while time slips away.

But despite the fact that these realities, these irresistible forces, have the capacity to destroy you and me, none of them is unduly hazardous if recognized, respected, and, above all, dealt with. We possess the knowledge and the technology to confront the challenges. What we lack is the will, and what we are losing is the time.

Let me draw an analogy. Imagine yourself with a friend gliding peacefully down a river in a canoe without paddles. The spring weather is pleasant, the river is swift and cold. The lack of steerage is of some concern, but the long trip has been successful and the sun's rays are hypnotically warming. Suddenly you see, on the distant shore, a man jumping up and down, frantically waving his arms and shouting. The voice carries poorly, but you think you hear the word "waterfall."

Your companion assures you that although he's never been down this stretch of the river, all is well. Why would there be a waterfall beyond that wide bend ahead? Besides, the only alternative is to jump into chilly water and swim ashore, and who wants to do that?

So you lean back in the canoe and face the sun. Eventually, both you and your companion will notice or hear the waterfall. One characteristic of a waterfall, however, is that it is best seen and its danger best appreciated as one is about to go over it. It provides no real warning.

Our mythical canoeist eventually reaches a point of no return, the area closest to the waterfall where it's already too late to swim ashore.

In terms of this book, the crucial area—the "decision zone"—is that portion of the river where one can still reach the shore. Its most crucial characteristic is time—time to make an unpleasant, chilly, exhausting splash for survival. Obviously, the sooner the decision is made within the decision zone, the less difficult and less hazardous the venture.

Then why not do it? Why not do it before the point of no return is reached?

If you are concerned with the existence of the waterfall, your survival instinct will respond, and the warmth of the sun and chilliness of the water become irrelevant. Obviously, if you doubt the existence of the waterfall, the warm sun and chilly water dominate the decision process.

Eventually, the relative certainty of the waterfall triggers a response. Fine, but where are we? Is there still enough time to deal with our problems? And that becomes the issue: not how strongly we can swim; not the closeness of the shore; not how experienced we are at swimming. If we have crossed the point of no return, these issues (critical to our survival when there was time) are now beyond us.

I believe that with the passing of the 1960s and early 1970s, we drifted into a decision zone. I also believe that somewhere ahead we will cross a point of no return. I don't know when that will be, and I won't know when we cross it. My heart tells me we haven't crossed it yet.

If we are strong enough to swim ashore, and we are; if there is still time to swim ashore, and there is; then all that remains is to shout out a warning before it is too late.

If we give in to our creature comforts, if we drink from the wine of dogma or ideology, if we refuse to be what we can be, we will —dare I say it?—perish.

To perish after having discarded the chance for survival may be judged a fitting end. Darwinian, divine retribution, fate? Perhaps we deserve it. But what of our children? They discarded nothing; they decided nothing.

We must recognize the proximity of the waterfall ourselves. We must plunge into the icy waters. We must do these things so that we can give our children what every generation has given to its children—and what has been given to us—the gift of survival.

The Road From Here

1/The Road to Reassessment

In 1975, the House of Representatives faced up to the question of Wayne Hays's chairmanship of the House Administration Committee. Hays was a raw, tough, skilled Democrat from Ohio, who would later become publicly embroiled with his secretary. Her typing skills, or lack thereof, would be front-page news.

Many congressmen strongly disliked Hays, and when the Democratic Caucus met to decide whether to deny him his chairmanship, there was considerable anticipation of his demise. I hadn't been a congressman long enough to feel strongly about him, but I had heard the stories of his abuses of authority, his treatment of House employees, his Napoleonic conduct while on foreign tours.

I sat in the back row, fascinated, as the debate raged on. Reform ers called for his scalp, while old-school Democrats recommended tolerance.

Then, incredibly, standing up to speak for Hays was Edward Koch (now mayor of New York, but at that time a liberal congressman representing one of Manhattan's most progressive and reformist districts).

Koch faced two hundred dumbfounded colleagues. He looked us over, paused, and with ill-concealed mirth said: "You're probably wondering what a nice liberal Jewish boy like me is doing defending someone like Wayne Hays?"

The caucus erupted—it was *exactly* what everyone had been thinking. Koch had disarmed the hostility.

In the months since I began raising the issues in this book, I have often been received with the same look of incredulity. "Now, to speak on Soviet expansionism, a gasoline tax, productivity, and the

need for nuclear power is our own liberal senator, Paul Tsongas."
What's going on here?

I am often tempted to resort to Koch's disarming quip, and I
have succumbed to that temptation a couple of times. It is, however, cold comfort. For despite the shrewdness of his comment, its
timing, and its delivery, I can remember nothing else that Koch
said. More relevantly, when the vote on Wayne Hays and his chairmanship took place, I voted to take it from him.

Any attempt to redefine a political philosophy carries with it the
certainty of reaction. The inevitable doubts as to my intention and
its apparent threat to established turf could seriously detract from
the message. So let me first explain my motives.

I have always considered myself a liberal. My distaste for conservatism runs deep because I cannot tell where legitimate conservatism ends and reactionary dogma begins. But I admit that I tote
certain bits of conservative baggage. Perhaps some personal history
will help to define my motivation and purpose.

My roots are ethnic Republican conservative. My father was
born in Greece, and emigrated to America at the age of four with
his brothers and sisters to join his father, who had gone ahead three
years earlier. My grandfather may have been the classic example of
an immigrant seeking a better life in America. Sleeping on newspapers in Lowell, Massachusetts, during the winter, however, was
made more comfortable by knowing that if he went back to Greece
he'd probably be arrested for having sold sewing machines for a
bankrupt German company. In any case, he was one tough customer—a prototypical "bootstrapper."

As children of immigrants, my father and his siblings grew up
with all the disadvantages of being poor; English was a foreign
tongue at home, and the community was often hostile to their kind.
Here was a textbook case of disadvantage and discrimination—a
foundation bloc for the Democratic Party coalition. Well, not quite.
My father went to Harvard, my two uncles to M.I.T., and my three
aunts to Simmons College, and most (including my father) became
conservative Republicans.

My father was a small businessman, who rode the waves of the
free enterprise system through good times and bad. The bad occurred during my adolescence as Lowell's economy declined. As a

boy working in my father's dry-cleaning store, I suffered two firm rebukes from him. One came when I used an obscene word that had fascinated me but whose meaning I only vaguely sensed. The other was when he overheard me ask a long-time employee what a union was, and whether there was one at the store (there wasn't).

His vehemence in both situations scared the hell out of me; but I made a mental note to find out someday why each caused such an uproar.

Lowell, my once, present, and future home, is no suburb. It's an old mill city—a typical blue-collar, mostly Roman Catholic, New England city. It is now in the process of resurgence as a National Historical Park and high-technology center, but during the forties, fifties, and sixties, it was as depressed as any other American mill city.

These influences left me with a deep respect for hard work, education, and "bootstrap" thinking, mixed with a scarred sense of what it means to be on the down side of the free enterprise system.

The early years in an ethnic, blue-collar conservative city (I vaguely remember rooting for Eisenhower against Stevenson, although I don't know why) were followed by ten years that read like the travels of a limousine liberal's youngest son. Dartmouth, Peace Corps in Ethiopia, Yale Law School, congressional intern, Peace Corps in the West Indies. Somewhere during that time, I went from non-political to liberal. My guess is that it began during the presidency of John Kennedy and crystallized during my two years in Wolisso, Ethiopia.

Living in a village in Ethiopia was the formative experience of my life. After twenty-one years in which my farthest trip had been to Annapolis, Maryland (when the Dartmouth team swam against Navy), I found myself 7,500 miles and several cultural light-years away from home. I learned to care deeply about Ethiopia. The people I lived among sustained me emotionally. I came to know what it meant for an Ethiopian to be poor, to die from a lack of medical supplies, to live under a system of authoritarian rule, and yet to be gracious to strangers, to show affection to a white, to absorb education like a sponge, and to honor the elders of one's community.

Stepping through the looking glass into a totally different culture for an extended period of time leaves its mark. I discovered how to see America through Ethiopian eyes. I also found out how difficult it was to explain to Ethiopians why an American President for whom the Ethiopians felt a strong affection was killed, and how race riots could be happening in America.

The three years at Yale Law School were notable not for my yearnings to be a good lawyer (there were no such yearnings), but for two outside events. First, I spent two summers working as an intern for my congressman, F. Bradford Morse, a liberal Republican, later the head of the United Nations Development Program. This was my initial exposure to politics. As a result of the association, I registered as a Republican, and in 1965 worked for the election of John Lindsay as mayor of New York.

I might add here that my registration as a Republican back in the mid-1960s would have been an acute embarrassment early in my political career. So for the first eleven years of my political life that fact was guarded like the family jewels—not even my priest knew about it.

The second event was the Vietnam War. In retrospect, it is hard to sort out my early reaction to that national trauma. I recall watching the evening news and being pleased about South Vietnamese military victories. In my second year at Yale, I began to wander into the library stacks to read about guerrilla fighting in Indochina during World War II. I read every firsthand account written by a guerrilla leader about the struggle against the Japanese. And I was drawn to it.

By the end of that year I had decided to leave law school and join the Special Forces as a medic. This fact invariably astounds people who have known me only since I entered politics. Implausible as it may seem, my theory was that I would be a medic in a village, helping to protect its inhabitants. The prospect of being in war intrigued me, but as a medic I could feel that my purpose was humanitarian as well as military. I made moves in that direction during the summer of 1966 until I had a chance meeting with Jack Vaughn, the director of the Peace Corps, who tactfully let me know I was crazy—a medic in the Green Berets was no Peace Corps volunteer in fatigues.

He suggested that if I wanted to pursue Vietnamese interests—

I had already begun to learn the language—I should join the Agency for International Development (AID) instead. After some thought, I agreed. During my subsequent interview at AID, I said that I wanted to go to a remote area of Vietnam. For "remote," read dangerous. To my surprise, I was turned down. I'm sure they saw me as a naive, foolish Ivy Leaguer with a death wish. Given my utter confusion as to what I wanted to do, their decision was clearly in the interests of all concerned.

Anyway, I returned to law school wondering about the currents running deep inside of me. The desire to fight, later to be expressed in political campaigns, was much more powerful than I had imagined, and I began to understand it in others. Having spent eight months thinking about and reading about war, I felt my last year at Yale to be largely an exercise in irrelevance.

After graduation, I returned to the Peace Corps in paradise—the West Indies, with a base in the Virgin Islands. The job was to coordinate Peace Corps training programs in the Caribbean countries. But paradise eventually proved boring, and when Lyndon Johnson announced that he would not seek a second term, I decided to return home and get involved in politics. My last days in the sun on the beach at Magens Bay, St. Thomas, were spent dreaming of running for public office. (I have spent the subsequent years in public office yearning to lie in the sun on the beach at Magens Bay.)

In May 1968, I took a bar review course and the bar exam, hoping to join the Robert Kennedy presidential campaign afterward. His death ended my interest in that political year. I had no affinity for Eugene McCarthy, although my wife-to-be, Niki Sauvage, was one of McCarthy's original workers in New Hampshire. I saw McCarthy as an intellectual lacking in political judgment. Kennedy's feelings struck me as more visceral, more rooted—more combative than ethereal. And I could perceive little difference between Hubert Humphrey and Richard Nixon; needless to say, I would later learn to regret that sophomoric attitude.

By the fall of 1968, I had moved back to Lowell from the suburb of Chelmsford, where my parents had gone in order to find a better school system for my younger sister. Nine months later I was a candidate for the Lowell City Council, pounding the streets and knocking on doors. During that period, there was time for occasional participation in anti-apartheid meetings and anti-war demonstrations. I had become strongly opposed to the war by then. That opposition wasn't exactly politic, given the strong support of the war by the local newspaper, the Lowell *Sun,* and by the population of Lowell generally.

Service as a Lowell City Councillor and as a Middlesex County Commissioner left me with a strong dislike of systems dependent upon political patronage. Public money was nobody's money, so therefore it was fair game for abuse. No-shows and favoritism in hiring in the county were examples of non-accountability. As county commissioners, my reformist colleague and I proceeded to reduce the size of the county bureaucracy significantly. During these five years, I saw myself as a defender of the public purse (a traditional Republican instinct) and as an opponent of the job-providing function of government (a traditional Democratic instinct).

In 1974, I ran for Congress against a young Republican incumbent, Paul Cronin, who was a moderate liberal. In that Watergate era the issues were tax disclosures and Richard Nixon, and although I was more liberal than Cronin, I still was able to win with 61 percent of the vote. In 1976, I was challenged from the right by a Republican conservative and won with 68 percent.

During four years in the House, I was rated among the most liberal members. My Americans for Democratic Action (ADA) ranking, environmental voting ranking, labor ranking, consumer ranking, tax reform ranking, senior citizens ranking—most were above 90 percent. Correspondingly, I received a zero from the Conservative National Security Council, due, among other things, to consistent voting against defense authorization bills that stemmed from my opposition to the B-1 bomber.

In 1978, I decided to run for the Senate. One of the precipitating reasons was the hesitancy of Senator Edward Brooke to endorse the Panama Canal Treaties. Faced with a primary challenge by a hard-right candidate, Brooke felt imperiled by his liberal stance on many issues. He barely survived the primary and entered the general election against me weakened in his own party. Both of us were weary, however, since the Democratic primary involved five candidates, two of whom were far ahead of me in the first polls. My candidacy was dismissed by one Boston *Globe* columnist as that of "an obscure first-term Congressman." That was incorrect: I was an obscure *second-*term congressman.

Brooke had also endured the revelation of his personal and financial difficulties. Because of a solid record of support for liberal issues, however, he received enthusiastic support from traditional progressive political bases—labor, women's groups, Jewish groups, and minorities. Many key liberals endorsed him: Joseph Rauh of ADA, Gloria Steinem of NOW, Jesse Jackson of PUSH, among others. In addition to political support, he received financial assistance as well—some $90,000 from labor unions alone. Although these organizations approved of my service in the House, Brooke was the incumbent in the contested seat, and that was determinative.

The polls showed the race to be close. Despite the state's heavy Democratic registration, Brooke's grip on the liberal community had seen him through in previous statewide races. What followed was strange in its development. The campaign began to focus on Brooke's support of the neutron bomb, his alleged hesitancy on SALT II, and my voting record on defense spending. I was accused of being "against the Army, Navy, Air Force, and Marines," and criticized by conservatives on behalf of a candidate who had most of the liberal endorsements.

The emergence of these issues proved to be critical. The liberal /academic/high-tech communities swung to my candidacy, as did traditional blue-collar cities that could identify with my Lowell roots. In essence, the fact that I was perceived as significantly more liberal overcame the hesitation on the part of most Massachusetts liberals about voting against the only black U.S. senator.

That hesitiation was almost my Achilles' heel. The liberal voters of Massachusetts were proud of having elected a black in 1966. I know because in that year I wrote to Congressman Morse urging him *not* to run against Brooke in the primary so that a black could be elected to the Senate. I voted for Brooke for that reason in 1966, and again in 1972. So, the law student who urged his congressman not to run against Brooke was to be Brooke's opponent twelve years later—a situation some would call ironic and others crudely ambitious.

Many thoughtful liberals and many black leaders felt that my running against the only black in the Senate was illiberal *per se*. The endorsement of me by Senator Edward Kennedy was to cause him problems in the black community later on. I argued that to reelect Brooke for a third term because he was black was in 1978 (unlike 1966) by definition discriminatory. I felt he should be judged on his record if we were to be truly color-blind. However those arguments were debated, the result was that Brooke won the black vote, I won most of the liberal vote, and the Senate became once again lily-white. (I admit to occasional pangs about this fact, but I know that, given the same situation, I would run again.)

I thus came to the Senate in 1979, bucking a wave of conservative victories in other states. (Most people don't remember that the Senate liberal defeats in 1978 were almost as widespread as in 1980.) Although I had defeated a respected colleague, the graciousness of Brooke's concession speech gave me an enormous amount of good-will.

In the Senate, I continued my liberal House voting record. My labor rating in 1979 was 100 percent, and my ADA, consumer, tax reform, environmental, and women's rights rankings were all highly supportive of their concerns. Perhaps most telling, the Committee for the Survival of a Free Congress, the most comprehensive of the conservative rating services, listed me as the most liberal member of the Senate, edging out Ted Kennedy.

Why, then, am I espousing the positions contained in this book? Part of the reason can be explained by conflicting personal influences and experiences. Some conservative friends assert that I have been a closet conservative all along. That is simply erroneous. And given my unbending views on social issues, it is a conclusion completely contrary to the facts.

Rethinking—1979 to the Present

Several events that took place after I entered the Senate forced me to rethink my political assumptions. But first I should probably deal with what did *not* inspire the reassessment.

It has been said that many liberals have moved to the right in order to survive politically. This may or may not be true. The 1980

Senate races provided evidence of candidates who moved right and lost, and of candidates who remained liberal and lost.

In my case, considering the circumstances in Massachusetts, a shift to the right carries no particular advantage with it. My liberal views on capital punishment, abortion, gay rights, civil rights are not about to change, so there is no placating the Moral Majority. The progressive vote in Massachusetts is substantial, and attacking traditional liberal stances is rife with hazards. (Unlike George McGovern, who won Massachusetts eight years earlier, President Carter lost the state because of the defection of the basically liberal John Anderson vote.) Further, the most significant "conservative" sector in Massachusetts is the business community, and business people have always been supportive of me, given my extensive efforts on economic development issues that affect the state. (Most of my election contributions in 1978 came from conservative business sources in my congressional district.)

So, with a blue-collar city political base, support in the business community, and a "natural" constituency among the liberals, why rock the boat?

Simple. Because the boat is leaking.

Now let me talk about the four main events that inspired this reassessment.

The Chrysler Dilemma: Economics 101. I had been consistently critical of Detroit's automobile industry. Heavily involved with energy issues, I had grown to detest Detroit's hawking of gas-guzzling comfort machines that appealed to the macho instinct, not America's needs. Watching Lee Iacocca's Ford ads urging consumers to "get a full-sized car" when General Motors began its scaledown left me almost apoplectic. In 1977, I introduced an amendment to the Energy Act prohibiting the manufacturing of fuel-inefficient automobiles (it was ruled "non-germane" to the act when challenged by a Michigan congressman).

During town meetings in Massachusetts, I cited Detroit as the prime example of special-interest lobbying in America: the industry worked the Republicans and the United Auto Workers (UAW) worked the Democrats to kill legislation that would affect them. In 1975, there was an attempt to pass the Fisher Amendment providing for a tax on gas-guzzlers and a rebate on fuel-efficient cars. The pincer lobbying technique defeated the amendment, helping the auto industry in the short term, and exacerbating America's vulnerability to imported oil. Detroit first, America second. What was good for General Motors was not good for America, but who cared?

This was particularly galling, since it undermined the credibility of the UAW, one of the most progressive unions in America.

The industry succeeded in protecting its right to build gas-guzzlers, but it turned out to be a Pyrrhic victory. The American consumer was already changing to fuel-efficient cars, and Japanese and German car sales soared while American sales fell off. In the late 1970s (the post-1973 Arab oil embargo period), the best small cars were foreign-made. Having owned a Volvo and a Volkswagen in the early 1970s, I was appalled by the quality of the Vega and Bobcat I bought later. At Massachusetts town meetings, I said that the energy crisis was our paramount national concern and if my constituents wanted to buy a Rabbit or Honda, it was all right with me.

My animus against the auto industry ran deep. By 1979, Chrysler, the weakest of the Big Three, had begun to crumble. Its management team was sacked, and new blood (read Lee Iacocca) was brought in to save the company. It soon became obvious, however, that the company's cash flow requirements were such that bankruptcy was inevitable by late that year or early 1980. What does the captain of a free-enterprise vessel do when shipwreck looms? He heads for Washington, of course. Lockheed paved the way with its loan guarantee legislation in 1971. Blaming its troubles on government regulations (despite the fact that the Japanese and Germans had to meet the same standards), Chrysler came to Washington for a bail-out. The Carter administration supported the request and submitted to Congress the Chrysler Loan Guarantee Bill. It was referred to the Senate Banking Committee, where I was the most junior Democratic member.

I had no special interest in the bill, so I used the hearings to vent my disrespect for the industry's decisions over the past decade. My contribution was not positive. What I said was particularly uncomfortable for Michigan Senator Donald Riegle, a close friend, who was the sponsor of the bill, and who knew a solid Democratic coalition would be needed to get it out favorably, given the opposition of Chairman William Proxmire and most Republican members of the committee. Vote counts varied, but our office believed that the bill would be defeated in committee by at least an 8 to 7 margin, if I were to vote No as I intended.

But the more I attended the hearings, and the more I researched the issue, the more my emotions faded and gave way to concern. A chance trip to Michigan (to speak at the University of Michigan on South African apartheid) gave me my first glimpse of Detroit itself. The projected unemployment and dislocation—especially among minorities—troubled me. I had seen Lowell devastated by the exodus of the textile industry. (The other city in my old congressional district, Lawrence, lost 25,000 jobs in three years in the 1940s, the worst job loss relative to population base in American history.) To act as the swing vote in doing the same thing to Detroit was a heavy responsibility, and I resolved to examine the issue with more objectivity.

It became obvious that the rhetoric surrounding this issue was both insufferable and inconsistent. Republicans who had voted for Lockheed and opposed Chrysler had to find a distinguishing feature, and fell back on the argument of "national security"—Lockheed built military aircraft. Senators who voted for the loan guarantee to New York City and opposed the Chrysler package took refuge in the "public versus private" distinction. Steel state senators who had helped arrange legislative assistance for Jones and Laughlin Steel and who opposed Chrysler had their burden of reconciliation as well. On the other side, there were those who supported Chrysler for constituent reasons, but who had opposed at least one of the three above-mentioned bills. Even Bill Proxmire, one of the brightest people in elective office, was caught in this dilemma. He talked about Detroit's desire to "free-enterprise its profits and socialize its losses." However, when Riegle pointed out that Proxmire had legislatively helped American Motors, whose main plants are in Wisconsin, Proxmire acknowledged the inconsistency.

After much discussion, one dominant fact emerged: by the fall of 1980, Chrysler would have the best line of fuel-efficient cars of any of the Big Three. The Omni/Horizons would be in full U.S. production and the K-cars would be state-of-the-art fuel-efficient.

It made no sense to help Chrysler if it was going to fold anyway —the move would be expensive to the taxpayers and illusory to the employees. But equally, it made no sense to allow Chrysler to collapse and incur all the economic and social costs of that bankruptcy if its future product line would give it a reasonable possibility of economic survival.

The Omni/Horizon and K-car production schedules appeared to me viable enough to warrant the risk. Despite the economic recession and high interest rates, the sales of these cars have been promising at the time of writing, and the revenues to the Treasury in taxes paid by Chrysler employees, suppliers, and dealers have already exceeded the amount of the loan guarantee.

The second major conclusion was quite different. The cash flow requirements of Chrysler were a function of two assumptions: how many cars would be sold in America and what percentage of those would be Chrysler-made. The administration bill was less optimistic than Chrysler's. It assumed a range of scenarios in which Chrysler's cash flow needs peaked out anywhere from $2.3 billion to $3.8 billion. The administration's package decided upon a $3.0 billion cushion. My view was that, given an energy crisis or economic downturn (both of which were later to happen), the cushion would be inadequate. The Banking Committee projected the company's needs up to $5.6 billion. The administration's bill would help for a while, but its protection against adverse economic conditions was skimpy.

Looking at the projections, I decided that $4.0 billion was a more desirable figure. This represented an annual production of 10 million autos—with Chrysler getting 10 percent of the market. It allowed for more economic adversity in the general economy, although it did not provide for a worst-case scenario. (A worst-case scenario would have seen Ford in trouble as well.)

Given two assumptions—first, we should help Chrysler, and second, a bigger cushion was required—the issue then became: where will it come from?

Part of the additional cushion would come from greater contributions from suppliers, dealers, bankers, and other sources dependent on Chrysler's good health. The only other possible source was the estimated $1.1 billion in the package that represented the UAW's three-year wage increase pact, which had been recently signed. The more I looked at that provision, the more I thought it incredible. It was—as inflation czar Alfred Kahn pointed out—"unconscionable," considering the circumstances.

What if Chrysler's needs for survival were $3.4 billion? Under the administration bill, the union members would have received a pay raise and the company would have folded. Would that be in the interest of the workers? What possible purpose would be served by providing $1.1 billion in wage increases to workers whose livelihood hung by a thread because of the company's financial dilemma? Would it not make more sense to forego a wage increase, as Eastern Airlines workers had done, to enable the company to have a better chance for survival? Wouldn't it be more intelligent to provide wage increases on a schedule that reflected Chrysler's economic recovery? What about wage increases in the form of stock—so that the company would not have the cash flow drain, and the workers, upon Chrysler's resurgence, would reap an economic windfall?

These notions seemed obvious to me, and I set about to draft an alternative bill. On November 27, 1979, I reserved time on the Senate floor to express my concerns about the administration's bill and to propose my ideas. The bill was scheduled to be considered by the Banking Committee two days later. Also reserving time that morning and speaking just before me was Senator Richard Lugar of Indiana. Lugar, who was the most junior Republican on the Banking Committee and whose state had some Chrysler plants, took virtually the same approach in his speech. Without either of us knowing the other's position, we had arrived at exactly the same conclusion: in order to maximize Chrysler's chance of survival (and therefore to protect the taxpayer's investment), a wage freeze would be necessary. As we listened to each other's fifteen-minute speeches that morning, it was clear that we had grounds for collaboration. We agreed to work together, and by the next day had produced an alternative, the so-called Lugar-Tsongas substitute, which provided for a $4.0 billion cushion ($1.0 billion more than the administration) by requiring a wage freeze coupled with stock issuances.

The reaction to the proposal was swift and sure: the administration opposed it, Chrysler opposed it, the UAW opposed it. The wage freeze concept in particular was anathema to organized labor.

Normally, this kind of opposition would kill a piece of legislation. However, there was an unusual set of circumstances. First, Lugar and I were the deciding votes in the committee; given the division within it, if we voted against a measure it would be defeated. Second, the *New York Times* endorsed the proposal just in time to provide us with some credibility. Third, Senator Proxmire decided to argue for our version over the administration bill.

After much debate, Lugar and I moved to substitute our bill for that of the administration. It passed 10 to 4, receiving the votes of Lugar, myself, and those who, supporting Chrysler, realized it was better than nothing.

The introduction of the wage freeze–cum–stock concept two days earlier had started rumblings among unionists, liberals, and traditional Democrats. The victory of the concept in committee, however, apparently was a surprise, and the reaction was intense. In fact, all hell broke loose.

Since Lugar was a conservative Republican, his sponsorship of the substitute was not surprising. But for a liberal Democrat with an impeccable union voting record, my position was regarded by some as treasonous. With his conservatism and my liberalism, we bracketed the Senate ideologically and thus gave plausibility to the proposal.

While some Senate Democratic colleagues expressed suppressed shock over my actions, some were not so subtle and weighed in bitterly. To their credit, Chrysler's main sponsors—Riegle, Carl Levin of Michigan, Birch Bayh of Indiana, and Tom Eagleton of Missouri—reacted with great restraint. From home in Massachusetts, the calls began. Why was I being anti-labor? Why was I turning my back on a union, one of only two that had supported me in 1974? What kind of a Democrat was I, anyway? Several friends and congressional colleagues sent word that they were receiving a lot of heat to try to get me to reconsider.

This was my first major step outside of the expected cadence— and people were upset. Although I had been criticized for particular votes in Congress, the criticism had almost always come from the right. (The conservative home-town newspaper regularly lambasted me editorially and called me a socialist.) When I tried to explain the merits of the substitute and the complexities of Chrysler's cash flow needs as reflected in various economic assumptions, the details were lost in the horror of the term "wage freeze."

The Lugar-Tsongas substitute was compromised as it went through Congress. The final package contained $500 million of additional cushion as compared to the administration proposal, but $700 million less in wage contributions than the Lugar-Tsongas substitute.

The reality of the final version was as follows: If Chrysler's cash flow needs proved to be less than $3.0 billion (the original administration bill), Lugar and I had wasted our time. If they fell between $3.0 and $3.5 billion (between the administration bill and the final package), Lugar and I, by being so "anti-union," had in fact saved the company and the jobs of the UAW members. If the figure was between $3.5 and $4.0 billion, then Chrysler would go under and the UAW members would be laid off precisely because Lugar and I had to compromise with pro-union congressmen.

I realize that others have a different perspective on this issue. Some argue that a straight wage freeze was not workable for such reasons as retention of employees, quality control incentives, and so on. But a stock package/wage freeze thawed only by the company's revival seemed to me clearly the wiser course.

Yet the arguments were submerged in the emotion of the moment. The "reality" of Chrysler's dilemma—and by definition, therefore, the workers' dilemma—was ignored in the name of ideology, to wit: Thou shalt not endorse a wage freeze. And the political fallout from my advocacy of this position continued.

Fourteen months later, in January 1981, the UAW endorsed a wage freeze package in order to help Chrysler through the turbulence caused by high interest rates and the recession. The reality had not gone away, and ideology had to yield. (This development was, of course, subsequent to the debate of late 1979, and was not part of the common wisdom available at the time.)

As a result of the Chrysler episode, I was left wondering. To have been so out of step with my philosophical confreres on such a critical issue was odd. To have teamed up with a conservative Republican to determine legislation was unusual. To have been fulfilled by the process was surprising.

I began thinking about matters that hadn't occupied my mind for a long time, such as whether liberals weren't trapped in rigid dogmas.

Later, I bought a Chrysler-made Plymouth Horizon. Sometimes I think about the people who put the car together; I happen to believe that my "aberrational" behavior served them well. In retrospect, that entire incident served me well because it began the cutting of an umbilical cord.

The Lowell Plan: Private Sector 202. Lowell, Massachusetts (my home town), was the first planned industrial city in America. Attempting to break free from the horrors of the English industrial experience, its founders set up a total community based upon the labor of Yankee farm girls and an environment necessary to attract them. The city became a source of great interest, and many nineteenth-century travelers from abroad visited it to observe the great experiment. It was the textile capital of the world.

In the twentieth century the textile companies went south—to be closer to the raw material, cotton, and to take advantage of lower wage scales. Mills closed down, people were unemployed, investments in the community ended, and the city settled in for decades of decline. Lowell, along with many other New England cities, was an example of the problems of the free enterprise system. When the economics were with you, there was prosperity. When the economics were against you, the system was brutal.

Growing up in a declining city takes its toll.

The children of Lowell, Lawrence, Fall River, Brockton, and Chicopee had to work at being proud of their cities. Many didn't try, and simply left. The higher a person's standing academically at Lowell High School, the less likely it was that person would later live in the city. Those communities lost the head of their body politic.

Left to their own decaying resources, the cities started to implode. Downtowns were characterized by tacky stores and poor merchandise that couldn't compete with suburban shopping centers. Neighborhoods declined as the socioeconomic fabric of the populace unraveled.

Under the free enterprise system, useless items are discarded in favor of more productive ones. How do you discard a city? Very simply—by allowing it to decay. Who makes such a decision? Everyone. Corporate decisionmakers pull their companies out. Individual professionals take their skills to the suburbs. Parents move to better school systems. Workers flee to the Sunbelt in search of opportunity.

Thirty thousand people left Lowell between 1920 and 1970, reducing the population to 94,000.

Watching a city decline is like watching a fire dying out. The critical mass necessary for continued dynamism is no longer present: even while there is still both heat and light, the eventual outcome is obvious.

The federal government rode in with theories and urban renewal. Tear down the old and historic, put up the new and faceless. Little Canada, the French section of Lowell, was designated an urban renewal area. As the land was cleared, the population in that area dwindled dramatically. A coherent, cohesive neighborhood was blown away, only to be replaced by cement rental units.

Downtown cores in other cities were left gap-toothed or leveled. In many places, cleared land remained just that. The bureaucrats moved on to other theories, and the cities were left bleeding more profusely.

I ran for the city council in 1969, believing that federal funds were the answer. The words themselves suggested a kind of gift from above—imported salvation. The private sector had abandoned us in pursuit of its own self-interest, and the government was going to make us whole again.

The federal funds arrived: Model Cities, aid to education, revenue sharing, and so on. And the decline continued. In the late 1960s, the city's visionary, Model Cities Director Patrick Mogan, worked with Congressman Brad Morse to dream up the notion of an urban national park: Don't tear down the old mills, make them a tourist attraction. Don't demolish the historic downtown, preserve it. Don't fill in the canals for roadways, put tourist barges on them.

There was much effort on the part of Morse and his successor, Paul Cronin. Then, four years after my election, the Lowell National Historical Park was signed into law by President Carter in

1978 at an estimated cost of $40 million. We had our parades and parties.

Upon closer examination, however, it became obvious that the park would consist of five restored nineteenth-century structures surrounded by a city still reflective of twentieth-century decay. The good ship *Federal Funds* had docked, yet the future was not secure at all. Another reality became apparent. Government money does not by itself create a sustainable dynamic (except, of course, in extreme cases such as a space center or a military base, where massive amounts flow uninterrupted).

The only source of new logs for the fire to achieve this dynamic is the private sector.

In August of 1979, Lowell City Manager Joseph Tully and I sat in a dark corner of a local restaurant and on the back of a placemat devised the Lowell Plan. It was a blueprint for a collaboration between the public and private sectors. Bankers and businessmen were to be allies, not adversaries. Industrial leaders—Wang Laboratories, most notably—were to be assisted in every possible way and were expected to make massive reinvestments in return. The private sector responded, part with great enthusiasm, part with reluctance. But it responded. The investment of private dollars began in earnest. Federal funds continued to stoke the fire, but it was the promise and the reality of private money that caused the city to achieve Walt Rostow's well-termed "takeoff."

Look at the revitalizing Massachusetts cities and you will find a wedding of public cooperation and private investment. Boston, Springfield, and Worcester—the largest cities—have begun their renaissance and in each case private sector leadership was critical.

Remove the economic stimulus caused by private sector investment growth and you have continued decline. Government money has but one purpose: to foster an environment that will attract private money, giving disadvantaged sectors of society a chance to reap the rewards provided by economic growth. The future is not urban renewal. It's the urban development action grant (UDAG) program, enacted under the Carter administration (public monies for leverage in private investment), and initially and inexplicably rejected by the Reagan administration. It's the free enterprise zones (tax incentives for industry to locate in distressed areas). It's the

Massachusetts revenue bonds program (less expensive money for industrial investment using the government's capacity to sell bonds). If we are to restore our urban centers, there must be leverage to make the private decisionmakers see a chance for profit. The good old profit motive works as nothing else can or ever will.

As the primary deliverer of the Lowell National Historical Park, I remain highly enthusiastic about its impact on the city. Since its delivery, however, I have come to understand its very real limitations.

The trick is to encourage the private sector, feed it, and channel it, without getting bitten. The private sector is robust and cruel. I have been the victim of its cruelty (in the decline of both my family's business and that of the city I grew up in) so I will forever feel a distance from it. But I know that it's a necessary component. If this fact is ignored, efforts to revitalize—whether directed at regions, cities, neighborhoods, or individuals—will not be sustained.

Liberals intent upon the resurgence of older urban centers will have to lure industries that have left (or are thinking about leaving) for more profitable environs. This "reality" has taken my home city out of its doldrums, and has caused me to regard corporate America with a different perspective.

The Energy Plan for Massachusetts: Nuclear Power 303. My predecessor in the House, Paul Cronin, predicted an ever-increasing energy crisis and gasoline prices that would soar to the unheard-of price of $1 a gallon. He was ahead of his time politically, and few people, including myself, took his warnings very seriously.

When I defeated Cronin, I sought out the Interior and Insular Affairs Committee in order to pursue the Lowell National Historical Park legislation. By chance, the committee also had an Energy and Environmental Subcommittee on which I served. Soon I found myself absorbed by the energy issue, which became and remains my major legislative focus.

My efforts in the House involved conservation, renewable energy sources, and nuclear safety standards. Upon election to the Senate, my first choice for committee assignment was the Energy and Natural Resources Committee, then chaired by Henry Jackson of Washington—and I was so assigned.

I have continued to pursue my previous interests and have filed several related bills: the Community Energy Act (as co-author with Harrison Williams of New Jersey), the Conservation Bank (author with Edward Kennedy of Massachusetts and John Durkin of New Hampshire), and the Solar Bank (co-author with Durkin and Robert Morgan of North Carolina); and I was also the sponsor of various successful amendments supporting conservation and renewable resource efforts. I had become one of the more reliable spear carriers for the conservation and solar energy adherents.

It was soon apparent that the energy issue was not going to be seriously addressed without a real crisis. President Carter's fine April 18, 1977, speech ("the moral equivalent of war") was followed by congressional disinterest, despite leadership efforts, and the administration's ardor for the issue cooled. What passed out of the Congress during the Carter years was adequate in structure but woefully inadequate in scale. When polled, the public indicated that it barely believed we imported oil, and did not believe we had an energy crisis.

Yet several studies in 1979 emphasized the seriousness of the crisis. *Energy Future: A Report of the Energy Project at the Harvard Business School* got the most attention, but others said virtually the same thing (the Ford Foundation, Resources for the Future, the Mellon Institute, and the National Academy of Sciences). In 1980, reports such as *Global 2000,* a joint State Department and Council on Environmental Quality effort, carried a similar message.

By spring 1980, I had decided that federal action by itself was likely to be too little, too late. Thus, it would make sense to develop an energy plan for Massachusetts. If energy was to be the major determinant of life in America—absent nuclear war—then it was about time that a Northern state like Massachusetts began to protect itself.

I worked with my staffs in Washington and Massachusetts to draft the Massachusetts Plan (Mass Plan). Specialists in housing, economic development, transportation, agriculture, education, recreation, and environment joined forces with energy experts. By early April, I was prepared to announce the Mass Plan, after briefing editorial boards, community groups, utilities, and others.

The 61-page Mass Plan contained over 250 recommendations in

every conceivable area related to energy (the Mass Plan is printed in the Appendix). It was promoted as a challenge to the state to control its own destiny. The plan was thorough, and I saw it as a major contribution to the economic future of Massachusetts.

It was received with a big yawn. In newspaper after newspaper, it either made page 21 (Boston *Globe*), was subordinated to editorial comments on the Kennedy presidential campaign (Boston *Herald American*), or was well covered and then promptly dropped (by most non-Boston newspapers).

The Mass Plan died before it reached Broadway . . . all except for one relatively minor subsection.

In reviewing the long-term projections of supply and demand, I had concluded (as had the aforementioned reports) that the peaking of world oil production before the year 2000 due to physical limits would create a serious supply shortfall—assuming that vulnerability to political interruption did not do so first.

To produce electricity in the middle term, there are two alternatives for baseload generation: nuclear energy and coal. Even after conservation and the use of renewable resources have been maximized, there may be no escaping the nuclear/coal dilemma. Having chaired hearings on the issue of the "greenhouse effect" (carbon dioxide overload of the atmosphere) and having been involved with problems like acid rain and strip mining, I viewed coal with some hesitation. While accepting its use, I came to feel that nuclear energy (the light water reactor, not the breeder reactor) might well be better than coal environmentally. I considered nuclear energy superior to oil because the supply problems are less difficult and because liquid fuels like oil should not be used for electrical generation, but rather should be saved for transportation.

Consequently, the Mass Plan argued for the retention of a nuclear option. As can be seen by reading the plan, it was an alternative only after the full realization of conservation and renewable sources of energy. Indeed, the plan was above all a comprehensive, functional blueprint for conservation and renewables.

The details were lost in the furor. The influential anti-nuclear community in Massachusetts felt betrayed. Although I had never come out against nuclear power, it was assumed that I was opposed to it, or was at least neutral. To advocate its retention was just too much: an outspoken environmentalist had given nuclear energy unwarranted credibility.

Since the utilities were ignoring the renewable energy sources and pushing ahead to construct nuclear power plants such as the one at Seabrook, New Hampshire, a precarious and important East Coast estuary, the anti-nuclear movement did not lack adherents. The anti-Seabrook Clamshell Alliance had supporters throughout the state, including many who had helped in my campaign.

The morning after the announcement of the Mass Plan, my wife, Niki, called me over to the window at our home. On the lawn was a large wooden NO NUKES sign, and our American flag had been taken from its pole. Clearly, accepting nuclear power was un-American to some.

At airports, commencement speeches, town meetings, and factory tours, I would be approached by someone saying sternly: "No nukes, Senator." Environmental activists were part of my natural constituency. Explaining my position in detail sometimes resulted in emotional disagreement, and cries of "Remember Three Mile Island!" Remembering Three Mile Island (or Brown's Ferry, for that matter) was not difficult. Figuring out the sources of energy if nuclear plants were abandoned was a different task—and in my opinion, an impossible one.

As yet, we cannot generate substantial amounts of electricity from the sun at a reasonable cost. Wind machines, hydro sites, and solar cells are important and should be developed, but they can't do the job alone in the next several decades. Oil is finite and too dependent on the whims of volatile foreign leaders. Coal involves a carbon dioxide problem, acid rain, strip mining, coal ash disposal, particulate pollution, and transportation difficulties.

There is no way out of a nuclear option in the middle term. The fact that it is a controversial source of energy (and potentially uneconomic, due to delays, engineering problems, etc.) does not lessen its practical inevitability. Otherwise, we are back in the oil or coal bind, which is potentially worse. In the face of such a set of Faustian choices, it seems clear that we need a mix of energy sources, and neither nuclear energy nor coal can, or should, be eliminated at this point.

But nuclear energy carries with it a sensitive psychic response.

The word "nuclear" is associated with human destruction, radiation, cancer. Americans are constantly reminded of the bombings of Hiroshima and Nagasaki and their terrible aftermath. It is difficult to separate the issues of nuclear warfare and nuclear energy.

The NO NUKES sign remained on my lawn for several days next to the unflagged flagpole. When I left for Washington, I asked my father to save it. I wanted to hang it in my garage in Lowell to remind me of the vagaries of politics. He had different ideas, and gave it to a neighbor, who chopped it up and used it in his wood stove—an appropriate non-nuclear energy source.

In the weeks that followed, I spent a great deal of time reevaluating my position. I decided that I had not been in error. To eliminate any option, given the uncertainty about our energy future, without a practical alternative was ideological shortsightedness. In their unwillingness to consider the wider and longer-term perspectives, opponents of nuclear energy were, despite the best of motives, ignoring a larger responsibility. The energy supply-demand dilemma was a genuine one that would not go away just because it was unpleasant.

By anyone's standards, my opponents were well intentioned. But if they succeeded, they could conceivably create far more havoc in the future. Indeed, some thoughtful observers have contended that the world is far more likely to witness nuclear devastation from an energy-starved world than from nuclear power plants.

I wondered why this conclusion was so clear to me and so ludicrous to them. I also wondered why the difference gnawed away at me. Taking on the narrow-mindedness of the oil companies, auto manufacturers, or utilities on energy matters was a matter of course; there was an economic impetus for those decisionmakers, and most of their "errors" could be so explained. But disagreeing with the environmentalists on such a gut issue was uncomfortable. Many of these people were my close allies on the Alaska Lands issue.

One thing was sure. As in the Chrysler case, we couldn't both be right.

The 10¢ Gasoline Tax: Consumerism 404. The final chapter of my reassessment also involved energy, and related to the consumerist-populist constituency. As a loyal consumerist, I was always rated by the Consumer Federation of America at either 100 percent or close to it. In October 1980 it was the highest, along with Howard Metzenbaum's, in the Senate. My record of support on these issues was so consistent that some might call it knee-jerk.

The consumer often was the victim of an unfettered free enterprise system, and consumerism was needed to provide safeguards. Sometimes consumerism was over-zealous (car ignition systems linked to seat belts), but generally it played a positive role.

When it came to the energy crisis, however, consumerism became a double-edged sword. The struggle against the excesses of the oil companies probably saved the consumer hundreds of millions of dollars. But while protecting the consumer against OPEC was virtually impossible, shielding the consumer from government-imposed gas taxes was viewed as mandatory by liberal Democrats as well as Republicans.

Is defending the energy consumer from higher energy prices good for the consumer? Obviously so, in the short term.

What about the long run? Couldn't it be argued that holding down American energy prices has been harmful to the consumer? Considering the enormous financial drain of $70 billion in 1980 for imported oil, wouldn't it be in the interest of everyone, including the consumer, to price oil at its replacement cost? Indeed, the Mellon Institute study stated that had we decontrolled prices years ago, we would have had a program that could have reduced the cost of energy today by some 17 percent from its actual present level.

America's per capita consumption of gasoline (440 gallons per year) is far and away the highest in the world. Oil is a finite, diminishing resource. Our need for foreign oil is our major national weakness.

Given these facts, can it not be argued that America must consume less gasoline?

Two ways of accomplishing this goal are rationing and higher prices. Voluntary conservation hasn't worked, is not working, and will not ever work satisfactorily.

Effective rationing would not be passed by the Congress in the absence of a serious shortfall. Under current law, rationing would be imposed only after a 20 percent shortfall. It would take about nine months to implement fully a program that would oversee 123 million cars, 35 million trucks, and an endless list of special-interest groups who feel strongly that they should have priority allocations. If the Persian Gulf were to be closed off tomorrow and supplies fell for the United States, for Japan, and for western Europe, the entire Western industrial system would collapse six months before our government could establish a working rationing program. As currently conceived, rationing is a cruel hoax.

That leaves us with rationing by price. The argument for the decontrol of crude oil was simple—the United States was keeping the cost of this resource artificially low, thus encouraging consumption and discouraging production. Decontrol was endorsed by the Carter and Reagan administrations and is now the law of the land. This congressionally approved and Reagan-accelerated plan to raise the price of energy was enacted, and the ripples of protest soon dissipated. These actions, coupled with OPEC increases, sent the price of gasoline soaring from 70¢ to $1.20 by early 1980. In real dollar terms the price has doubled since 1973.

These increases were realized by the oil companies and the OPEC states—in billions. And no one lost his seat in Congress as a result.

What about an increase whose monies would be used for mass transit, energy conservation, aid to the poor to pay fuel costs, and balancing the budget? Rather than monies going to Exxon or Kuwait, they would be channeled to the Treasury or recycled to the taxpayer. In addition, such an increase would encourage conservation, with the consequently positive balance-of-payments and national security benefits.

But a gas tax is always going to be very difficult to pass. Ever. It doesn't make any difference whether it's a 4¢ gas tax (killed 370 to 52 in 1977), a 10¢ import fee (killed 376 to 30 in the House, and 73 to 16 in the Senate in 1980) or a 20¢ stand-by gas tax (killed 345 to 72 in 1975). It doesn't make any difference who proposed them (both Ford and Carter). It doesn't matter whether the money is recycled back to the consumer or earmarked for energy-related expenditures. There is a shortsighted political reaction that is triggered every time. Such a reaction is a survival response politically, but for our country it makes survival less likely.

Senators who grit their teeth and vote for the politically sensitive Panama Canal Treaties wouldn't consider supporting a gas tax. Congressmen who would risk their careers over a whole range of issues feel the same way. No one wants to pay more for gasoline. Members of Congress receive a great deal of mail on the notion of a gas tax—all opposed to it. The only national political figure to suggest a sizable gas tax (to be rebated through lower Social Security taxes) was John Anderson, who received 6.6 percent of the vote in the 1980 presidential race.

I believe that the strongest argument against a gas tax is that it would hurt poor people, and thereby harm those who can least afford it. That argument collapses if the tax is rebated. In fact, it could be validly claimed that under a recycling tax plan many poor Americans would achieve a net economic gain. Indeed, most citizens would not suffer a dollar loss unless they used a great deal of gasoline.

If the object is to protect the consumer, especially the poorer consumer, how do we accomplish that without reducing our dependence on OPEC? The more we import, the more dependent we are, and therefore the more vulnerable to OPEC price increases, as history has shown.

If there is an energy crisis, who is most likely to be ravaged by that crisis? *Poor people.* The consumer. A nation that has not addressed the energy issue has placed its poor people in severe jeopardy. A nation that allows its citizens to be dependent upon gasoline cannot protect those same citizens in a crisis.

Almost every country in the world understands this and has imposed gasoline taxes accordingly. In early 1981, the price of gasoline in Great Britain was $2.67, in West Germany $2.55, in Italy $3.19, in Japan $2.25, in France $3.16, in the Soviet Union $2.85, in Greece $2.65, in Spain $2.68, in Norway $2.98, in Sweden $2.69, in Denmark $3.23, in Poland $2.10, and in Switzerland $2.77. Of the industrial nations, only Canada has cheaper gasoline than the United States.

What do these countries know that we don't? They realize that gasoline waste and gasoline dependence would jeopardize their security and weaken their economies. They also are aware that the best way to protect their consumers is to publicize the reality of the crisis and at a minimum to price gasoline at or close to its real cost. But we have schemed to delude our consumers. When the severe crunch comes, as it inevitably will, the consumer will be devastated.

In 1980, President Carter, knowing that the Congress would not impose a tax, took executive action using the import fee to install a 10¢ gasoline tax, representing an 8 percent increase in cost. The tax required no congressional action, sparing legislators the agony.

But Congress seized the moment. Here was a chance to save the country from the ravages of a 10¢ gas tax. Resolutions were filed in both houses to repeal the tax. It became a holy war, and one that was led by the liberals.

What would be nicer than running for reelection in 1980 on the grounds of having defeated a gas tax? I understood the sentiment. Having voted for every gas levy that came before the Congress in my seven years, I have been confronted with the issue in my campaigns, and learned from firsthand experience that no one relishes such a tax.

No effort was made to salvage the gas tax in the House, and administration efforts focused on the Senate. To forestall an override of his veto, the President needed only 34 votes to sustain his position.

Meetings were held to gather support among senators, who basically divided into three groups. The first felt strongly that we had to begin addressing the harsh realities of the energy crisis. The second were dead set against any such politically suicidal move. And the third acknowledged the need to do something, but preferred different approaches.

The third group usually took the tack of saying, "I would vote for a tax if it did X, not Y," or, "I would vote for a tax if . . ." It soon became obvious that these senators would support any tax except one that came up for a vote.

A senator who said, "Look, if I vote for this tax, I will be defeated," was at least being honest.

The "it's-not-fair-to-the-poor" group was made up mostly of good friends of mine, especially in the House. One congressman told me he would strongly support a 50¢ gasoline tax if it were rebated back to the consumers. Neither he nor any of his like-minded colleagues has since breathed a word about such a proposal in public, nor has he filed such a bill.

The only liberals who voted for the tax in the Senate were those whose concern about the potential havoc of an energy crisis over-rode their normal consumerist instincts. They were in a minority. (One, Gary Hart, barely survived his 1980 reelection bid.)

The 73 to 16 vote against the tax was widely regarded as a victory for the consumer. I believe it was a defeat for America, and for consumers.

The ADA Speech

These four events rattled my political assumptions. There were other less significant experiences and issues that also triggered this rethinking. And my personal experiences, detailed earlier in this chapter, made me sensitive to a wider perspective.

In any case, I spent a great deal of time in late 1979 and the beginning of 1980 feeling that something was askew. The early political events of 1980 certainly did nothing to discourage that conclusion. Conservative Republicans with simplistic solutions were riding roughshod over moderate Republicans in presidential, gubernatorial, and congressional primaries, and liberal Democrats were fighting for their political lives.

The question was: Why? What makes a nation move collectively like a flock of migrating birds that changes direction without any perceived signal or leader?

One could dismiss these trends as simply irrational, or as unfor-tunate aberrations. But if you can identify a collective behavioral pattern, you can usually discover an underlying rationale. I have never seen a city whose geographic location made no sense. People originally settled in certain places for very real reasons.

National characteristics? Particular events take place, leave their marks on a people's psyche, and affect their behavior thereafter. You can better understand Germany's phobia about inflation and its corresponding discipline on fiscal matters if you study the coun-try's economic chaos caused by runaway inflation between the two world wars. And you can better understand the anti-nuclear proliferation attitude of the Japanese if you think of what happened at Hiroshima and Nagasaki.

America is behaving in a particular way, in reaction against existing assumptions and ground rules. The operative majority (the Democratic Party and its philosophical legacy) was perceived to have wandered off the path. It had lost its sense of the realities. In rejecting the Democratic approach (and in the process ousting a President and several outstanding senators), the nation was embracing the simplicities offered by the conservative Republican tide. A vacuum existed that liberals had created, and into that vacuum rushed the only other product available in the political marketplace.

In the spring of 1980, while I was presiding over the Senate one afternoon, a long quorum call was in process, which is the technique used to kill time until something is decided upon. Unable to leave the chair (presiding is a function reserved for the most junior members) and with nothing to observe on the Senate floor, I phoned my office to find out whether there were any messages.

One of the calls was from Leon Shull, executive director of Americans for Democratic Action. When I later reached him, he invited me to give the keynote address at the ADA's national convention in mid-June. I accepted—I had always enjoyed a good relationship with the ADA, its Massachusetts chapter, and particularly its president, Patsy Mink, a former colleague in the House.

I was pleased by the invitation and rearranged my schedule to accommodate it. The original draft of my speech was a typical litany of liberal Democratic values and programs. Liberalism had significantly enhanced the lives of ordinary Americans over the past fifty years, and I wanted to pay homage to that legacy.

The day before the convention I read the speech and it left me cold. I have heard so many politicians, both liberal and conservative, tell audiences what they want to hear that I've become almost Pavlovian in my reaction against such mutual backscratching. Rarely will an industry group, for example, seek out a senator for a speech whose views will clash with its accepted party line. Audiences generally want reinforcement of existing views, not challenges to them.

So I retired to the quiet of the senators-only Marble Room off the

Senate floor, and wrote what I was actually feeling. It was strangely liberating, and when I finished, I felt the ADA would hear a speech that would serve them well. They were my ideological brethren and I hoped they would listen as well as hear.

The next morning the convention was discussing issue positions when I arrived. They had been addressed earlier in the morning by my Massachusetts colleague, Ted Kennedy, and from all accounts it was a stirring message. The issues discussion that followed was not stirring, and eventually it was interrupted to allow Patsy Mink to introduce me.

I told the convention what I felt had gone wrong with liberalism. After reiterating the tremendous strides made by traditional liberal Democratic programs in the 1960s, I went on to explain why I felt the momentum was dissipating. (The text of the speech is given in the Appendix.)

Liberalism, I argued, was living off its legacy—basically the New Deal. From FDR to LBJ, there had been a rich flowering of our philosophy, and as a result, the Democratic Party had dominated American politics. That very success, however, had locked us into a stereotyped mentality, much like a baseball player who never developed a slider because his fastball was so successful. Now, years later, that fastball was being jumped on and hit out of the park. There were a host of new concerns challenging the mentality.

A mentality geared to protecting workers in the workplace and promoting unionism was now being asked to worry about productivity.

A mentality geared to stopping the war in Vietnam was now being called upon to ponder a Soviet arms buildup and Soviet aggression in Afghanistan.

A mentality geared to keeping consumer prices down was now called upon to worry not about the price of gasoline, but its supply.

A mentality geared to opposing nuclear power was now being urged to concern itself about the source of electricity in an era of reduced oil production.

A mentality geared to ever more government programs to meet real needs was being forced to choose between equally worthwhile programs.

This new era was going to be *very* uncomfortable.

I concluded the speech with a plea for the kind of innovative thinking that would appeal to Americans and forestall the possibility of a conservative tide based on unworkable ideological simplicities.

The reaction was not what you would call an ovation—there had been little applause during the speech. But neither was the audience hostile. They had listened (anyone accustomed to public speaking knows whether his audience is paying attention), and that was what I had hoped for.

Two convention delegates criticized me over the gas tax and nuclear power. Others, most of them young, thanked me for saying what needed to be said. Most were noncommittal. The next day the speech was paraphrased in the *New York Times,* based on an interview I had given earlier.

The next week the speech reached a national audience when it was the subject of a David Broder column that appeared in forty-four newspapers. Broder, perhaps the country's most respected political columnist, had interviewed me in connection with a book he was writing about what today's leaders had been doing in the sixties and seventies. That interview and the speech itself resulted in his article.

The syndicated column, however, had a dynamic that went beyond the substance of my speech, as can be understood by the headline in Broder's home paper, the Washington *Post:* "Politically Passé?" and that used in the Boston *Globe:* "End of Kennedy-Style Liberalism?"

Broder's interpretation of what I had said was reasonably accurate. But the not-so-subtle implication of the headlines was devastating, serving to blur the intent and content of my argument. Needless to say, the column certainly didn't help the Kennedy candidacy, which I was supporting. When I spoke to Ted later that morning, he was concerned about the article, given Broder's excellent reputation, but he showed no irritation toward me or Broder. He had read the ADA speech earlier and we had discussed it over lunch in his office the day before.

The reaction of his staff and his supporters in Massachusetts, however, was anger. My staff members, three of whom had taken leaves of absence to work for the Kennedy campaign, as well as my sister, received the brunt of that hostility. Many of his backers thought I was hitting Ted at a point of vulnerability, after his losses in the 1980 primaries. Some even suggested I was trying to undermine Kennedy's political future so that I could run for the White House in 1984.

If I hadn't realized it before, I came to understand fully what it means to be the other senator from Massachusetts. Whatever I said would be analyzed and interpreted for its "Kennedy angle." I wondered what would have happened had I been born eight miles farther north (in New Hampshire) and elected to the Senate from that state. How differently would the content of the speech have been interpreted?

An excerpt from the speech was printed on the editorial page of the Washington *Post,* and I wrote an op-ed piece that appeared in the *New York Times,* the Boston *Globe,* and other leading newspapers. Unlike the Massachusetts Plan, the ADA speech was to contain its own dynamic.

My office was deluged with requests for the original text. There was also a great deal of reaction. To my surprise, conservatives like former Defense Secretary James Schlesinger telephoned to praise it. Other conservatives, such as Senators Richard Lugar of Indiana, Alan Simpson of Wyoming, and James McClure of Idaho also had kind words. Moderates like Senators Daniel P. Moynihan of New York, David Boren of Oklahoma, David Pryor of Arkansas, Alfred Kahn, and Jack Watson of the White House gave me support. (Moynihan declared it was the best speech given to the ADA since his own in 1967!) Among liberals, I received positive comments from Senators Gary Hart of Colorado and Howard Metzenbaum of Ohio, and ACTION head Sam Brown.

Apparently, the speech had struck a chord. By October, it was in its fifth printing (some 2,500 copies). Two weeks before the presidential election, Vice President Mondale's office asked for a copy, as did John Anderson's running mate, Governor Patrick Lucey.

All this commotion was fine, except for two problems. First, the Kennedy angle persisted. Even a year later, the pre-publication speculation in the press about this book would invariably refer to its impact on Ted Kennedy's 1984 presidential chances. Being interviewed about the "New Liberalism" involved awaiting the inevitable "Now, Senator, how do these ideas square with those of your good friend and Massachusetts colleague . . . ?" Second, the liberal constituency (as opposed to liberal officeholders) felt that I was betraying the cause in the face of adversity. This response was best summarized in Ellen Goodman's September 11, 1980, column printed in the Boston *Globe* and other newspapers, entitled "Repentant Liberal."

Her article, which mentioned no names, was clever but blunt. It painted a portrait of liberals who, sensing the change in the wind, ran around discovering new truths and ignoring old values.

Other liberals went much further. Several longtime supporters claimed that I was "selling out," although much of this was said to my staff and not to me personally. Some notable old JFK hands weighed in with criticism in guest editorials, led by Arthur Schlesinger, Jr., in the *Wall Street Journal* and Richard Goodwin in the Boston *Herald American.*

It was soon obvious that the ADA speech by itself was inadequate. It had no conceptual beginning, being just a reflection of an attitude. It had no ending, and was largely a criticism of what existed. I had not adequately explained why liberalism was in trouble. Worse still, I gave no indication of what was to replace it. I had not been constructive.

This book, then, is an effort to put my thesis into a coherent framework. It is meant to provide a sense of direction that stems directly from my personal experiences. These experiences basically have left me observing events and asking "Why?" Why do certain political ideas take hold, and others not? What is it that causes a nation to embrace, then reject, particular ideologies? The answer, it seems to me, lies not in the ideas or the ideologies, but in the world to which we attempt to apply these notions. The concepts work *only* if they are congruent with the realities confronting us. Square pegs are worthless when you have round holes, but if the holes evolve into squares over time, they will fit. Equally, round pegs will not fit after such a transformation, and there is no use in lamenting the situation.

In 1980, some liberal round pegs no longer fit into the square realities of our world, and the conservative square pegs prevailed.

I believe fervently that the transformation continues unabated. As we journey into the 1980s and 1990s, the need will be for oval pegs, and neither the rounds nor the squares will do. Whichever political party is capable of a transformation consistent with the evolving realities will achieve electoral success.

What then are these "evolving realities"? In the analogy used in the preface, we must have the capacity to see the realities (the waterfall) early and to move to meet them, free of the baggage of dogma. Getting ahead of these realities is very difficult in a democratic society because realities (like waterfalls) are always sensed by the non-ideological voting citizen long before they are recognized by the ideological special interests that make up the adherents of either party. Thus you have a situation where evolution follows only after rejection, because rejection alone can shake off the constraints of the dogmatically smug.

The successes and failures of prominent liberals over the past fifty years can tell us something about their capacity to recognize realities and to fashion a philosophy that took these into account.

From FDR to the Present: A Liberal Perspective

It is a given in today's political discussion that Franklin Roosevelt was the creator of the coalition that propelled the Democratic Party into the prominence it has enjoyed for the past half century. Thus in the 1980 presidential campaign, Democrats considered it blasphemous for Ronald Reagan to quote FDR in his acceptance speech at the Republican Convention.

Reagan tried to project the impression that President Roosevelt was a fiscal conservative. His mechanism was quite simple—to cite FDR himself.

Although Reagan's quotes were accurate, they were so contrary to popular perceptions that they sounded hollow. Hanging out on a credibility limb, Reagan was an easy target, and Edward Kennedy ravaged him eloquently at the Democratic Convention.

Reagan's researchers, however, were correct; it was the analysts who failed him. To organize a coalition, FDR responded to the realities of his time and discarded previous ideology. He created a philosophy of political action that accomplished many things—and above all, it worked. Its working was central to the philosophy, not vice versa.

Roosevelt did not impose a set philosophy (as quoted by Reagan) upon a world and nation whose circumstances had changed radically. Herbert Hoover did that. Hoover believed that the budget should be balanced irrespective of conditions. So when the country started its economic slide, Hoover vetoed direct federal relief to the unemployed and backed tight credit measures by the Federal Reserve, exacerbating an already weakened economy. Hoover's insistence upon being true to his ideals cost him the presidency. It also almost cost us our economy.

By being untrue to his initial rhetoric of fiscal restraint, FDR probably saved the country. It is ironic that this revisionist, this ultimate realist, should have been the instigator of a political philosophy departure from which would now be viewed as revisionism.

There are, obviously, as many views of FDR as there are students of his era. For myself, I believe that he approached his time armed with a set of human values and with a mind capable of dealing with the realities that confronted him.

His realism was his most interesting characteristic. In 1932 and beyond, he was faced with a grim set of facts that don't apply today to the same degree. Many people were have-nots struggling to survive. The spread between rich and poor was staggering. Urban workers labored in factories characterized by long hours, poor pay, unsafe conditions, and no job security. Rural farmers clung perilously to the soil, vulnerable to weather calamities and commodity prices, neither of which they could control. Much of the East Coast was populated by immigrants and their children, whose lives were scarred by such notions as "Irish need not apply."

The majority of Americans perceived themselves to be on the outside looking in, poor and/or discriminated against and/or abused by prevailing conditions. This majority (later to be identified as a coalition) had very real needs, and FDR moved to meet them. Electrification of rural America to aid the farmer; Social Security to protect the elderly; jobs programs to assist the unemployed. By the end of the 1930s, a new reality emerged—international fascism —and Roosevelt moved in turn to meet that adversary.

The advantages he possessed were two events that gave him the consensus necessary for action: the Great Depression and Pearl Harbor. These events saved him from the endless national discussions and debates generally required to allow shifts in direction in a democratic society.

Opposing FDR were a number of forces. The budget balancers, the America-Firsters, the radicals, all tried to challenge FDR's realism with ideology and failed. Roosevelt was able to fashion an invincible coalition because his ideas were right for the times. Were he alive now, I believe he would be equally attuned to today's realities, not tied to traditional dogma.

Harry Truman followed in like style. The man who ordered the bombing of Hiroshima and Nagasaki also promoted the greatest and most effective foreign aid program in the history of the world: the Marshall Plan. He believed both to be in the interests of America. This man who is today honored by Democrats gave us as well a good dose of the Cold War, presiding during the evolution of the doctrine of "containment" of the Soviet Union (of which the Marshall Plan was a part). And he responded instantly to Communist aggression in Korea. The last two policies are now viewed by some as illiberal, but it is hard to argue that they were inappropriate then.

Truman was followed eventually by a triumvirate who reigned over the full flowering of Democratic and liberal values—President John Kennedy, President Lyndon Johnson, and Senator Hubert Humphrey—accompanied by others who adapted and refined their values—Senators Eugene McCarthy, Robert Kennedy, George McGovern, and Edward Kennedy.

The 1960 campaign and its immediate aftermath represented a clinging to the ideological legacy of President Eisenhower's hard-line Secretary of State, John Foster Dulles. Kennedy campaigned on the existence of a "missile gap"; he and Nixon debated whether we would be prepared to engage in full-scale war to defend Quemoy and Matsu, and Kennedy was to approve the fiasco known as the Bay of Pigs. These events were not the Kennedy legacy of party litany; they represented the failure of applying ideology to a changing world. The flowering of the JFK/LBJ/HHH era involved the addressing of real-world issues, and the fashioning of the responses to meet them.

The emergence of the Third World inspired the Peace Corps and Alliance for Progress.

The Soviet attempt to tip the nuclear balance resulted in the blockade of Cuba.

Racial discrimination in America led to the Civil Rights Act and the Voting Rights Act.

Limited economic opportunity in America brought the War on Poverty and the Great Society.

The breakdown of the extended family caused the creation of Medicare and Meals on Wheels.

Sometimes a response was devised to meet a real need but was simply misguided; for example, urban renewal to address the problem of decaying cities.

Sometimes a response was created to meet a perceived need whose reality had been superseded by a newer reality; for example, the war in Vietnam was waged to combat Communism while ignoring nationalism in Vietnam and the Sino-Soviet split.

Some realities would be addressed in the 1970s: the urban crisis saw the enactment of revenue sharing, the community development block grant program, and the urban development grant program. The crisis in the environment inspired the enactment of the Clean Air Act and the Clean Water Act. In both these instances, the laws naturally followed the governmental activism that began ten years before.

These latter programs were the legacy of the Nixon years just as much as Watergate. Nixon and the Democratic majority in Congress continued the tradition in fashioning programs to meet real (and perceived) needs. Nixon also responded to the reality of the breakup of the Soviet-Chinese monolith when he sent Henry Kissinger to reestablish relations with China. Here Nixon's realism was a genuine contribution, accurately cited by him as his greatest achievement. (One can imagine the reaction of the right wing if George McGovern, for example, had been the President to open up China. Yet today few, if any, reject the realism of that move; even Ronald Reagan, the President, has assumed a posture different from Ronald Reagan, the candidate, who talked about a Two-China policy.)

The JFK/LBJ/HHH triumvirate enjoyed great success. It represented a high watermark of the Democratic Party just as assuredly as FDR had some thirty years before. Its momentum was derailed for three reasons.

First, in failing to understand Third World dynamics, the leaders stumbled into the quagmire of Vietnam. They viewed Ho Chi Minh as a Communist, while many Vietnamese saw him as a nationalist. They regarded a succession of South Vietnamese rulers as bulwarks against communism, whereas the Vietnamese considered them corrupt and ineffective. They assumed a war of "national liberation" could be won with firepower; the Vietnamese believed the war could be won only by appealing to the "hearts and minds" of the people. Young Americans went to fight and die for a country whose people sized them up with distance and even hostility. The Americans in turn considered the Vietnamese as somehow unworthy of the effort. It was a marriage of convenience doomed from the start, because it was caught up in a swirl of complex realities—nationalism, racial awareness, self-determination—that overcame the assumed reality, international aggression. This tragedy was virtually unavoidable. Given our missionary beliefs, our concern about Communist takeovers (epitomized by the "domino theory"), and the total lack of Third World experience among key American decisionmakers, there simply was not, and could not have been, any "feel" for the realities that existed in that unhappy land.

This dichotomy between expectations and reality caused a profound national trauma. During the Fulbright Senate Foreign Relations Committee Hearings on the war, one senator asked plaintively: "Are we the international good guys or are we the international bad guys?" The confusion was rampant across America.

A new reality existed, and we were not dealing with it. We were responding with an outmoded ideology inappropriate to the time. It was a foreign-policy counterpart to Herbert Hoover and the dogma of the balanced budget during a worsening recession.

Nothing in Lyndon Johnson's political life had prepared him for such a situation. He had no antennae for the Third World, which to him meant a Pakistani camel driver he could bring to the United States and shower with affection. He could like Third World leaders, but he could not give them what they wanted most, the respect of equality. LBJ was basically patronizing. He was comfortable dealing with Third World citizens as a dominant, not co-equal, partner. It is ironic that Kennedy instituted our substantial involvement in Vietnam. No American leader, before or since, has established such an identification with Third World peoples. (I vividly recall finding pictures of Kennedy alongside those of Emperor Haile Selassie on the walls of Ethiopian homes in remote areas.) The goodwill felt toward Kennedy was almost tangible.

Would this "touch" have eventually turned Kennedy away from the old assumptions and caused him to reverse the policy of U.S. intervention? Would he have been able, given this enormous reservoir of goodwill, to wage a battle for the hearts and minds of the Vietnamese as opposed to seeking higher body counts? Would he have been able to envision a unified Vietnam, truly non-aligned and enjoying fruitful relations with the United States? No one knows. What we do know is that the new reality was never understood by Johnson, and his policy in Vietnam didn't work.

The appreciation of the new reality took root, ironically, in Johnson's own party. The Republicans were still imbued with assumptions reaching back to the legacy of John Foster Dulles. They did not perceive the changing scene. Many interventionists argued for the obliteration of the reality by more and more bombing. To this day, many of the "best and the brightest" still don't understand what happened. Three senators, however, did. Robert Kennedy, Eugene McCarthy, and George McGovern put together a phalanx of activists and changed the course of history—bringing down LBJ in the process.

The second reason that the triumvirate lost its way was also a function of the war in Vietnam. Following the emotional outpouring that marked this country's response to the death of President Kennedy, Johnson skillfully began the trek toward the Great Society. The War on Poverty was something he understood in his gut, and it was to be his great achievement.

Guns or butter? Nonsense. Guns *and* butter—he would wage the War in Vietnam and the War on Poverty at the same time. Few challenged Johnson on this assumption. We are reminded now of this by Ronald Reagan's campaign pledge to provide massive tax cuts, huge increases in defense spending, and a balanced budget at the same time. In both cases, saying it didn't make it so. Johnson's determination became a resistible force that met an immovable reality—it just was too much for the system. The attempt to exercise his will over reality began the inflation that is still a major force in America today. What makes the situation in the mid-1960s particularly interesting is the fact that LBJ was blessed with an ever-expanding economy and a low underlying rate of inflation. Had he been faced with a stagnant economy and double-digit inflation—as we are today—his room to maneuver would have been much more constricted.

Ignoring the monetary and fiscal constraints was easily done. Avoiding the result of that policy was impossible.

The third reason for the end of the JFK/LBJ/HHH era was the sheer success it achieved in the domestic arena. By the time this momentum had consumed the sixties and seventies, there were programmatic approaches (if not solutions) to most problems.

In addition to the programs mentioned earlier:

The concern about hunger and education spawned the food stamps, school lunches, the Higher Education Act, the Secondary Education Act, and Head Start. There were the Occupational Safety and Health Act, Affirmative Action programs, housing for the elderly, and the Older Americans Act.

Programs were devised to deal with black lung disease, the handicapped, nurses' training, historic preservation, the arts and humanities, rural housing, law enforcement, hospital construction, and mass transit. There were programs for rental housing, owner housing, rural housing, family housing, housing for the handicapped.

As Congressman Morris Udall affectionately and wryly said once in introducing Hubert Humphrey: "He has solutions to which there aren't even problems yet." Or as Congressman Peter Rodino remarked to me: "Sooner or later we're going to realize that you can't pass a law to take care of every hurt."

The transition was just about complete. The majority of have-nots had become transformed. An expanding economy, unprecedented opportunities for advancement, and social programs at every turn had opened the door wide. By 1980, the average American owned his own home and 2.0 cars, 1.5 television sets, and a washer/dryer, worked in relatively safe conditions, and enjoyed most weekends off. The goal was not to get his, but to keep it. The instinct was for the status quo. The have-nots were not a majority, whose needs had to be accommodated; they were a minority, whose desires seemed seriously to threaten the achievements of the newly arrived middle class. The reservoir of social anger directed upward toward the privileged that had fueled FDR now turned downward as the economy stopped expanding and the middle class began to view the poor with resentment.

The New Deal and Great Society worked, but all too well for the political survival of their doctrines. The children of the coalition who had revered FDR were voting for Proposition 13 in California, Proposition 2 1/2 in Massachusetts, and Ronald Reagan all across the nation. Government became not a provider of the good life but an obstacle to it. Lower taxes, less government, became the cry. The classic example of the "taken-for-granted" attitude exhibited by recipients of social programs was found in South Dakota. During his 1980 campaign, George McGovern was castigated at a supermarket by two elderly women for his support of government programs. When they finished their discussion, they paid for their groceries with food stamps, a product of McGovern's own efforts. At that point, he knew he was caught up in a crosscurrent that he couldn't control.

In addition, by 1980 the average American was forgetting about the war in Vietnam and was worrying again about Soviet expansionism. And he was concerned for good reason, because there was the reality of a Soviet military buildup. A political movement based upon the economic opportunity and war resistance of the 1960s was bound to encounter rough sailing.

The average young person seeking a political identity in the 1980s was experiencing a very different set of circumstances than liberals realized.

Rather than reading about hunger, he was reading about food stamp abuse.

Rather than following American involvement in Vietnam, he was following Soviet aggression in Afghanistan.

Rather than worrying about safety in the workplace, he was worrying about productivity there.

The old FDR coalition is gone. The have-nots have become the middle class, and their mindset is the status quo. The national advantage enjoyed by the Democrats has vanished. It is now a whole new ballgame and a remarkably level playing field.

The Democrats must put together a majority the same way FDR did—by dealing with the realities that confront us. Conversely, if we don't and the Republicans do, we will be relegated to minority party status for a long time—and properly so.

After the 1980 presidential election, I was traveling through the Sumner Tunnel from Logan Airport to the center of Boston. On the back of a cab in front of me was a bumper sticker that read BEAT INFLATION, VOTE REAGAN. That cab driver was supposed to be one of the foundations of the FDR coalition—and he was hawking Reagan. He was reflecting the realities that intruded on his life. It would do the Democrats no good to browbeat him; they must understand the reasons instead of lamenting the results.

As the cab driver goes, so, in many respects, will go America. If President Reagan does beat inflation without reducing the college loan funds the cabbie's daughter needs for her college tuition, then that cabbie's vote is lost to the Democrats forever.

If the Reagan approach takes away advantages expected by the cabbie (such as college loan funds) and does not halt inflation, that bumper sticker will be removed all the more rapidly. And if that happens, the Democrats must offer a program that speaks to his future. If we can do no more than repeat the liturgy of New Deal and Great Society, we will still be round pegs unable to find the right-shaped holes.

Democratic Instincts, Republican Instincts

Before dealing with the realities of the 1980s and 1990s, it would be well to invest a moment on the issue of instincts. It is the instincts of public officials that determine from which direction they are likely to misjudge the realities. The more ideological the value system, the more pronounced will be the misjudgment.

Politicians are human beings with the same tendency to engage in group behavior as anyone else. I have always felt that if you want to learn about elected officials, you should observe what they do when no longer in office or when engaged in private activities. They will swiftly revert to their natural behavioral characteristics. There are "instincts" that are Democratic in nature and others that are Republican in nature. Republicans are generally more hawkish than Democrats on such issues as the B-I, SALT II, and defense. The anti–Vietnam War contingent in the Republican Party was a distinct minority. Thus, Republicans are apt to see a Soviet arms buildup before it happens, and the Democrats after it happens.

Republicans are more likely to view the world in East-West Cold War terms than Democrats, on issues such as aid to Central America or lifting sanctions against Rhodesia. Thus, Republicans will ask a Third World leader whether he's pro- or anti-American; a Democrat will study his human rights record.

Democrats are more sensitive to social issues, such as racial discrimination and women's rights. They are more likely to tolerate waste in social programs because they are more committed to the programs in the first place, whereas Republicans tend to ignore excessive military spending. A recent compilation of General Accounting Office studies that showed the existence of $34 billion in extravagance found it evenly distributed between social and military programs. It is not difficult to guess which party criticized which areas of waste.

Democrats mostly believe in governmental activism, Republicans in the free market forces. Thus, Democrats are more likely to indulge over-regulation (such as some of OSHA's excesses), while the Republicans are more likely to tolerate private sector abuses (industrial pollution of the environment).

Democrats look at urban unemployment, see injustice, and devise job programs like the Comprehensive Employment and Training Act (CETA); Republicans see normal market fallout and devise tax schemes to encourage private sector investment in urban centers.

These characteristics suggest that the *average* Democratic and *average* Republican political leader are different in fundamental ways. And this difference in turn is reflected in the electorate as a whole. Thus, each party has a natural base from which to operate.

Which approach more truly represents what America stands for? Obviously, the answer to this question is a function of which party one belongs to, or which characteristics a citizen has.

My view is that the Democratic Party, with its liberal tradition, offers a base of compassion essential for the functioning of any democratic society. It represents a barrier against the kind of social and economic inequities (both domestic and international) that lead to violent dislocation, be it the burning of Watts or terrorism in Chile. Without this sense of compassion, a society is merely a Mount St. Helens awaiting its time and place to explode. Compassion is what cushions the predatory instincts that mar the free market system—instincts that gave us the slave trade, child labor, and the robber barons.

In January 1980, I visited Africa and traveled to the northwest corner of Tanzania to meet with Julius Nyerere, the country's first and only President. He is a revered figure in Tanzania and all over Africa, and internationally respected for his intellect; he is considered the father of African socialism.

We met in his home village of Butiyama, in the simple and unassuming setting that has marked Nyerere's personal living style. After the appropriate courtesies, we got caught up in a discussion about competing economic systems. I said that socialism (or Marxism) was a system doomed to failure; that it required a collective fervor and devotion that was simply not sustainable over a long period of time; that capitalism was based on the reality that man operates in his own self-interest and therefore can capture the incentive and work habits that are natural to him. I predicted that even the most Marxist of African states would eventually turn to a more free enterprise–oriented system, such as was being tested in Mozambique. I tried not to sound like the U.S. Chamber of Commerce, though probably without success. I said that I did not feel threatened by African Marxism, because I believed it would wither away and be replaced by a mixed economy.

Nyerere heard me out with interest. He knew from my background that I was not a reactionary, but this adherence to the capitalist "party line" was probably familiar. "The issue," he said slowly, "is justice." Capitalism to Nyerere was too susceptible to greed and injustice. He had seen it during the British colonial period. The crass exploitation of his people by educated, cultivated, and well-groomed British gentlemen bespoke an inherent defect in the system.

I agreed that unfettered free enterprise led to exploitation. Fettered socialism, however, leads to stagnation. The trick is to keep the reins loose enough to allow people's strivings to better their lot, but to have the reins prepared to pull back if that advancement comes at the cost of someone's undue exploitation.

Free market forces softened by compassion.

Realism—some of it Republican in its origins—combined with the value system of the Democratic liberal tradition is the objective.

Compassionate realism requires a clear-eyed analysis of the world welfare, followed by a decision about how best to deal with that world in a way that works, but always filtered through the prism of simple justice.

I believe this is not only the preferred approach but the only one that will work. The unavoidable realities that confront us in the 1980s and 1990s will require clear-headedness, free from ideological constraint. It will not, however, be the clear-headedness of a theoretician, but rather of a practitioner of human contact.

I think these realities do represent the waterfall referred to in the preface. The task ahead is to recognize the existence of the waterfall, and to begin the process of dealing with it. This task can be accomplished only if there is a firm understanding of what motivates us as human beings and the boundaries beyond which policies cannot go without inviting a severe backlash.

The Realities—An Introduction

Obviously there are many issues we will have to face before the turn of the century. What follows is a discussion of eight that seem to me inescapable and significant. The list is by no means exhaustive, and I'm sure there are other issues whose importance cannot be grasped at this point.

I have attempted here to avoid likes and dislikes. I happen to admire the kind of people who buy wood stoves, for example, but I disagree with their probable views on nuclear power. I find many corporate chief executive officers remarkably removed from the day-to-day problems of the poor, but that does not affect my belief that those executives should be helping the poor.

I would ask the reader to absorb these next eight chapters with an ideological clean slate. The question should not be whether I am consistent with liberal or Democratic traditions, but rather whether my analysis of reality is correct or not. Later, the matter of philosophy can be considered.

2/Energy:
The First Reality

There rages a great debate among scientists as to how the world began and when. In addition, there is continuing discussion in some religious communities as to whether the biblical description of our beginnings is correct, or whether Darwin's theory of evolution is to be believed.

In any case, I think it's fair to say that almost all parties to these discussions would agree that the amount of oil in the ground is finite. Neither the laws of physics nor the laws of theology allow for the "production" (i.e., the creation) of more oil and other fossil fuels.

What is in the ground, then, is in the ground. Unless we experience divine intervention, at some point in the foreseeable future there will be no more. To the extent that we use that finite resource, we diminish it. Since the world has collectively decided to consume a finite resource at a rate of some 60 million barrels a day, it is clearly a diminishing resource, temporary oil gluts notwithstanding.

Oil is a finite, diminishing resource.

These six words tell us almost everything. The preservation of America and the world requires that the facts be known and understood by every schoolboy and schoolgirl—and their parents. It's no easy task.

In 1976, my second year as a member of Congress, I was conducting a town meeting in my district. By then I had invested a great deal of time on the energy issue, and was using the town meeting as a means to convince my constituents of the severity of the crisis. After a prolonged presentation, a woman rose to declare: "Congressman, God would not have put us on this earth if he wanted us to run out of oil." So much for my powers of persuasion. Nevertheless, the reality remains and will have to be dealt with.

To the extent that we construct a world society whose viability and stability depend on a finite, diminishing resource, there are serious problems when it becomes a finite, diminished resource. By "diminished," I don't mean that 60 million barrels a day will diminish to zero barrels a day. But eventually, increasingly less than 60 million barrels per day will be practicably produced—or an amount far below the needs we have built into our society. (Consumption of oil at the 60-million-barrel level presumes "cheap" oil, i.e., $10 to $40 a barrel.)

Since there are oil deposits that are recoverable if the price rises to $100 barrel or more, it is often pointed out that the petroleum shortage exists only for "cheap" oil. This is a self-deluding argument that overlooks two obvious facts: first, even expensive oil is finite; and second, for some uses, $100 a barrel for oil is the same as no oil.

The 1973–74 energy crisis was caused by a cutoff of only 2.0 million barrels a day of oil production by the Arab states. The 1979 energy crisis was caused by a shortfall of only 2.0 million barrels a day. There is an excruciatingly limited capacity in our world to endure even minor blips in energy production. This addiction of the world to its oil "fix" has all the characteristics of any other addiction. A heroin addict is incapable, for example, of avoiding the shock of withdrawal if he cuts back on his intake.

The dilemma, however, is not only our inelastic demand for oil. In addition, there is the logistical problem of where it is and who controls it. In this case the problem is the OPEC nations of the Persian Gulf and elsewhere.

Close off the Persian Gulf long enough, and the free-world economy would collapse. It's as simple as that. The area is the source of only 30 percent of world oil production, but the lack of this 30 percent would absolutely devastate the global industrial base.

In 1979, 32 percent of our imported oil was shipped from that region, 73 percent of France's, 40 percent of West Germany's, 62 percent of Italy's, and 72 percent of Japan's. Indeed, the overall U.S. dependence on imported oil (38 percent in August 1980) is far less than that of France, Germany, Belgium, Italy, Greece, Spain, and Japan (100 percent). Among the industrial nations, only Great Britain and Canada are better situated.

Yet, these are the good old days. Current U.S. oil production is 10.2 million barrels a day, down from a peak of 11.5 million in 1970. By the year 2000, even counting Alaskan oil, offshore development, and enhanced oil recovery, daily production will range between 4 and 7 million barrels, depending on whose numbers you believe.

The non-Communist world oil production of around 52 million barrels a day will peak by the end of the century. By the year 2000, it is likely to range between 40 and 60 million barrels a day, again depending on which source you believe. In any case, the *demand* for oil will continue to increase as more and more developing nations seek to industrialize their economies, and, as many believe, the Soviet Bloc becomes a net importer of oil in the 1980s.

Obviously, we cannot get there from here. We have structured a world that is petroleum-dependent; but unfortunately, it is dependent on a petroleum base that is finite and diminishing.

Oil is a finite, diminishing resource.

Each gallon of gasoline consumed by a motorist is a gallon that is gone forever. It is a gallon of gasoline that will not be available for the children of that motorist.

Each barrel of American oil that is consumed is one barrel of oil no longer available to our country for the future.

The Arab embargo in 1973–74, the fall of the Shah in 1979, the Soviet invasion of Afghanistan in 1979, the Iran-Iraq war that began in 1980, the Israeli attack on Iraq's nuclear facility in 1981—these events make up a chain of circumstances that threatens our oil lifeline. The Persian Gulf is absolutely vital to our national security interests. The Western countries, out of necessity, have pledged themselves to keeping the Gulf open. Many nations cannot survive as industrial powers without Persian Gulf oil; therefore to cut it off would be the functional equivalent of attacking their national security, thus compelling an act of war to prevent such a catastrophe. It is often said that we would have to go in to protect "our" oil. While the urgency of such an act is accepted, the use of the possessive "our" is not. Imagine our reaction if the Russians went into Canada to protect "their" wheat!

This vulnerability to foreign oil, this fragility of our industrial machine, is unprecedented in American history. It is real. And it is a national security tripwire of the most serious consequences.

I would go one step further than President Carter's statement that the energy crisis is the moral equivalent of war. The energy crisis *is* war. And we should treat it as we would any war: with top priority, complete mobilization, total commitment.

This talk of national security and linkage of oil and war may seem overstated. In my town meetings in Massachusetts, I often encounter skepticism. Here is one way I have used to make it seem more concrete.

Suppose you are the chief military planner in the Kremlin. You are instructed to prepare a war plan that will result in the destruction of the West. You have to analyze the options available and make a recommendation. The Politburo has decided to abandon its "time is on our side," "target of opportunity" strategy. (More on this in Chapter 3.)

After careful analysis, you decide that you have three main options:

First: To engage in a first-strike nuclear attack, hoping to catch the United States by surprise. It would require launching the Soviet ICBM force against America's land-based missiles, airfields, submarine bases, and command centers, and holding the less capable Soviet submarine and bomber forces in reserve. The attack would theoretically wipe out America's ICBM's, and leave the United States with the sole option of attacking cities in the USSR, because all of our highly accurate counter-silo missiles would have been lost to this first strike. The assumption is that no American President would decide to retaliate, knowing that if the United States did so, American cities would then be obliterated by the remaining Soviet nuclear force.

This Soviet plan carries with it obvious risks. If the United States is not surprised, it will retaliate with its nuclear strike force. Even if the United States is taken completely unawares, and America's land-based ICBM and B-52 forces are rendered 100 percent inoperative (virtually impossible statistically), there remains America's submarine-based nuclear strike force, which would retaliate with

656 missiles and 5,120 warheads. Each warhead carries with it a destructive force equivalent to between two and forty Hiroshimas, depending on the particular warhead.

Second: To engage in a conventional force sweep across western Europe, deploying the Warsaw Pact nations against the NATO allies. This option would take advantage of the Warsaw Pact's numerical superiority in tanks, armored personnel carriers, and troops. The objective would be to conquer Europe and render the United States isolated and impotent.

This plan also carries risks. Such an attack would galvanize America and western Europe into a grimly determined response, as did Pearl Harbor. Battlefield victory would by no means be certain, given the advantages inherent in defensive technology (e.g., an antitank missile costs much less than a tank), given the fervor with which people defend their homelands, and given the very real question as to the willingness of eastern European soldiers to die for Mother Russia. In addition, there is the likelihood that Soviet success in battle would cause the NATO allies to resort to tactical nuclear weapons, thus beginning the unpredictable and uncontrollable escalation up the nuclear ladder and leading the combatants back to the first option.

Third: To launch Soviet fighter bombers to destroy the oil-exporting capability of the Persian Gulf states. The action would be completed swiftly, few if any Americans would be killed, it would involve no U.S. or European homelands, and the Arab states would be unable to retaliate. How would the United States respond? Would it attack the Soviet Union with nuclear weapons and invite a devastating exchange? What *is* certain is that destruction of Persian Gulf oil would ruin the Western economies. Japan would fall first, finally becoming victim to its barren energy resource base. Western Europe would also succumb, with Germany and France grinding to a halt first, and Great Britain last. Plunged into a depression caused by the economic collapse of its allies, and cut off from a significant portion of its own oil requirements, the United States would be left to wither.

There are obvious risks for the Soviets in this third option also, but of the three, which would you recommend as a Soviet military planner? To my mind, the third represents the clear choice, and is the one generally chosen by my constituents when put in this hypothetical situation.

There are other possible scenarios, of course, and other considerations. But if you ponder these three—and their relative probability of occurrence—long enough, one thought stands out. How is it that we consider the first two as serious, as war, and spend tens of billions of dollars to reduce our vulnerability, while we hardly ever speak about the third with equal gravity? How is it that we pump iron to strengthen our biceps, do sit-ups to toughen our gut, yet hardly ever pay attention to our Achilles' heel? It makes no sense.

The energy crisis *is* war.

Now how does the political structure deal with this nasty reality? Let me resort to simplistic generalizations that, despite their overstatement, do represent reasonably accurate summaries of the two stances of our political parties.

The Republican approach can be summed up as: "Production, production, production." We should, as Ronald Reagan would have it, unleash the oil companies. How do you produce more of a finite diminishing resource? You don't. You extract it. A massive search for and extraction of U.S. oil is just fine for you and me. Try explaining why it's such a great idea to your children and grandchildren. For them, it is a catastrophic policy because reserves will be that much lower. To concentrate on domestic production is to bring even closer the day of depleted U.S. reserves. It is, in fact, a "Drain America First" approach.

In November 1979, despairing of the likelihood of convincing people of this reality, I resorted to satire and proposed a Dinosaur Oil Production program. If we insisted upon "producing" oil, then we could only do it the way nature does. We would breed dinosaurs, bury them, and after 2 million years, we would have "produced" oil. Because of its absurdity, the idea received a reasonable amount of notice and, ironically, made a point that my serious discussion had been unable to get across.

Any commonsense view of resource management would tell you to husband your scarce resources, not exploit them. Fossil fuels should be viewed as a vehicle of transition to a non-fossil energy economy, not as an end in themselves. The case for more production has enormous political appeal, and I understand that. It offers the solace of continuation of current habits. It avoids the need to confront the fact that since 1968 we have consumed more oil than in all the preceding years of human history. (If every other country in the world used oil at our per capita rate, world reserves would be gone in five years.) It also ignores the need to ponder a serious and disturbing generational question. Do we do what is best for our generation, knowing that it makes all the more hazardous the survival of our children? Can maximum domestic energy production be squared with concern for our offspring? I don't think so.

The bankruptcy of this approach is evenly matched by the approach of the Democrats.

It is standard and effective political strategy that nothing serves a politician better than a good enemy. If you can identify a villain, you can generally get elected merely by lambasting him. The same principle applies in non-democratic societies. President Nasser used Israel for that purpose for years and shirked Egypt's problems.

Few institutions fit that role as neatly—and deservedly—as the oil companies. These corporate entities are on the whole insensitive, powerful, and removed. They make enormous amounts of money and they take it from everyone. Their leadership has grown accustomed to wielding considerable political and economic power. Oil company executives I have encountered are almost unfailingly brusque, exhibiting the impatience of people used to getting their way in government.

So, when faced with harsh realities, none of which will be favorably received by the constituents, what better course than to blast the oil companies? There is no pro-oil constituency to worry about, except in a few production states like Texas and Louisiana. Attacking them is a sure-fire applause getter. Thus, the Democrats rail against Exxon and Mobil and Gulf, which allows them to evade the real problem—that oil is a finite, diminishing resource.

I have almost always voted against the interests of the oil companies. I have not, to my knowledge, received 5¢ from any oil company political action committee in my political life. Nevertheless, the fact remains that the oil companies, for all their avarice and deception, are not the basic problem.

Even if the Archangel Michael were in charge of Exxon, or

Mobil, or Gulf, the energy crisis would not be solved. There would not be one more gallon of oil produced; there would not be a significant decline in the price of gasoline; and there would not be a change in the demand for energy.

But blaming the oil companies is good politics for any Democrat, just as calling for more production is good politics for any Republican. Damning the oil companies and unleashing the oil companies are both formidable political lines by any reckoning.

The energy crisis threatens our survival and both political parties give us bumper sticker "solutions." What's discouraging is that these "solutions" are well received by the voters. They are accepted because the reality of oil as a finite, diminishing resource has yet to penetrate public consciousness seriously. This is shown in countless ways.

Let me mention a rather common occurrence, one that appears to be benign, one that happens every day. A builder clears a tract of land that will contain twenty homes. He will make several decisions critical to the viability of his project. He will make one decision critical to the viability of his country: the energy efficiency requirements of the homes.

For some years, we have had the capability to design and build homes that require minimal fossil fuel energy. By employing passive solar design techniques, optimal insulation, and a wood stove, a builder can provide homes that need no oil or other fossil fuels. (Indeed, today there exist "superinsulated" homes that can be heated primarily by the warmth generated by people and appliances.) The homeowner will be protected against any decision by an oil sheik, oil company, or oil dealer. The home and its occupants will be virtually energy-independent—and significantly better off financially.

But the builder decides instead to construct houses in the same Garrison, or Cape Cod, or Ranch, or Federal style that he is familiar with. He installs an oil burner that will consume twenty barrels every winter. Each year that one decision will mean the consumption of four hundred barrels of oil in that twenty-home tract, or the export of $14,000 each winter from that neighborhood to OPEC.

Should war occur, the builder will be outraged at the arrogance of the offending Middle Eastern nation, will curse the Ayatollah (or whomever), and demand strong action. If his son is drafted, the matter may take on a different perspective.

The homebuilder is not likely to recognize the linkage between his decision and America's dilemma. He won't feel unpatriotic. Yet his decision, made without malice, and based on the economic signals he perceives, has hurt his country. And if you ask him to identify Americans who have made their nation vulnerable to Persian Gulf politics, it would never occur to him to name himself.

There is a dimension to this irony beyond the national security implications. If asked to designate the issue that troubles him most, the homebuilder will probably refer to the economy: inflation and stagnant economic growth. Asked who is to blame for these conditions, he will answer big government, big business, big labor, the multi-nationals, or whatever. Again, he will not think of himself. But his decision takes $14,000 out of our country each year and sends it to OPEC, thus weakening the dollar by adding to our balance-of-payments deficit. A weakened dollar means more inflation. In addition, the greater the dependence on foreign oil, the more likely there will be further price increases in the future.

As to the stagnant economy, if the $14,000 were left in the national economy, it would have multiplied twice in the course of a year and the national economy would have been $28,000 less stagnant. Over the fifty years of the tract's lifetime, the value today of the full cost to the economy of the homebuilder's single decision is some $1.4 million.

If that same homebuilder robbed the U.S. Treasury of $1.4 million and sent the money to a hostile foreign government, the reaction would be immediate. The country would be mobilized against him, he would be arrested, and his disloyalty to America recounted on the front pages and in the evening news programs. The only difference between the two events—the theoretical robbery and the real decision—is intent. The effect is exactly the same.

The point of this example is not to single out homebuilders as a group. They are no more or less patriotic than you or I. When it is more convenient or less expensive to consume energy than to conserve, we use it. The result is the precarious and, to my mind, intolerable position in which this country finds itself. Everyday acts, including many of my own, have serious implications for national security and economic viability.

And yet these consequences are unappreciated. The consumer who buys a gas-guzzler does not believe he is hurting America. A restaurateur who keeps his place at a cozy 72°F in the winter does not feel unpatriotic. A teenager who goes cruising in a car does not regard this as an act hostile to his country. A homemaker who installs an electric trash compacter does not perceive that creature comfort as aiding and abetting our enemies. A business executive who drives to work when he could take a bus or train doesn't view this action as a drain on national resources.

Is it fair to so characterize these acts? To the extent that they contribute to our dependence on foreign oil, the answer is Yes.

We are engaged as a nation in behavioral patterns and policies that can please only the Ayatollah Khomeini and Chairman Brezhnev. What we are doing is weakening America—not intentionally, but weakening it nonetheless.

Is the situation hopeless? No, there is a possible course of action, and we are beginning to see the first signs of public awareness.

With the 1973–74 oil embargo, energy research and development began to be taken seriously. At the end of the decade, a steady stream of reports and studies were published that were to sound depressingly similar. The first popularized report was the one entitled *Energy Future: A Report of the Energy Project at the Harvard Business School* (released in June 1979). It and other reports confirmed our worst fears. World oil production would not and could not keep pace with world demand, and we were heading toward a serious crisis.

Energy Future had a remarkable impact. It said things that others had been arguing for years, but since its source was the Harvard Business School, the book had the ring of authority. The authors appeared before congressional committees, Secretary of Energy Charles Duncan made a point of reading it, and mostly positive reviews appeared everywhere.

Its publication was an important step toward the process of educating America as to the realities of the energy crisis. It was followed by reports issued by Resources for the Future, the Ford

Foundation, the Mellon Institute, and the National Academy of Sciences—all identifying the seriousness of the crisis.

In September 1980, the Council on Environmental Quality and the State Department issued a comprehensive and controversial report on the future of global resources, *Global 2000.* Its conclusions were even more devastating. It projected that during the 1980s world oil production would approach geological estimates of maximum production capacity. Put another way, even with rapidly increasing prices, oil consumption would exceed new additions to reserves.

The next month, the Office of Technology Assessment published an even more detailed and thorough report, *World Petroleum Availability 1982–2000.* It concluded that there would be little or no increase in world oil production from conventional sources. Oil production in industrial non-Communist nations would begin to decline as soon as the early 1980s and by as much as 50 percent by the year 2000; OPEC nations would not be likely to increase their output; Eastern Bloc countries would become net importers of oil; and oil produced by the non-OPEC Third World would be exceeded by increased Third World demand.

Reading these reports is a particularly depressing exercise. They suggest clearly, as President Carter pointed out in his April 18, 1977, speech, that the energy crisis is "the moral equivalent of war." It is, in the terms used in the preface to this book, a "waterfall." The avoidance of this "waterfall" must become a national mandate.

There can be no spectators in such a call to arms. It's not Monday Night Football. We need a nation of G.I. Joe's and Rosie the Riveter's. I realize how corny that sounds, and how subject to ridicule it is. But we haven't experienced a truly national crisis since World War II.

In October of 1980, I stood in the arcade of a Beverly Hills hotel and watched the parade of Jaguars, Bentleys, Cadillacs, Mercedes, and Rolls Royces—and I wondered how those owners would react to the notion of less consumption (conspicuous or otherwise). Except during a "Pearl Harbor" crisis, chances are they would scoff. Why worry when you can "produce" your way out of this dilemma by "unleashing the oil companies"? But the waterfall is still ahead.

All this is most ironic, because (as will be argued later) the energy

crisis is not a crisis of technology but of management and collective
will. We know how to deal with it. It's like a runner facing the
prospect of an early morning jog. The running is not easy, but he
knows how to do it, and he knows that doing it is beneficial. The
hard part is getting out of a warm bed.

A Plan for Transition

Any war requires a strategy. A plan.

Conceptually, the plan I have to offer is quite simple. We are
living in a fossil fuel economy. We are dependent upon a resource
that is finite and diminishing. Since we certainly do not see ourselves as the last or next-to-last generation, we look to a future
where the finite resource has in fact diminished substantially. In
terms of oil, that worldwide process of decline will commence
before the year 2000.

That's the good news. The bad news is that any number of
political events, especially in the Middle East, can bring the day of
reckoning much closer. Other fossil fuels such as natural gas and
coal are more plentiful, but will be depleted at an increasingly rapid
rate as well. The same applies to synthetic fuels, for the obvious
reason that they are fossil fuel–derived.

A future world economy, then, must by definition be based on
inexhaustible energy sources if it is to survive. What are those
sources? Renewables and nuclear fusion. (The reader will note that
the reference is to *fusion,* not conventional nuclear energy. The
difference will be explained later.)

There are a host of renewable energy resources: active solar
collectors for heating water or space, passive solar design systems,
solar photovoltaic cells, hydroelectric energy, wind energy, geothermal energy, ground water systems that use the 55° temperatures
of the immediate subsurface, biomass, wood, gasohol, trash to energy, other resource recovery plants, ocean thermal systems, tidal
power, wave power, and others that will be discovered as time goes
on. All except the resource recovery plants tap into enormous
natural energy flows.

Then there is the fusion process and its various design systems (such as magnetic fusion and laser fusion). These systems ultimately will use isotopes of hydrogen derived from sea water and are virtually limitless sources of energy generation.

If the inexhaustibles are where we are going, how do we get there? The answer should be clear. We have to fill the gap in the meantime with fossil fuels and conventional nuclear energy.

But while the answer is obvious, the perspective is not. The prevailing perspective today argues that we should utilize the capacity to stretch these resources. We can stretch fossil fuels by tapping the so-called unconventional sources, such as tar sands, oil shale, and geo-pressurized methane. And we can extend conventional nuclear energy by using advanced converter reactors and breeder reactors. This is correct, although the processes are both technically difficult and very expensive. But there remains the basic reality—we need to begin relying on inexhaustible energy sources.

We have a "window," to use the terminology of the space program. That window will someday close—and we sure as hell better have made the transition before it does.

The consumption rate of these transitional fuels should be a function of the amount needed for transition. To oversimplify, if it will take fifty years to achieve transition, then each year we should consume only one-fiftieth of the fossil fuel and uranium reserves—assuming we could burn them all.

If it takes fifty years for transition, and we have consumed the fossil fuel and uranium reserves in thirty years, then we have Armageddon.

To take a more pedestrian example: Suppose a person is unemployed: he has $6,000 in a savings account. Now, if he knows he will have a job in six months, he can understand quite easily that he must draw down on that savings account no more than $1,000 a month. If he decides he would be happier spending $2,000 a month and proceeds to do so, the first three months will be delightful, the second three catastrophic. Unfortunately, the catastrophic nature of the last three months will be best understood only during those last three months. The key to survival is to understand it early on and to act accordingly.

The same principles apply to a world depleting its finite resources at far too rapid a pace to allow for transition.

To make matters even worse, let us assume that our unemployed friend spends $2,000 a month (or even $1,000 a month) and at the end of six months still has no job. The same disaster looms for a world depleting its finite resources and blithely ignoring the necessity of fully developing its inexhaustible resources.

Thus, we must focus our efforts on three goals. First, to find a job (i.e., accelerate the development of renewables and nuclear fusion); second, to spend only $1,000 a month (i.e., deplete the fossil fuel and conventional nuclear resources at a rate consistent with transition); and third, to get the most out of that $1,000 (i.e., take conservation and energy-efficient technologies seriously).

Finally, let me apply this discussion of resource depletion to the United States specifically. In 1979 we consumed some 79 quads of energy.* President Carter's National Energy Plan II projected that by the year 2000 we will consume 114 quads, or a 43 percent increase over current levels.

There is no way that can happen.

Given the fact that we are stretched thin to supply current needs, and given the 40–60 percent decline in U.S. oil production by 2000 and the peaking of world oil production by the end of the century, a 43 percent increase in current levels of U.S. consumption is impossible. Even if it were physically or politically conceivable to increase U.S. imports from 6 to 17 million barrels a day (and it is neither), such an import schedule would bankrupt us financially. The cost could exceed half a *trillion* dollars per year, a hemorrhaging of our resources that clearly could not be tolerated, representing about $10,000 per family per year.

Supposing the increased production of synthetic fuels and natural gas could substitute for the U.S. oil production decline (an accomplishment virtually beyond reach), it still would allow only for current levels of consumption, and then only if we could import our current levels from a world market characterized by greater demands and lesser supplies than exist today.

---

*A quad is equal to one quadrillion (one million billion) BTU's. One BTU is roughly the energy you would get from burning a single flat toothpick.

But these severe problems only begin to scratch the surface of the difficulties.

The amount of capital and manpower and effort needed to meet the 114 quad energy demand, using other fossil fuels and conventional nuclear energy, is staggering, even if one assumes (and many don't) that the task is physically possible.

And if we managed to meet that demand level, we would have done so by draining all those economic and human resources from someplace else. That someplace else is renewables and nuclear fusion. The six months passed, and there was no job.

Clearly, then, our present course won't work. It is a straight line from here to the waterfall.

How do we structure a policy whose basis is *transition*? What follows is a proposal meant to offer guidance rather than specifics. The goals outlined are technically feasible, and would be rendered infeasible only by the lack of collective will.

By the year 2000 . . .

1. We must learn to maintain economic growth without consuming more energy than we use today. This requires a commitment to conservation and the serious pursuit of energy-efficient technologies.

2. We must maximize the use of renewable sources of energy, achieving the 20 quads of energy (25% of current demand) that is technically feasible and the technological demonstration of nuclear fusion.

3. We must employ a mix of oil, gas, coal, synthetic fuels, and conventional nuclear energy production to make up the difference between supply and demand.

By the year 2030, we should be well into the transition, with the inexhaustible sources supplying most of our energy needs. Fossil fuel would be used as a secondary energy source and in applications where its chemistry is so far irreplaceable, such as plastics and feedstocks.

Although there are technological difficulties in this approach, the consensus in the scientific community is that none is considered beyond the capacity of our science and technology. It is the economic, organizational, and social adjustments that loom as the major obstacles to this transition. We are dealing here with a new world, and no one looks forward to making the change. But one factor may make the change a little more comfortable—we don't have a choice.

If the goal is transition, achieved via the various sources of energy, we need a framework for managing that objective as smoothly as possible.

There are three basic elements to that framework: the capacity for emergency response, a pricing policy, and the role of government.

Emergency Response. Suppose we have accepted the reality of the energy crisis and are proceeding toward transition. Reason has triumphed over dogma, and the nation has avoided the "waterfall." Then, suddenly, the government of Saudi Arabia topples, or is toppled—with its oil-exporting capacity eliminated. At that point, transition becomes a secondary issue. Survival in the short term is now the primary concern. We need an emergency response capability, a strategic petroleum reserve in place to buy us precious time to adjust. There must be standby allocations to ensure the equitable distribution of available supplies, such as military forces, ambulances, food producers. And there should be plans for federal, state, and local efforts to coordinate emergency conservation measures. Not one of these mechanisms exists today.

Pricing Policy. It is difficult for liberals to accept, but fuel must be priced at its replacement cost, and that means decontrol of oil prices. Such pricing should be tied to what is charged by OPEC, since each extra barrel of oil used in America costs the import price. A lower figure imposes an artificial price mechanism, whose unreality will be reflected in unrealistic practices and behavior.

Let me put this in perspective.

There is no question that America is now consuming less than it has in the recent past. Annual per capita consumption in 1980 fell to the lowest level since 1975. That year oil imports dropped 1.7 million barrels per day. The burning of home heating oil and diesel fuel was down 13.2 percent, and industrial boiler fuel 11.4 percent. The use of gasoline, which had always been thought to be unresponsive to price levels, declined 12 percent during 1979–80.

People are driving smaller cars, buying wood stoves, and installing insulation, largely because the cost of not doing so is increasing. Many Americans, it is true, are conserving because of their concern over the severity of the energy crisis; they feel strongly about conservation as a matter of principle. But the determining factors impelling most savings have been, unquestionably, gas lines and the quadrupling of prices. The growing sales of small cars have had a direct relationship to the availability and price of gasoline.

In most respects, we will be better off if the price of energy begins to approximate its true value. I realize this statement will seem preposterous to a Third World inhabitant whose country is being crushed under the weight of oil payments. It will seem equally absurd to someone who can no longer afford to heat his house.

But from a larger societal perspective, the point is valid. If we were to crush OPEC and lower the price of gasoline to, let's say, 80¢ a gallon, it would be a short-term bonanza and a long-term disaster. We would enjoy the immediate benefits and forfeit all chance of transition. There would be much less expenditure on the exploration of remote oil fields; much less development of solar panels; much less pursuit of synthetic fuels; much less serious conservation; much less emphasis on small cars. Transition would be rendered impossible.

So decontrol serves us well in a rather savage, Darwinian way.

But what of decontrol on its own, as preferred by the Reagan administration and the oil lobby—what of decontrol without a windfall profits tax and programs, like low-income assistance, to cushion the blow and provide time for adjustment?

The issue of economic equity will be raised in Chapter 10. Here I want to focus solely on the transition implications of decontrol, with and without the attendance of the windfall profits tax and related assistance programs.

What we are aiming for is transition, not maximum "production." There is no question that decontrol by itself will maximize production. At the $80 a barrel price level, for example, half of America would be buying drilling rigs and puncturing their backyards in hopes of hitting a bonanza. So you have a production policy (and a "Drain America First" policy) of monumental proportions. But that's all you have.

If the policy is transition, the objectives are to conserve, increase production to provide transition energy, and develop inexhaustible resources (higher prices accomplish all of these objectives). But does decontrol by itself insure the transition? The answer is no. Price-induced conservation, without the dissemination of information—energy audits, appropriate literature—will lag far behind potential. Price-induced conservation without the financial means to conserve—weatherization programs for the poor, and the Conservation Bank for the middle-income—will by definition not take place. The development of mass transit to conserve energy, the commercialization of solar heating, the widespread use of wind machines, the construction of community resource recovery plants, will all remain theoretical responses to higher prices. The marketplace works imperfectly when capital and the access to that capital are limited.

Thus it serves the transition policy to employ a windfall profits tax and direct those monies to the long-term necessity of maximizing conservation and developing inexhaustible resources. A policy of maximum fossil fuel production that drains funds from this objective is *transitionally* bankrupt.

The Role of Government. Imagine, if you will, being a U.S. senator who has actively and successfully pushed for legislation involving conservation, renewables, and nuclear fusion because you believe in transition and the need to avoid the "waterfall." The Reagan administration espouses the twin doctrines of "getting government off our backs" and "letting the marketplace prevail." In pursuit of those doctrines, the Solar and Conservation Banks are to be killed; the conservation and renewable resource programs in the Department of Energy are to be eviscerated; and the program objectives enumerated in the Magnetic Fusion Engineering Act are scaled back. You don't like it. You don't agree with it. You think it's rigid ideology—and shortsighted. The Secretary of Energy responds to your concern by saying that these cuts do not reflect energy policy but are simply budget cuts. We are getting government off our backs so that the free market system can work its magic.

Well, you don't subscribe to the substance, but at least there is an identifiable approach.

Earlier, however, a staff member had whispered in your ear the rumor that the administration was going to spend some $250 million to proceed with the Clinch River Breeder Reactor. Your reaction is one of deep skepticism, since in 1977 a similar request had been described, in the words of a Republican congressman, as "totally incompatible with our free market approach to energy policy." Here was a case of a heavy federal subsidy to a multibillion-dollar industry for the commercial demonstration of a technology that would not be needed for decades, if ever. The congressman in question was David Stockman, now Director of the Office of Management and Budget, and the architect of President Reagan's financial program. How does the Secretary of Energy respond to such an inconsistency? Well, he tells us, we need to establish U.S. technological leadership. Ask about conservation and solar energy, and he says we've got to cut the budget to reduce inflation. Ask why the government wants to spend $37 million to help Metropolitan Edison clean up Three Mile Island—a perfect example of a public dole to private enterprise to rectify a private-sector error—and the Secretary replies unabashedly, "It's research." Ask why conservation and solar research and development are cut 70 percent while nuclear power gets increases, and the answer is unintelligible.

An impossible case? A wild hypothesis? It happened to me in February 1981.

So where does that leave us? Right back where we began. Forget the slogans. Let's ask the hard questions about how things work in the real world, not how they sound at dinner parties.

The unfettered and well-informed marketplace is a very efficient instrument. It adjusts rapidly and performs at a level generally more productive than government. It is not without its flaws, however. And one serious flaw is its time horizon: its focus is short-term (more on this in Chapter 4).

When you deal with rates of returns, annual reports, quarterly dividends, and payback periods, there is a limited capacity to see far ahead. So transition is not a matter of serious discussion, let alone serious decisionmaking, in the free market of today. Almost no one in the corporate boardroom is worried about the sources of energy in 2020. To survive in the immediate term, executives have to worry about enough profits to keep stockholders at bay.

But since the need to develop inexhaustible energy sources is still with us, the incapacity to perceive it does not lessen its reality.

Let me use a metaphor: A car is traveling at night at a given rate of speed. The laws of physics require 300 feet to stop the vehicle; the headlights, however, provide only 200 feet of illumination. In the road is an obstacle that won't go away. At 200 feet, the driver (the free market system) will see the obstacle. All that's required then is to repeal the laws of physics.

Assuming that one wishes to avoid crashing into the obstacle, one needs the capacity to see into the distance. This is the area of greatest weakness in a short-term–oriented free market system.

So who's going to provide the focus? There is only one other player—the public sector. The objective should be to "unleash" the free market system to perform the tasks it can do more efficiently (allocation of resources, production, marketing, etc.) and "unleash" the public sector to do those things that are necessary for transition but that the private sector won't get around to doing adequately (long-term research and development, mid-term demonstration and commercialization, short-term public education, market stimulation).

It is essential that we keep our eye on the objective, transition. To do that—and we have no alternative—requires the jettisoning of rhetoric, no matter how much applause it generates.

These are the guideline policies for transition. Now I am going to review the specifics.

Conservation

Conservation is like Hank Aaron. Sure, steady, reliable, long-term, effective—and unexciting. In a time of Willie Mays, Mickey Mantle, and Reggie Jackson, Aaron holds the home-run record; but unlike them, he endured years of relative obscurity. It was not until he overtook Babe Ruth that most people noticed.

Conservation is simply not congruent with modern American attitudes. When was the last time you heard anyone say, "Waste not, want not"? We are "into" bigger, better, flashier, and easier. The ethic of understatement and frugality went out long before today's generation of decisionmakers formed their basic attitudes.

Conservation doesn't appeal psychologically. It's perceived as a weak alternative for those who don't have the capacity to do something else.

We are bedazzled by the energy options that challenge our greatness, rather than by the one option that works best.

In 1974, the Ford Foundation study entitled *A Time to Choose* concluded that conservation was as important as supply; that future economic growth was not tied to future energy growth; and that after 1985, economic growth could be sustained without increased energy use.

The report was scoffed at and then ignored.

The Harvard Business School Energy Project, the National Academy of Sciences, the Mellon Institute study, and others, all rediscovered conservation. The advantages of conservation are impressive: it is obtainable at costs lower than increased supply, thus leaving more income for economic growth; it is more benign environmentally than supply alternatives; it can be implemented with shorter lead times than supply technologies; and it creates more jobs than increased supply.

Faced with this crescendo of scientific data and a growing American awareness of the need for conservation, President Reagan declared: "Conservation means being colder in the winter and warmer in the summer." So much for science.

But reality will win out; in fact, it has already begun to do so. Back in 1972, conventional wisdom suggested that U.S. energy demands would be 160 quads by the year 2000. The guru of conservation and renewables, Amory Lovins, predicted a 125 quad level. He was considered foolish. Today, conventional wisdom is moving to and below the 100 quad level. Indeed, some studies are showing that we could support our current lifestyles and economic growth with 30–40 percent less energy use, and by the year 2000 we could be at today's energy use level with no loss of economic growth and virtual elimination of oil imports.

The problem with this design is that it represents the thinking of science. And science does not equal national policy, which is often determined by image, special interests, and rhetoric.

To take one example: the catch phrase of 1980 was synthetic fuels: by transforming coal, tar sands, and oil shale into liquid fuels, we could move toward energy independence. So we poured billions of dollars into the concept. It was big and mighty and exciting. Conservation never had a chance.

Advocates claim that synthetic fuels refined into home heating oil will cost around $40 a barrel. Applying conservation techniques to a home results in savings that require a one-time investment of $200 to save a barrel every year thereafter. (These figures can vary, but those quoted here are within reasonable limits of estimates.) At least to begin with, then, synthetic fuels seem by far the better investment. Over time, however, the picture becomes a little different. In year one, the figures read:

> 1 barrel of oil conserved—$200
> 1 barrel of synthetic fuel—$40

In year two, synthetic fuel still looks good:

> 2 barrels of oil conserved—$200
> 2 barrels of synthetic fuel—$84
> ($40 for barrel #1, and $44 for barrel #2, assuming a 10% increase in costs per year)

By year four, the picture has changed quite noticeably:

> 4 barrels of oil conserved—$200
> 4 barrels of synthetic fuel—$186
> ($40, $44, $48.80, and $53.20 for each barrel)

By year ten, the reversal is complete:

> 10 barrels of oil conserved—$200
> 10 barrels of synthetic fuel—$617.80

And by year twenty, the reversal has become a rout:

> 20 barrels of oil conserved—$200
> 20 barrels of synthetic fuel—$2,291.30*

From the viewpoint of fiscal conservatives, consideration of this picture should have resulted in an immediate adoption of conserva-

---

*This figure is not in constant dollars, and would be smaller if that were the basis of calculation.

tion. It hasn't happened. To the contrary, the Conservation Bank* was eliminated and the overall conservation budget authority heavily reduced, from $817 million to $195 million in the Reagan budget. If all this seems incredible, let us look at one more example. The United States Congress appropriates $1.8 billion a year to assist poor people in paying their fuel bills—a worthy expenditure, and one I have voted for. But the $1.8 billion leaves the Treasury and goes eventually to OPEC, with steps in between. Why is spending $1.8 billion this year, next year, the year after, and the year after that acceptable, and spending adequate funds for conservation, which does *not* go to OPEC, unacceptable? I'll never understand it.

What would constitute a viable conservation program? First, the economic attractiveness of conservation must be stressed by pricing oil at its replacement cost. Second, we should have major programs to speed conservation efforts in the areas of housing, automobiles, and industry:

1. A massive program of retrofitting existing residential and commercial buildings should be begun—savings of up to 50 percent in fuel use are both possible and practical. The homes of the poor should be insulated by a comprehensive weatherization program (Reagan would cut it); the insulation of middle-class homes should be encouraged by the interest subsidies in the Conservation Bank and home audits (Reagan would eliminate both); and the insulation of homes of the wealthy should be encouraged by conservation tax credits (Reagan would leave that intact).

2. The Congress should pass legislation setting automobile fuel efficiency standards after 1985. Existing cars on the road average a mere 15 mpg; even the 1981 models average only 22 mpg. This is enormously wasteful. The fact is that 50–70 mpg automobiles are possible, and they should be the major part of our new car fleet by the late 1980s.

3. "Co-generation" should be pursued by industrial users. Although industrial output rose by 12 percent between 1973 and 1978 and energy use dropped by 3.4 percent, the conservation potential

*The Solar Energy and Energy Conservation Bank would provide subsidized loans for conservation and solar investments in residential and commercial buildings.

is largely untapped. Since electric utilities discard two-thirds of the heat they generate to produce steam, and since industry uses steam in its processes, the coupling of these two activities (co-generation) is a natural. If this were accomplished, we could cut energy conversion losses by more than half. Co-generation is the norm in Europe and should be here as well.

These programs represent a sample of the multitude of suggestions detailed in the Massachusetts Plan in the Appendix.

Conservation is the *sine qua non* of transition. The threat is time and only conservation can buy time. To return to the metaphor used in the preface, conservation extends the decision zone and delays our entry to the point of no return. The fact that it helps our gross national product, our balance of payments, and our national security as well should not be lightly dismissed either.

If conservation buys time, its purchase is meaningful only as it relates to a transition to the inexhaustible sources of energy: renewables and nuclear fusion. And the most familiar, practical, and benign of these sources are the renewables.

The Renewables

Renewables are energy sources that utilize natural "energy flows." Energy from the sun hits the earth at the rate of 170,000 million megawatts. Mankind uses energy today at the rate of 10 million megawatts, a fraction of what the sun provides us. Some of the sun directly strikes the surface, some of it heats the atmosphere. It is this unevenness of impact that creates winds. Of that which hits the surface, some evaporates water, which falls as rain and creates our rivers; some hits plants, which photosynthesize the sun's energy and turns the carbon dioxide (CO_2) in the air into biomass (trees, plants, etc); and some reaches the oceans, creating warm surface waters. The winds create waves and, with the earth's rotation, ocean currents.

These are all huge energy flows that dwarf mankind's puny use of the finite resources. Their sheer size mocks those who regard them as somehow inadequate. The amount of solar energy hitting the earth every two weeks is equal to all the energy in known oil, gas, and coal reserves available to us forever.

Even more important than the overwhelming magnitude of these energy flows is their inexhaustibility. They occur whether we tap them or not; and our using them does not generally diminish the flows at all. (The obvious exception here is the depletion of fuel wood forests, due to poor management worldwide—see the *Global 2000* report.)

Renewable sources of energy possess inherent strengths and advantages that make the case for them overwhelming on their merits, if not on psychological grounds. More and more decisionmakers outside of government are taking renewables seriously; these include private citizens as well as scientists, homeowners as well as industrialists.

The chief advantages of renewables are:

1. By definition, a renewable resource is infinite in its supply. There is no need to worry about solar, or wind, or biomass being a finite, diminishing resource.

2. The economy of renewables is totally American. There is no need to import them, and therefore the United States gets to keep its energy dollars to strengthen the domestic economy and increase the GNP.

3. The supply of renewables is also totally American, so there are no national security concerns about dependence upon hostile foreign powers for supply.

4. Renewables, like conservation, intrude least on the biosphere. These resources are for the most part environmentally benign, and don't present society with a Faustian choice between energy and the environment.

5. Renewables provide more flexible and diverse options because they come in all forms. Thermal energy (heating) from direct solar energy; electricity from photovoltaics (solar cells), wind machines, and hydroelectric plants. Liquid and gaseous fuels from biomass. These sources are resilient, decentralized, and require short lead times to plan and construct.

6. Renewables are more labor-intensive than conventional sources, thus providing a better impact on employment.

Given the fact that fossil fuels and nuclear energy do not offer these advantages, a visitor from another planet would guess that the United States is investing heavily in renewables and somewhat less so in other forms of energy. The truth is that as a nation, we have allotted $200 billion of public funds for the development of fossil fuel and nuclear energy, and around $15 billion for renewables and conservation (almost all of which is accounted for by large hydroelectric dams). This historical record is not just a matter of past decisionmaking. Although the solar budget has grown dramatically over the last five years, the Reagan budget would kill the Solar Bank and would cut the solar budget by 60 percent.

The arguments made against renewables are several. First, it is maintained that renewables are too intermittent and inconsistent to contribute to baseload (continuous) electrical generation capacity. This contention is not entirely valid. Hydroelectric power and biomass are suitable baseload sources. Wind power and solar energy can contribute to intermediate and peak loads, as several utilities have shown.

It is also argued that renewables are too costly and impractical. But there are a variety of renewable technologies, some at early stages of development, others that have been known for ages. One hundred years ago, our nation ran almost entirely on wood, water, and wind. Passive solar energy, active hot water heating, and wood stoves are economical today. Some technologies such as photovoltaics, solar process heat, and wind may still be too expensive for widespread use, but as the price of conventional energy sources rises, as hidden subsidies are removed, and as manufacturing experience is gained, these technologies are beginning to emerge.

Lastly, it is said that renewable resources don't provide very much energy. If we consider each such resource individually—for example, low-head hydro—this argument is accurate. But if we take all the renewables collectively, it is simply not correct. Fifteen to twenty quads by the year 2000 is technically possible. Even today, wood supplies more energy than nuclear power.

The real difficulty with renewables is one of attitude. Solar energy has usually been viewed as something advocated by a fringe element. Its champions have been customarily regarded as bearded hippies smoking grass, chewing sunflower seeds, and living in communes, and joined by liberal suburbanites who espouse various impractical notions. The attitude here comes very close to that encountered by conservation. It's undramatic. A multibillion-dollar synthetic fuels program is the stuff of legend—and TV commercials; a resource recovery plant is not. Reinforcing this attitude are a variety of institutional barriers: Renewables are diverse and decentralized. Their implementation can't be brought about by seven oil companies or four reactor vendors; instead, it will take the combined efforts of 100,000 builders, 60,000 architects, two million craftsmen, thousands of engineers, bankers, local officials, corporate energy managers, and utility executives. Unfortunately, these groups tend to be conservative, avoid risks, are slow to innovate, and do very little R & D.

These attitudes are gradually being turned around—not in Washington, but throughout the country, as the rationale for renewables strikes home to ordinary citizens and corporate leaders alike. The solar industry, for one, is growing at the rate of 35 percent a year. But there is still a long way to go.

What kinds of renewable energy sources should we pursue? The fact is that all of them involve technologies that are either currently applicable for wide-scale use or are within reach of that stage. A range of options follows:

Passive Solar. A passive solar building is designed to stay warm in winter and cool in summer with minimal backup heating. The design can be as simple as putting extra-large windows on the building's south side to collect the low winter sun and overhangs to shade these same windows from the high summer sun. These techniques are now being amply demonstrated (30,000–50,000 homes currently use passive solar energy as a principal heating source), are effective even in cold northern climes, and need only be applied on a broad scale.

Active Solar. Active solar collectors are typically placed on or near a building, and use either air or water to capture the sun's energy and transfer it to the building's heating system. While active space heating is not quite competitive as yet, solar hot water systems can generally be purchased with confidence and are economically competitive almost everywhere. Today, there are 215,000 active solar energy systems in the United States, while in Japan, more than 450,000 were sold just last year.

Solar Photovoltaic Cells. The widespread economical generation of electricity from photovoltaics is still a few years away, owing in part to the low level of federal funding. My amendment to promote photovoltaic development passed in 1977, but the project was poorly funded and desultorily pursued by the Department of Energy. Nonetheless, the cost of solar cells dropped from $24 in 1976 to about $6 in 1980. (A rate of 70¢ per peak watt is needed to compete in the residential market.) Currently, photovoltaics are being used in a variety of special applications but, given recent progress, many analysts see photovoltaics as being competitive by the late 1980s.

Hydroelectricity. Hydropower provides 12 percent of our electricity today, mostly through large dams. But there is significant energy potential at existing small dam sites as well. Hundreds of these "low head" hydro sites have been surveyed and evaluated, and the number of permit applications filed by private developers is growing rapidly. Existing requirements that utilities purchase power, and the availability of tax credits, have provided strong incentives for development that should be further encouraged by state and local government.

Wind Energy. There is now a growing market in small wind machines, and several utilities have been gaining experience with larger demonstration models. No major technological breakthroughs are needed, and engineering development and mass production are continuing to lower construction and operating costs. As conventional energy prices continue to rise, clusters of wind machines (wind farms) in favorable locations should begin to make a significant contribution to our electrical supply.

Biomass. This resource covers a large variety of organic feedstocks, primarily forests and crops. Many current biomass projects utilize wood and crop wastes (tree bark, mill waste, sugar cane residue). There are also projects designed to cultivate fast-growing trees, such as the eucalyptus, and certain crops with high energy content, like sugar beets.

Biomass can be used directly in solid form, distilled into alcohol, or gasified. At present, direct burning of wood accounts for more U.S. energy production than nuclear power; residential wood-burning has increased sixfold since 1977. There are 15 million wood stoves in the U.S. (including one in the author's home). Wood is also being used as an industrial boiler fuel.

Alcohol from crops and grains, ethanol, can be mixed with gasoline to form gasohol. In countries like Brazil, gasohol is widely used as an automobile fuel. Two problems need to be resolved prior to its large-scale production here. One is technical: In producing a given amount of alcohol, inefficient oil-fired distilleries can use more energy than is contained in that amount of alcohol. The solution is to derive process heat from renewable sources and develop more efficient processing technologies. The other factor is moral and philosophical: how does one balance the needs for energy and food in a world where tens of thousands are literally starving to death?

Alcohol from wood, methanol, is less problematical than ethanol. It can be employed as an oil substitute in utility and industrial boilers, and used in vehicles whose engines have been modified.

Municipal Solid Waste. The use of solid waste to produce process heat and electricity has been successful in several areas, both abroad and in American communities like Saugus, Massachusetts. These systems are particularly attractive to densely populated communities without other energy resources. Such communities are in danger of losing their energy-intensive industries, since those industries are becoming increasingly worried (and properly so) about the reliability of energy supply. Solid waste systems can provide electricity, process heat, steam, and a solution to waste disposal, all at the same time. In Europe, 3 percent of all trash is now converted into energy, as compared to 1 percent in America. Considering that we produce 170 million tons of trash each year, and a ton is equal to 1.2 barrels of oil, the potential is significant.

Geothermal Energy. An energy source that could be significant in areas where geothermal reservoirs are near the earth's surface. The hot water or steam can be used to directly provide heat for buildings or industry, or to generate electricity. Improved exploration, drilling, and utilization technologies should expand the use of this resource in favorable locations.

Ground Water Heat. This resource involves the use of the constant 55° Fahrenheit temperature of the immediate subsurface water of the earth. In much of the country, buildings have such an energy source beneath them, at reasonably close depths. Since the water is always constant in its temperature, a heat pump can use that temperature to keep buildings warm in winter and cool in summer.

Ocean Thermal Energy. This system involves the difference in temperature between warm surface and cold deep ocean waters that are found in equatorial waters such as the Gulf of Mexico, the Caribbean, and the Pacific near Hawaii. A heat engine can use this temperature difference to drive a turbine and generate electricity. Several prototypes are operating, but additional engineering development is necessary before this technology will be commercially viable. The significant potential of this resource could be tapped by ocean thermal energy conversion plants moored offshore which would transmit electricity to the shore via cable, or by roving plants that, for example, generate ammonia, which could be delivered to the shore by tanker.

This list of renewable resource systems is by no means exhaustive; there is also tidal power, wave action energy, solar industrial process heat, and central station solar repowering, among others. The range of applications is impressive. Equally impressive is the fact that when combined, these resources offer a significant solution to our energy requirements.

What is needed is the will to develop renewables. The task clearly can be done. In the 1960s, we decided that putting a man on the moon was in the national interest—and we did it with the Apollo Program.

President Carter's 1979 Domestic Policy Review of solar energy found that the technical limit of solar penetration by the year 2000 was 25 to 30 quads. A practical effort would yield 18 quads, or around 20 percent of the nation's energy in 2000, according to the administration's projections. The Carter administration set the goal at 20 percent. Given actual progress and the present government's commitment, however, even 12 percent would be a major miracle.

What possible reason can there be not to reach a 25 percent goal by the year 2000? Renewables save fossil fuels. They don't add to the balance-of-payments deficit, they add to our GNP. They help reduce inflation caused by a weakened dollar. They reduce dependence on foreign crude oil and so strengthen national security. They offer the least damage to the environment.

Yet we don't take them seriously.

Someday when the energy crisis worsens, those families dependent on renewable resources provided either by themselves, their municipality, or their utility will be considerably better off than those who have clung to fossil fuels. At that point the feasibility of renewables will be beyond debate.

Nuclear Fusion

The inexhaustible sources of energy are an odd couple indeed. Renewables are basically decentralized—fusion is highly centralized. Renewables are supported by environmentalists—fusion is viewed skeptically by many of them. Renewables are denigrated by many of the people who endorse fusion; yet these two alone occupy that magic category entitled the "long-term future." When all the other sources to be described later have faded and/or disappeared, these two will remain. It's an unholy alliance, but an alliance nonetheless. And like all marriages of odd partners, the sooner they learn to accept each other, the better off everyone will be.

Fusion is the fundamental energy process that powers the sun. It involves the combining of isotopes of hydrogen, which can be extracted from water, to form helium. To make this reaction occur, it is necessary to heat the hydrogen gas to hundreds of millions of degrees and confine it with a very strong magnetic field. It is a terrifyingly complex problem of both science and engineering. Although great strides have been made in the last few years on the fusion process, much still remains to be done. It is a high-risk, high-gain process.

Fusion has the potential for achieving a relatively high degree of safety with an acceptable level of social and environmental impact. Its fuel is low-cost and abundant. It has a much less serious accident potential and nuclear waste problem than that associated with conventional nuclear energy. While the ultimate economic size of fusion power plants cannot be estimated with any certainty, fusion could complement decentralized renewable energy sources, providing centralized power where appropriate and substituting for coal and conventional nuclear power plants.

The problem with fusion is that it will not be a cheap source of power. Indeed, if we can't solve the many engineering challenges, fusion may never be an economic energy source. Some radioactive materials have to be used in a fusion plant and these must be handled very carefully. Parts of the fusion device may become radioactive and will have to be disposed of. All of these problems need to be resolved through an accelerated program of research, development, and demonstration, so that the commercial potential and the social and environmental issues can be assessed.

Fusion is an option whose potential should be maximized. Congress and President Carter approved the Magnetic Fusion Engineering Act of 1980, which I sponsored. It set specific targets for the operation of a magnetic fusion engineering device (1990) and the operation of a commercial demonstration plant (2000). The Reagan administration is wavering in its commitment to these targets.

Transition—The Gap Fillers

Having maximized efforts in conservation, renewables, and nuclear fusion (none of which is currently being done), one proceeds to the transition period. To fill the gap between the present and the era of inexhaustibles, the options are oil, gas, coal, synthetic fuels, and conventional nuclear energy.

In fact, all of these are necessary. The strain during transition will be great, so we need a wide range of options.

How do we choose from among these options?

The way to go about it is certainly not the way it's being done at present, by interest groups. If you add to the political mix an unending stream of oil companies, natural gas producers, coal miners, oil dealers, investors, environmentalists, stockholders, offshore-drilling rig builders, refiners, pipeline manufacturers, gasoline station operators, petrochemical companies, public officials, and expect the mix to make decisions, you've got a problem. Such decisions become a function of relative degrees of entrenched power, not rational needs.

The other approach is to analyze the constraints and the realities we face, and then decide the best way to fashion a response to them.

The constraints are serious. We must reduce the importation of oil for all the reasons referred to earlier, and we must face the shortfall in *liquid fuels* and be prepared to provide substitutes.

The reality is that domestic oil supplies will continue to decline.

If the transition period has a point of extreme vulnerability, liquid fuels are it.

An important way to substitute for liquid fuels during the transition is with synthetic fuels and biomass. Synthetic fuels require the liquefaction of coal, oil shale, and tar sands. Biomass requires the liquefaction of grain stocks, crops, wood, and solid wastes. These unconventional liquid fuels vary in their environmental desirability, their economic feasibility, their finite versus inexhaustible nature, and their relationship to other parts of the energy package.

In approaching these fuels, several questions arise:

1. Is an additional dollar spent on synthetic fuel development economically feasible if it comes at the expense of a dollar that would otherwise be used for conservation?

2. Is an additional dollar spent on the liquefaction of coal (a finite resource) sensible if it comes at the expense of a dollar that would otherwise be used for liquefaction from biomass (an inexhaustible resource)?

3. Should the development of liquid fuels be pursued at the expense of the curtailment of programs for the renewables and nuclear fusion?

Such cost benefit analyses and the use of a comprehensive long-term plan are critically needed. Yet such questions are not being asked today by Washington's decisionmakers. In pursuing a liquid fuel strategy, the decisionmaker must ensure that choices reflect a wise allocation of capital rather than going by which alternative has a more significant lobby. The goal is transition—and liquid fuels are critical to that transition.

The second reality to be faced during transition involves the question of how one generates *electricity*. The first objective is to cease using liquid fuels for this purpose. While it's true that only 10 percent of our electricity is generated by burning oil, that 10 percent represents almost 1 million barrels a day that can be "backed out" if other means are utilized. There are particular regions, like New England, where the percentage approaches 60, and that is an unacceptable burden in terms of cost and vulnerability to interrupted supply. In addition, if there is a serious long-term shortfall of liquid fuels, especially for transportation, the only available alternative may be electric cars, which by definition require additional electrical generation. Finally, since there are uses for natural gas that cannot be easily replaced (for fertilizers, chemical feedstocks, home heating), it may eventually be necessary to cut back on the use of that fuel to generate electricity (it currently represents 15% of U.S. electricity).

So electricity becomes a central issue not only for its own sake but for its impact on the entire interrelated puzzle of transition.

I referred earlier to the generation of electricity from the inexhaustibles of today—wind, hydro, photovoltaics—and the inexhaustible of tomorrow—nuclear fusion. Those should be the highest priorities. Beyond that, however, there is an inescapable need to have baseload centralized electric power during the transition.

This need ties us to two equally undesirable alternatives: coal and conventional nuclear energy. Their undesirability is matched only by their inevitability. The sooner we accept that fact and deal with it, the sooner we can proceed rationally.

Coal. If you have wandered through an airport in recent years or listened to all-news programs, you have probably seen or heard the ad entitled "Coal Is the Answer." The ad is brought to you by "business and labor for coal."

But the answer to what?

If the question is, How can you provide baseload electric power?, then coal is the answer.

If the question is, What fossil fuel resource do we have that is most abundant?, coal is the answer.

But if the question is, How do you maximize the amount of CO_2 and acid rain in the atmosphere? (see Chapter 8), coal is the answer.

And, if the question is, How do you create a problem involving the disposal of massive quantities of coal ash?, then coal is indeed the answer as well.

Of course, business and labor for coal focus on the first two questions, and environmentalists on the latter two. So which questions do we ask? All of them. The fact is that coal—and conventional nuclear energy—confront us with Faustian choices.

Conservatives are fond of saying that when you go to bed with the government, you get more than a good night's sleep. The same is true of coal and nuclear energy. If you want the power, you've got to accept the morning after.

The litany of coal's hangover is compelling: acid rain, CO_2, strip mining, black lung disease, deaths in the mines, disposal of coal ash, and emission of pollutants that cause respiratory problems. Ironically, most of these problems have one characteristic: they are essentially scattered. The people who die each year from respiratory complications due to industrial and utility coal burning (estimated to be as many as 38,000 per year), the number of miners who die in accidents each year (around 250) or from black lung disease each year (around 1,000), the deposition of acid rain and CO_2—most are normally not reported on the front pages or in the network news. This is in sharp contrast to Three Mile Island, which dominated the news for weeks, where the risk was great yet no one died.

The negative side of coal is silent and insidious. It kills people, but it does so one by one. And since everyone's grandfather used to burn coal, it has the acceptance of familiarity.

All this is not to argue against the use of coal. Rather, it is to argue for an awareness of the balance sheet involved. In order to reduce the liability side of that sheet, we must accelerate the development of second-generation coal technologies (fluidized bed combustion, magnetohydrodynamics, coal gasification), which are more benign environmentally, and which mandate practices that minimize the dangers (coal washing, scrubbers, constant emissions policies). If we are going to burn coal—and we are—it does not seem excessive to demand that the cost to the environment and to our people be minimized.

Conventional Nuclear Energy (Nuclear Fission). The case for the nuclear option was made in Chapter 1 and will not be repeated here. Suffice it to say that I view this alternative with grave concern but recognize its role during transition.

What should that role be?

There are two components of nuclear fission: the conventional light water reactor (the power plants in operation today) and the breeder reactor. The first is generally a uranium-based process, the second is generally plutonium-based.

Their role is baseload electric generation, in order to provide power until such time as the inexhaustibles can take over. Their need and the decision to deploy the breeder reactor are a function of the demand for electricity, the supply of uranium, and cost effectiveness.

The rate of demand for electricity in the United States has dropped dramatically. In the 1960s and early 1970s, utilities projected a 7 percent annual growth in electric power needs. By the time the cost of electricity had skyrocketed in the late 1970s, growth had dropped to between 1 and 2 percent. At the peak 7 percent level, the need for power plants doubles in ten years; at the 1.5 percent level, the doubling won't occur for forty-six years. That means a lot of construction not required, capital not diverted to that need, and existing uranium supplies providing more years of service.

The uranium supply has, of course, never changed. What has changed is our estimate of known reserves. In the mid-1970s there was concern that the construction of new light water reactors would have to be stopped in the near future because there was not enough assured uranium for the lifetime of the power plant. Today, that concern is seldom heard. The known and anticipated reserves of uranium (coupled with the decline in the projection for new reactors) are such that the light water reactor will be serviceable throughout this century and well into the next. With the development of processes like the advanced converter reactor, that useful lifetime can be stretched even further.

It is the economics of conventional nuclear energy that to many people poses the most important question. Nuclear power plants are very expensive and they carry with them serious financial risks. This is reflected in federal policy. Despite the rhetoric of the Reagan administration about allowing market forces to prevail unencumbered by governmental intervention, the federal policy *vis-à-vis* nuclear energy has been and continues to be one of paternalism and subsidy. The Price-Anderson Act provides a subsidy by limiting utility liability to only $535 million per nuclear accident. The goverment has also poured billions upon billions of dollars into nuclear research and the financing of uranium enrichment facilities.

What would happen if these props were removed from under conventional nuclear energy the way they are being taken out from under conservation and renewables? Nobody knows for sure, but the intensity of industry lobbying for federal support gives us some indication. If nuclear power were allowed to compete unaided in the marketplace with other alternatives, its relative feasibility would obviously be reduced. Although nuclear power plants would still be built, they would constitute a lesser part of a portfolio of electrical generating sources. In time, as the utilities decided on which source to invest in, the cost-effectiveness of the renewables would make them seem more and more attractive.

The discussion on coal above referred to some of the environmen tal and health concerns involved. The same caution must be voiced about nuclear power. Here, the three major concerns are wastes, safety, and proliferation. The first of these will be dealt with in more detail in Chapter 8.

Nuclear safety is a bizarre issue in the sense that the industry views the public discussion of it as somehow inappropriate and threatening. In some respects, this reaction is based on the feeling that nuclear power has become a pejorative term, at which opponents and proponents alike lash out from firmly entrenched, inflexible positions. The confrontational nature of the discussion serves no one.

The light water reactor is relatively safe. We have had 585 reactor-years of operational experience without a fatality. The Kemeny Commission Report on Three Mile Island concluded that the principal failures were managerial, institutional, and organizational, in addition to some technological inadequacies. Commission Chairman John Kemeny, then president of Dartmouth College, described the problem as largely one of software, not hardware. The interface between man and machine had not been well thought out; reactor operators were not well trained; there was no effective coordination between the utility and the Nuclear Regulatory Commission.

The industry simply must do better. During my service on the Energy and Environment Subcommittee of the House Interior Committee, I tried to improve nuclear safety standards. But industry officials, as well as most Nuclear Regulatory Commission officials, were hostile to our efforts, and viewed us as intruders. Since Three Mile Island, however, such smugness has diminished. It ought to be realized that one more such incident and the nuclear option may well be dead. The fatalities caused by coal mining and coal burning are tragic, but a nuclear accident could cause loss of life on a scale that would be catastrophic. As a society, we are strangely immune to significant numbers of deaths as long as they happen singly, such as the numbers of people killed on the highways each year. But we do respond to death visited upon large numbers of people at one time. Nuclear safety is a critical issue to the industry, and the proponents of nuclear power should themselves be adamant in advocating it.

For me, the most troubling aspect of conventional nuclear energy is proliferation. When I think about the possibility of Iraq or Libya or Pakistan or South Africa possessing nuclear weapons, I am chilled. When I contemplate a terrorist organization with such a device, my world turns cold. What would we do if one day we were told that a nuclear device had been placed on a ship moored in New York Harbor or San Francisco Bay or New Orleans—and that a terrorist group was making demands? What would we do if one day such a device were detonated in one of our cities by terrorists angry at America because of some wrong, real or illusory? The world we know today, for all its problems, would in retrospect appear childlike in its innocence compared to the world we had just entered. It would be a time of fear, panic, outrage, and retaliation, in which individual liberties would be destroyed by the overriding need for physical security.

Nuclear proliferation *must* be minimized. While I realize that the genie of nuclear weapons technology is long since out of the bottle, and that domestic U.S. nuclear decisions are not the critical points of vulnerability, there is still a need for American policymakers to focus on the issue as a primary concern.

Specifically, this means the avoidance of a worldwide plutonium economy. The basic ingredient of a nuclear device is plutonium. In a light water reactor, plutonium is produced as a byproduct, but it is mixed with highly radioactive nuclear wastes that make it very difficult to handle. The danger arises when plutonium is separated out. Then it can be dealt with easily—and used to fuel a nuclear device. Any system that leads to separated-out plutonium should be avoided at all costs. If reprocessing of spent nuclear fuel is undertaken worldwide, we will have entered into a plutonium economy. There is no conscionable reason for accepting the risks. The United States should be *adamant* in opposing reprocessing.

All of this brings us to the last issue on the nuclear agenda—the breeder reactor—which requires reprocessing.

The debate about the light water reactor is a model of reason when compared to the controversy over the breeder reactor. The breeder reactor is based on the principle that particular nuclear reactions breed more fossil fuel than they consume. For example, in the Clinch River Breeder Reactor, the American prototype on which we've already spent $955 million, uranium 238 is bombarded with neutrons and converted into plutonium, which can be used as a fuel. Unlike the light water reactor, the breeder has a potential that is measured in centuries. This enormous potential has been acknowledged by many other nations, some of which are in the process of building breeders (Great Britain, France, Germany, the Soviet Union); others are in the market for purchasing them (Iran, Pakistan, Brazil, South Africa).

The safety considerations relating to the breeder are generally more serious than those relating to the light water reactor. Given the need for reprocessing, the same is true of waste disposal.

More important, our present breeder program ensures that two major concerns, the breeder's design and its economics—each of which is capable of delaying or eliminating the program—will remain unresolved. Both involve the Clinch River Breeder Reactor, which is being built in Tennessee.

The first argument against Clinch River is simply one of the design, which is now nine years old. We have progressed past it conceptually. Any advocate would today endorse a newer concept and a newer design. In a normal, unemotional atmosphere, amid engineers and scientists, the project would be scrapped, and alternative technology substituted, such as advanced converters, the thorium cycle breeder, and the once-through breeder. In essence, that was the decision made by President Carter.

But the pro-nuclear forces are so gun-shy that shooting down Clinch River was perceived as equivalent to killing the breeder program. In an atmosphere of severe polarization among those in the nuclear debate, there is no consensus, so everyone hangs on dearly to what he has. Congress voted to continue Clinch River and President Reagan strongly supports the project.

Ironically, there are even some anti-nuclear adherents who back Clinch River on the theory that since it is the worst of all possible breeder technologies, further investment in it will doom the entire program. They reason that a switch to a more "acceptable" breeder technology would eventually win wide support and thus save the program they are committed to terminating.

The second obstacle is more basic. If the uranium reserves are much greater than we thought; if the demand for electric power is leveling off; if the advanced converter reactor can stretch the use of existing uranium supplies; if renewable sources of electrical generation are coming on line; if the economic feasibility of the breeder is doubtful; and if the much more benign nuclear fusion process is being pursued, then why have a breeder with its myriad attendant problems at all? I don't think we should. The breeder should not be deployed when we can ride for many more years with the known technology of the light water reactor and its various improvements.

Unfortunately, we can't kill the breeder completely. Research and development (not of Clinch River but of the other, more advanced and less proliferation-prone breeders) should continue. If the goal is transition, we need a range of inexhaustibles. A breeder may still be necessary if fusion doesn't work, or proves so unreliable or uneconomic that it fails to be a viable alternative.

The moment of decision will come around the year 2000, when

the fusion process is demonstrated. By then we should be able to make a judgment on fusion and to determine the potential of the renewables.

American nuclear policy will require much thought and fine-tuning. We must have a clear vision of where we are going, why we are going there, how long it will take, and the risks we are accepting. The nuclear option must be constantly compared to all the other options—with cost-benefit and risk-benefit analyses doggedly applied.

The realities of the energy problem are a true test of our democracy. It is argued that democratic societies are inherently weak because they require consensus, and consensus is very difficult to achieve when the issue is both long-term and affects vested interests. At present, our energy policy is like a pinball, bouncing back and forth between powerful interests.

But the realities are very complex. They won't fit on a bumper sticker (NO NUKES). They won't fit on an airport billboard ("Coal Is the Answer"). And they won't fit neatly into the political platforms of the existing political structure.

What they require, above all, is a clear-eyed analysis of what we are currently doing. We must understand that our present energy policies are incompatible with the plan I have outlined. It might be said that current energy policies reflect the pursuit of another plan. But with oil being a finite, diminishing resource, is maximum oil production a genuine plan? With the serious safety, health, environmental, and proliferation risks involved in the transition fuels, is the denigration of conservation, renewables, and nuclear fusion a genuine plan?

They are plans, all right, and they will take us over the "waterfall."

3/War and Peace
and the Soviets:
The Second Reality

The primary function of any government is to provide for the physical security of its people. A government that cannot, or will not, furnish that security will fall. Man's instinct for survival is paramount. In many respects it is the ultimate reality. A government which threatens that instinct must be prepared for unrest and eventually political oblivion.

Man views man as aggressive, and that aggressiveness is in evidence in every walk of life. Sports are the most obvious example, but our entire free enterprise system is based on aggressiveness. The characteristic is also acutely applicable to politics. Incumbents usually move for higher office when they see an opening. How many well-positioned state legislators pass up a chance to run against a congressman who appears vulnerable? How many highly visible House members ignore the opportunity to challenge a senator whose seat seems attainable? How many nationally known senators will not run for a presidency that appears within reach? To a degree we all inherit a basic aggressiveness, and political philosophy must take this into account.

We are a people at odds with one another over what constitutes a rational defense policy. The struggle is a constant one because in coming to grips with our defense dilemma, we confront widely varying attitudes among Americans as to what our "nature" is all about. Just as critically, we cannot decide about the intent of the Soviet Union.

Hawks and doves disagree on defense because they cannot agree on what we "really" are and what the Soviets "really" are. More than an academic debate, this is, for all of us, an inner struggle

about the human and collective natures that we perceive in ourselves and others. Good will and fear, faith and hostility—each vies
for acceptance as the simple truth about our makeup. And as we
await final judgment as to that makeup, we steadily proceed to pile
up weapons of mass destruction.

If that struggle is lost by our intemperance, we will all be consumed in a self-imposed conflagration: my children, your children,
the fools who couldn't control nuclear weapons and the innocents
who never gave them a thought. Our hawks, their hawks, our
doves, their doves, the elderly in nursing homes and the newborn
in maternity wards—all incinerated because we as decisionmakers
were unable to control ourselves.

It is essential that we accept the reality of our rooted aggressiveness, that we assume it in others, and then attempt to structure a
policy that provides the aggressor no safe haven. In so doing, we
must not instill fear of our own combativeness in others. We have
to realize that rash actions and policies on our part will send signals
that can set off the survival instinct in friends and adversaries alike.

In every national election, each candidate pledges to be "second
to none" in defense. (Second to none: what a strange way to say it.)
We know there's no risk of being second to Paraguay or Finland
or Upper Volta. The competition is Russia, the Soviet Union. No
discussion of national defense operates in a vacuum, only in relation
to our major ideological and military adversary.

Most Americans view the Soviet Union as a threat to our collective survival. Most believe that the Soviets would, as Khrushchev
claimed, "bury us" if they were provided with a clear opportunity
to do so.

They are basically correct.

The Soviet political leadership is inbred with a doctrine of inevitable ascendancy, reinforced by several factors. One is the sheer
growth of confidence derived from a military buildup that has
approached equivalence with the United States. This momentum of
armament is made all the more significant because of the central
role played by the military in Soviet decisionmaking and the growing militarization of Soviet foreign policy.

Secondly, there is the phenomenon of nationalism. There is a
clear perception of, and feeling for, the rise of Mother Russia. It is

referred to as Great Russian nationalism, because it originates among the dominant Russians who constitute 50.5 percent of the population. This spirit of nationalism inspires a need to extend Soviet influence beyond the nation's borders. Thus it is a given that Soviet leaders desire a powerful international role.

Lastly, there are the teachings of Marxism-Leninism. The Soviet leaders and many of their citizens feel that capitalism is fundamentally exploitative, and that in time the vast majority of the people of the world will indeed "unite, and throw off their chains." There exists a sense of mission, a faith that history is on their side. To an extent that is not appreciated in America, the Soviet rulers and a good proportion of the Soviet people are firm believers in their role —and in the moral value of that role.

Now, certainly, before, during, and since the time of Marx and Lenin, there have been exploiters in the capitalist system. My home town of Lowell was built by "honorable" men who worked the farm girls, children, and ethnic immigrants without much compassion. These Yankee entrepreneurs were the stuff of history; they were also the precipitators of human misery. This point is critical, because Marxism-Leninism is basically a reactive philosophy—it requires exploitation to create its constituency. Find an exploiter and an exploited population, and Marxism-Leninism will take root. Without exploitation and the wellspring of bitterness and hatred it provides, Marxism-Leninism by its very origins has no serious appeal.

This reality is not understood by some hardline American conservatives who think that Marxism springs up *sui generis.* It is more than ironic that many of these conservatives invariably support conditions which lead people to consider the Marxist alternatives. We see this played out in Latin America, where conservatives who support right-wing governments ignore the enormous gap between the very rich and the very poor. The conditions of exploitation that have led to despair and unrest are a form of linkage that escapes them.

The Soviet leadership has always believed that an opportunity exists to exploit despair and unrest in the world. The Soviets concluded that unfettered capitalism (read colonialism and imperialism) in Third World nations would eventually provide the ingredients of its own demise. Give capitalism enough rope, and it will hang itself. The Soviet goal, then, is not only a function of traditional nationalism and militarism; it also seeks to lead the world away from the "horrors" of exploitative capitalism and into the "sunshine" of Marxism-Leninism.

Thus, to the Soviets, "burying" the United States would not only be a triumph of one country over another but the pursuit of a moral historical mission.

This sense of purpose is a form of "manifest destiny" that should not be lightly dismissed. It forms the basis of the Soviets' approach to defense issues. To be specific, they believe that history is working against their adversaries, that the wave of the future is represented by former colonies like Mozambique and Angola, wresting their freedom from European masters with the help of Soviet weapons, ideology, and political support. Therefore, they must avoid a military imbalance relative to the United States that might negate this inevitable decline of Western fortunes. The Soviets seek to achieve military parity—superiority, if possible—in order to prevent any U.S. "victory" (such as took place during the Cuban missile crisis) and to foster a politically beneficial perception of Soviet "ascendancy" on the part of non-aligned nations. They can then safely and skillfully exploit the inevitable "targets of opportunity" around the world. Then, in time, consistent with their dogmatic sense of history, they believe they will prevail. For the good of Mother Russia, yes, but also for the benefit of mankind. Consequently, the last twenty years have seen a dogged adherence to military buildup and the exploitation of perceived advantages.

This attitude displays all the inconsistencies and paradoxes of any fanaticism. Born out of Marxist-Leninist anger about oppression, its own internal trampling of individual freedom and human rights is accepted and condoned as necessary for the pursuit of the larger mission. The fact that the brutality of the czars has given way to the brutality of the commissars causes nary an ideological ripple. America has had all too much experience with this attitude: the Ayatollah Khomeini offers a recent example. The more fanatic of the Moral Majority exhibit the same narrow zealousness ("God does not hear the prayers of a Jew"). In the mind of the zealot, the end justifies the means. If, as in Hungary and Afghanistan, people must be killed in pursuit of these ends, then, the Soviets reason, "so be it."

A single-minded sense of mission is honored when exhibited by marathon runners or artists. But it can be very dangerous in international politics. That danger is well understood on Main Street U.S.A. If the Soviets are intent upon our destruction, most Americans reason, we'd better be ready for them. Unlike our period of manifest destiny, America is not expansionist today, and we seek no dominance, only stability. This lack of the need to "bury" the Soviets reflects our basically status quo attitude. As long as the Soviets don't encroach upon our friends, and don't frighten us with expansionism, we have no particular difficulty in co-existing. There have been several situations—the Glassboro talks, detente, etc.— when Americans had high hopes for better relations with the Soviets. But faced with a threat to our survival by this same Soviet leadership, we will respond. Or as Senator Pat Moynihan put it in his recent book, *Count Our Blessings,* "In a situation where the Soviet military always insists on more, the process will always end with the American military insisting on more as well." In a bizarre sense, our defense policy and foreign policy are written in the Kremlin. These policies cannot and must not reflect our hopes and desires about Soviet actions if those hopes and desires are not reflected in Moscow's decisionmaking.

By necessity, then, our approach is reactive. If the Soviets are willing to live in peace, so are we. If they seek to threaten us and our perceived spheres of national interest, then we must be ready.

The Soviets obviously dispute this view. They see us as aggressively expanding our interests around the world, using our economic power to gain dominance over other peoples. The Reagan administration's push in El Salvador, based on the now-discredited "white paper," raised the spectre of using military power as well. Since both countries have a tendency toward mirror image in explaining the motives of the other, neither enjoys perfect perception. And in an era of uncertainty, it is instinctive to assume the worst about the intentions and capabilities of one's adversary.

Thus, the Soviets' ideology is reinforced by their view of our "exploitation"; they, in turn, project a clear sense of challenge to us; we respond to that threat through our own mechanisms, which causes the Soviets to reinforce their mechanisms. And so on. Suspicion begets suspicion; military buildup begets military buildup. Two highly technological superpowers slide into an uncontrollable spiral of aggressiveness and fear. This slide is particularly uncontrollable if the principals are dealing in stereotyped perceptions of each other.

In the modern era, the United States has always had to gear up for war. We have diverted our vast resources to that end when necessary. Veterans of World War II are generally adamant about not ever being so unprepared as we were before Pearl Harbor. (The response after 1957 to the launching of the Soviet satellite Sputnik, which resulted in stepped-up scientific programs, is not without relevance here.)

The generation that came out of the Cold War of the 1950s is equipped with a psychic tripwire regarding the Soviets. Most Americans who grew up during that era are hard put to think of the Soviets in anything but overtly provocative terms. Stalin, Khrushchev, Berlin, Korea, Hungary—a litany of aggressive behavior.

The combination of these events and our resultant response mechanisms would eventually get us into Vietnam, which was perceived as simply another case of Communist aggression that had to be stopped. To those whose perspective was totally East-West (Cold War), there was no such thing as nationalism. "Neutrality is immoral," said Secretary of State John Foster Dulles. You're either for us or against us. Today, that view of the world is heard once again in Washington's corridors of power.

But Vietnam was not South Korea. There was no beleaguered Syngman Rhee with the support of most of his people. There were other forces at play, and we were not programmed to comprehend them. There were no basic training courses in "hearts and minds." Our forces could not understand why the Vietnamese did not appreciate what we were doing for them. Even the "best and the brightest" could not fit the round peg of Vietnam realities into the square hole of Cold War confrontation.

The result was a disaster: as has been stated earlier, applying dogma to reality never can work in the long term. Fifty-seven thousand Americans died "trying to help a people be free," and many of those people viewed that help with skepticism and mistrust. It was the wrong war in the wrong place at the wrong time for the wrong reasons. America was responding with an understandable Cold War mentality that had outlived its application and would blind us to the newer realities.

We were traumatized as violence broke out on campuses and in the streets. Berkeley. Columbia. The Democratic convention in Chicago. Kent State. The burning of draft cards. The marches on Washington and the Pentagon. Support your local police. Hard hats against the hippies. Haight-Ashbury. Lyndon Johnson's decision to retire. Spiro Agnew and his "nattering nabobs of negativism." America—love it or leave it. Give Peace a Chance.

When it was finally over, we were bitter, confused, and angry. Stung by an intervention that failed, we as a nation determined that we would not get involved again. There were attempts in Congress to pull troops out of Europe and South Korea. We recoiled against a military that saw nothing wrong with destroying villages to "save" them. We were repelled by the attempts to cover up My Lai. These actions did not reflect the America we believed in. And so, when our troops came home, we didn't try to acknowledge their luckless role. Unlike the freed American hostages in 1981, they would participate in few parades or White House ceremonies.

A mood of anti-militarism settled over the country. We had engaged our might in an inappropriate war, and the nation would not be so fooled again. During the 1975–76 Congress, military requests were regarded with great skepticism.

What happened among liberals was very understandable. We identified excess in military ventures with our foreign policy. It was the liberals, not just the conservatives, who became quasi-isolationists. Our hand had been extended in reactionary faith (according to the liberals) or in good faith (according to the conservatives), and had got slapped. Both felt hurt, and both wanted no more of it.

This feeling (quite understandable in context and one that I shared) expressed itself in 1975 when the so-called Watergate class of freshman Democratic congressmen arrived in Washington. Many of us were elected on reformist issues, and we went gunning for the seniority system. Among the targeted was F. Edward Hébert of Louisiana, chairman of the Armed Services Committee. He represented to us the hardline, give-the-military-whatever-it-wants mentality that had broadened our commitment to the Vietnam War. When he was removed as chairman by the Democratic Caucus, I and many of my freshman colleagues felt that we had dealt a blow to undue militarism.

Later that year the Congress would cut off funding to prosecute the war in Vietnam, and pass the Tunney Amendment prohibiting U.S. involvement in Angola.

Liberals saw their role as trying to keep hardliners who spotted a Communist behind every tree from stumbling into one fool's errand after another. Incapable of understanding the complexities of a multidimensional world, they wrapped the flag around themselves and got juiced up watching *Patton*. We liberals saw the Soviets gaining *because of,* not despite, these conservatives—no one, for example, wanted the United States Senate to reject the Panama Canal treaties as much as Fidel Castro and Leonid Brezhnev. But it was hardline conservative opposition to the treaties that would have delivered the goods to Castro and Brezhnev. Left to their own devices, the hardliners would perform all of the Soviets' heavy lifting for them. America had to be saved from its own superpatriots before they had undermined us around the world. I subscribed to this view—and still do for the most part.*

In focusing on the need to restrain the military, we were aided by the Pentagon's demand for the B-1 bomber. The B-1 was to provide a key point for skepticism over the hawks. The military argued that this $25 billion system was necessary because the B-52 fleet was too aged. As Ronald Reagan would say during his campaign for President, many of the planes were older than the pilots flying them.

There was, and is, no question about the need for overhaul of the air leg of the American nuclear force triad (land-based ICBM's, submarine-based missiles, B-52's). To the military, the B-1 seemed to be the obvious answer. Unlike the B-52, it flew low at supersonic

---

*On one issue, however, I dissented. After voting to cut off funds to end the war in Vietnam, I opposed the effort to withdraw U.S. troops from Europe as a message of undue isolationism that would surely be misinterpreted.

speed and thus, as a penetration bomber, was less vulnerable to surface-to-air missiles.

Upon closer examination, however, the B-1 had serious flaws. First, its ground-hugging proficiency would be compromised by the "look-down vectoring" radar capability of the Soviet equivalent of our AWAC's system and the Soviets would be operating their system by the time the B-1 was deployed. Second, it was questionable whether a penetration bomber was the specific vehicle needed to deliver cruise missiles since they could be launched far beyond the Soviets' border defenses. Given that mission, the B-1 was simply not cost-effective. Third, by committing ourselves to the B-1, we would then be unable later to pursue other, more advanced replacement alternatives. This third objection is now obvious, given the knowledge of the Stealth technology, but was not so plain at the time.

So liberals fought the B-1, and under the Carter administration it was scrapped. Lobbyists who pressured me to vote for it would later admit that they had major doubts about the plane all along.

There was, however, a down side to this anti-military attitude that would eventually come back to haunt us. We ran the risk of falling into the same trap that caused conservatives to believe fervently in the Vietnam War. The hardliners had seen North Korea attack South Korea, the attempt to strangle Berlin, Khrushchev banging his shoe at the U.N., and the placing of offensive missiles in Cuba. To them, Vietnam was the linear descendant of these activities. They could not comprehend the new complexities.

Liberals had witnessed the tragedy of Vietnam, the attempted intervention in Angola, and the push for the B-1 bomber, and thus witnessed the linear descendant of these activities in defense spending generally. Having been the guardians against American military adventurism, they found it difficult to react objectively to Soviet defense spending and the invasion of Afghanistan.

For liberals to claim that the Soviets were engaged in excessive military spending that required a response was to play into the hands of those conservatives who would say so whether the Soviets were engaged in a massive buildup or not.

To suggest that the Soviets were naked aggressors in Afghanistan

was to play into the hands of those same conservatives who habitu-
ally saw Soviet aggression even where there wasn't any.

Certain facts (realities) would not go away. Most important was
the commitment by the Soviet Union to a relentless rate of defense
spending that equaled approximately 4 percent real growth each
year. Although caused by the factors referred to earlier, it was
fueled by the acute chagrin felt by the Soviets when they had to
back down during the Cuban missile crisis. That national shame
would not be allowed to reoccur. And so they began to spend. We
allotted a smaller percentage of our GNP on defense each year, and
during the late 1960s and most of the 1970s we saw a real decline
in defense spending. This disparity was not in itself cause for alarm,
since the Soviets began quite far behind us. (Despite the "missile
gap" talk in the early 1960s, the Soviet capability was simply not
equivalent to ours.) Eventually, however, the momentum of this
rate of defense spending in five-year plan after five-year plan would
become disturbing. Many Americans assumed that there would
finally be a state of equivalence, which would provide a balance of
power, and then each country could try to meet its domestic needs.
Instead, the Soviets gave every indication that superiority, not parity, was the objective. (I should note here that the issue of superiority is more complicated than the term implies since one can achieve
conventional weapons superiority, for example, and still not have
strategic nuclear superiority. Or the Soviets can have numerical
superiority in a particular category, e.g., tanks, without taking into
account such real-life factors as reliability, antitank weapons technology, diversion of tanks by the Soviets to the Chinese border, and
our advantage of having West German, French, and English tanks
on our side versus Polish, Hungarian, and Czechoslovakian tanks
on theirs.)

Be that as it may, the rate of Soviet spending gave every sign that
it would not be deflected downward upon achieving parity, but
would continue its steady course. At that point, the U.S.-Soviet
differential would become critical. Not that the Soviets would necessarily use their advantage in outright aggression against the West,
but they could employ the superiority both to browbeat our allies
into distancing themselves from the United States and to convince

neutral Third World countries that the era of American supremacy was over.

This latter point is critical for liberals to understand. There are those who argue for what is termed "sufficiency." The rationale is that our capacity to destroy the Soviets is adequate to safeguard against any overt attack. That part of the argument is correct. However, the advantage of superiority to the Soviets is political as much as military. And we live in a time when other nations are guided by coldly calculated perceptions of relative ascendancy. That is where the doctrine of sufficiency, however desirable, fails, by not taking into account all the operative objectives of the Soviets.

The reality of the Soviet arms buildup was understood by more than just the hardliners. The Carter administration saw the conventional weaponry imbalance and began to move to correct it. At the summit meeting in May 1977, the NATO allies committed themselves to a 3 percent real growth above inflation in defense spending, reversing the decline that had prevailed during the Nixon and Ford years.

This approach did not satisfy some who were troubled by the Soviet policy. Perhaps representative of these critical moderates was Senator Sam Nunn of Georgia. Nunn had real concerns about the direction and vehemence of Soviet policy; above all, he was unsure of the steadfastness of the American will to continue substantial national defense expenditures over the long haul. Nunn's views were influential because he is regarded by other senators as both intelligent and thorough. While one can regard the extremism of some Senate hardliners as being mindlessly reactionary, there are clearly real political questions about America's military posture if the likes of Nunn are troubled.

The concern over defense policy thus reached well beyond the conservatives. The Soviet invasion of Afghanistan strengthened their position.* There were forces at play that had a life of their own. These various influences can be seen if one traces how the entire matter played itself out during the debate over SALT II.

---

*Ironically (to use a non-pejorative term), it would be Ronald Reagan who would argue for a strong stand against the Soviet invasion and then, after assuming office, lift the grain embargo against the Soviets while they remained in Afghanistan.

SALT II was the product of negotiations between the Soviets and Presidents Nixon, Ford, and Carter. Although there were issues to be raised and debated (such as that of verification, raised by Senator John Glenn), the treaty was a critical step toward arms control. In normal times, if there are such things, the treaty would have been viewed as more attractive than SALT I, which was negotiated by Presidents Johnson and Nixon, and the Vladivostok Accord signed by President Ford. These latter two documents were in my opinion no more vital to the United States than SALT II, and the SALT I Treaty passed the Senate by a lopsided 88 to 2 margin.

But 1979 was not a good year for treaties with the Soviets, irrespective of their merits. SALT II ran into the backlash of the invasion into Afghanistan and the contrived American blustering upon the "discovery" of the 2,000 Soviet troops that had been in Cuba for seventeen years. (On the latter issue, I recall the response of Senator Patrick Leahy, who when asked about his reaction replied simply, "I am confident that the Soviet troops could be quickly dispatched by the Florida National Guard." A touch of Yankee calm and common sense amid the hysteria.)

SALT II died when President Carter requested the withdrawal of the treaty from the Senate calendar after the Afghanistan invasion, and the casket was sealed by the subsequent election of President Reagan, an outspoken foe of it. But these events were determinative because of an atmosphere whose hostility to the treaty was a function of more than just a conservative mood.

I remember the testimony of former President Gerald Ford and former Secretary of State Henry Kissinger before the Senate Foreign Relations Committee. These men had negotiated much of SALT II and certainly had a stake in the resolution of the matter. Their ambivalent feelings of opposition toward SALT II were widely reported, and it was their position that made a two-thirds vote in the Senate impossible enough in 1979 to cause the treaty vote to be postponed until 1980, when it was caught up in other matters, including the election.

Why would these two men seek to undermine a treaty for which they were partially responsible when it involved the overriding issue of nuclear holocaust? True, Ford did harbor a resentment of Carter that would blossom forth during the 1980 campaign. And Kissinger was suffering severe withdrawal symptoms as he wandered in the wilderness of officelessness. Those easy explanations were not, however, the full answer.

Although neither Ford nor Kissinger embraced the provisions of the whole treaty, they were not necessarily opposed to it. As Kissinger said: "If we want equality, we must build to equality. We must reverse the strategic trends if we are serious about an equitable SALT treaty."

Their posture was remarkably similar to that of Sam Nunn, who was not ill disposed toward the Carter administration.

I believe that Kissinger and Ford's thinking went as follows: Hold up SALT II (which on its merits was arguably acceptable) until a national consensus had gathered to meet the Soviet challenge. They believed that if SALT II were to be passed, even though it was inherently worthwhile, Americans would tend to relax, to think that arms control had been achieved, and then be lulled into stagnant defense-spending patterns while the Soviets surged ahead. Thus the Soviets would be able to attain political objectives that were unrelated to the matters contained in SALT II itself.

The Ford-Kissinger-Nunn approaches presumed that upon the mobilization of the American will to meet the Soviet defense-spending threat, SALT II could be ratified, but certainly not before.

How ironic that to achieve arms control we needed to increase arms spending. And that without more arms spending there would be no arms control, and thus even more accelerated arms spending. (There is, of course, ample historic precedent for this dilemma.)

Yet the scenario was more complicated than it appears on the surface. It succeeded in raising the Soviet challenge issue, and in educating the public as to the very real concerns about American response mechanisms. Indeed, it was too successful, because it set in motion forces that could not be contained. Now that there is a consensus about the need to increase American defense spending to balance the Soviet rate and preclude the threatened "gap" (although fortunately no consensus as to the massive push advocated by the Reagan administration), the atmosphere has been poisoned to the extent that ratification of SALT II is no longer possible. The useful genie refuses to go back into the bottle.

The Soviets wonder about American intentions. They negotiated a formal treaty and that treaty died in the United States Senate without even a vote. They may well conclude that Americans are engaged in a charade. The events of 1980 must have confused their political analysts. Giving credence to Soviet doubts is their awareness of the consistent concern of our allies that Americans are prone to hardline rhetoric for its own sake, and go through periods of confrontation that are precipitated by domestic political interests, not international realities. The current European dismay at our move away from arms control talks is a case in point.

Recent history, then, does not provide much hope that reason will soon prevail on either side. The need is for a concerted effort to deal in realism, not misconceptions.

During each of my campaigns I have at times fallen into the trap of thinking of my opponents as 10 feet tall, rich as Midas, and popular as Santa Claus. If Jack Dever, or Paul Cronin, or Paul Guzzi, or Ed Brooke visited a particular town, I would lament the devastating impact of that event. If I went to the same town, I would feel that the schedule was inadequate, the crowds were small, the volunteers were few, and the press coverage awful. After the elections, I would talk to my opponents and they would relate how effective I always was, and how whenever they campaigned in a town the schedule was inadequate, the crowds were small, the volunteers were few, and the press coverage awful.

We do the same thing with the Soviet Union. If the President of Sierra Leone makes a state visit to the United States, it is treated as an event of no consequence and buried deep in the newspaper. If the President of Sierra Leone visits Moscow, it is reported on page one, and we lament the potential Soviet influence on Sierra Leone: "My God, Sierra Leone is going Communist!" If a Jordanian student is educated in the United States, no assumptions are made as to his ideology. If a Jordanian student is educated in the Soviet Union, it is taken for granted that he is a Marxist.

Axiom number one may be Know thyself, but axiom number two is Know thine enemy.

According to the polls, most Americans believe the Soviets are an ascending power. Most senators and congressmen think the same way. Jack Kennedy saw a missile gap in 1960, and Ronald Reagan discerned one in 1980. Chances are good that someone will spot one in the year 2000. Are these perceptions accurate? Are they shared by the Soviets?

Let's try to imagine how a thoughtful Soviet leader would view the state of his country. Would he regard his nation as a juggernaut free from the doubts and fears that plague the United States? Hardly. Let's take a look at some of his concerns through his eyes.

The Chinese "Menace." There are 1 billion Chinese to the East, who now have the ICBM capability to drop nuclear weapons on many Soviet cities. They are historically unhappy about the boundary drawn between the two countries, and border clashes occur all the time. They have aligned themselves with your enemy, the United States—an alignment that includes an oral agreement to receive American military equipment on a case-by-case basis—and have threatened to form a giant economic bloc with Japan. They try to undercut you at every opportunity all over the world, preaching the doctrine of the Soviet menace. (Imagine 1 billion Mexicans, with nuclear weapons, claiming the southern half of California, all of Arizona, New Mexico, and Texas, hating America and allied with Russia. It would make Americans very jumpy, if not paranoid.)

Oil. The Soviet orbit relies in part for its cohesion on Soviet oil. The various allies in eastern Europe, Cuba, and Vietnam are supplied by your oil at less than the world price. But because of problems of inadequate technology, sometime in the next decade you may well have to begin importing oil at the world price if you want to keep current practices intact. You don't have the hard currency to do that. Your satellites' dependence upon you will erode as the price charged escalates.

Food. As relentlessly as a mosquito in the night, you are plagued by poor harvests. No matter who your minister of agriculture is, the harvests don't get any better. You must periodically apply to Western nations, including the United States, for the food necessary to feed your people. This conclusively undermines your argument about communism being a better economic system. And importation of foodstuffs also requires hard currency.

Western European Determination. Events in western Europe are not going well. The wave of Eurocommunism that seemed inexorable in 1975 has since faded into a few ripples of bickering leftists. Mrs. Thatcher wins in Great Britain, and talks tough about standing up to you. Portuguese voters turn out the Socialists and install a moderate conservative government. Even the election of the Mitterrand government in France did not, as had been expected, weaken that country's commitment to NATO.

Islamic Fundamentalism. Your country is a nice set-up if you're part of the Great Russian majority (50.5%). The remaining 49.5 percent of the population has been quiet, but is enduring second-class status with a rising level of dissent. Their past quietude has been especially convenient while you accuse the United States of racism toward its minorities. On your southern flank, however, there looms the specter of Islamic fundamentalism, with its fierce abhorrence of the godlessness of communism. Some 18 percent of your people, most of them on that southern flank, are Islamic and are growing much more rapidly than the Great Russians.

Expensive Allies. Your surrogates in the Third World are expensive friends indeed. Fidel Castro is an example. After you have "liberated" Afghanistan, rather than being supportive, he talks only about his loss of credibility in the Third World. He also can't seem to get his economy in order—it requires a fix of some $3 billion a year. Subsidizing your Vietnamese allies in their Cambodian venture costs at least several hundred million dollars a year, and has solidified hostility toward you in China, the Philippines, Singapore, Malaysia, Indonesia, and Thailand. Subsidizing your surrogate Karmal in Afghanistan is costing you billions of dollars per year, in a nasty war that also has cost you Russian lives, and a 104 to 18 drubbing in a U.N. that never voted against you so strongly before.

Eastern Europe. While the United States has concerns about NATO, you are worried about the Warsaw Pact nations. Your guns-over-butter policies have caused the domestic sector to bear the brunt of sacrifice. In Poland, workers strike, not over ideology, but about the price of meat. And once begun, that strike spills over into more troubling issues. Their well-publicized activities constitute a fundamental challenge. They are practically goading you into some kind of retaliation; the Hungarian and Czechoslovakian situations seemed so much more controllable. The economic state of many of your eastern European allies is troubling—especially the increasing indebtedness to Western nations. The foreign debt of Poland to Western creditors alone in early 1981 was a staggering $26 billion. If you go into Poland with troops, you "win" that debt. Given your allies' oil dependence on you at about $15 a barrel, you will have to increase this price when you begin to import oil yourself. This hard-currency dilemma, added to existing indebtedness, will mean cutbacks somewhere. But where? In the military? In the consumer area? Neither is an attractive option, and both are fraught with hazards.

The Third World. There was once a time when you could actually feel the movement of the Third World toward Marxism. While you never were able to provide as large an amount of foreign aid as the West, you could deal in weaponry and ideology with those nations that sought self-determination. In addition, the United States would invariably support the wrong side in situation after situation, and that was of critical importance (in fact, sometimes you wondered if there would be much to cheer about if it weren't for the actions of people like Henry Kissinger in Angola and Senator Jesse Helms in Nicaragua and El Salvador). Now, however, the wars of national liberation are almost all over. The festering Arab-Israeli issue still offers you an entrée to the Middle East and apartheid in South Africa keeps the pot boiling, but it's not like the old days. And what happens when those two matters are resolved? You can't always expect to be rescued by a Somoza or a Reza Pahlavi or a Batista or a Trujillo. To make matters worse, the Americans got out of Vietnam and you got into Afghanistan. And even Marxist states like Mozambique, Guinea, and Angola are talking about trade with the West, and moving toward mixed economies. They need trade and technology and investment; you don't have these and the West does.

The United States. After years of agitation over the war in Vietnam, the United States has begun to reassert itself in defense spending, in areas like the Rapid Deployment Force and conventional weaponry. The Americans have become more conservative and the word "detente" has fallen into disuse. SALT II has been dropped, and the 1980 Republican platform plumped for nuclear superiority. Some of the people recently elected to the United States Senate remind you of your own hardliners.

The Economy. No issue troubles you, however, as much as the economy. The heady days of rapid growth in GNP (5.2% during the 1960s, and 3.8% through the mid-1970s) are apparently over. The projections for economic growth in the 1980s are expected to follow the more recent trend of a 2 percent annual rate. That is a virtually stagnant situation. Your capacity to fund your expensive friends, to keep oil at $15 a barrel, to provide a noticeable increase in the standard of living in Russia and in eastern Europe, to trade with Third World countries, will be severely limited. The constant 4 percent real growth devoted to arms spending will take a greater percentage of the stagnant GNP, especially with a need to import oil soon and no hard currency to fall back on. Any arms increase will mean serious cutbacks in domestic consumption, even beyond those caused by crop failures. You can always rally your people against a "hawkish" America, but how far and for how long? And with these hard-currency and stagnant economic growth problems, you won't be able to buy the Western technology needed to modernize the economy.

A Technology Gap. It is becoming obvious that the United States and other Western nations are pulling further ahead in the entire range of high technologies. A 1981–82 U.S. Defense Department report lists numerous examples of technology advances and the trend is accelerating. The recent statements by President Brezhnev calling for increased trade to purchase high-technology Western products confirm your worst fears. And the present structure of Soviet research is unlikely to reverse these trends. This results in both you and the Third World depending upon the West in an increasingly dominant area.

Labor Shortages. Your demographic trends are beginning to cause concern. Male and infant mortality are on the increase among the Great Russians. Since your society is geared toward control by the Great Russians, it becomes difficult to face the reality that population trends will mandate quantum increases in non-Russian participation in the labor force—and the army. It is hinted that either you will have to recruit your Muslim minorities or they will have to take the initiative and voluntarily seek greater involvement. Both options present very real political and social concerns.

This Soviet's view of his country is clearly that of someone who focuses on bad news. This is, I might add, a characteristic found in whichever party is out of power in American politics. While it tends to be one-dimensional, it also contains fundamentally correct warning signs.

Put another way, the Soviet Union offers an attractive domicile for any unemployed Cassandras.

The point is simple. The Soviets are faced with some crucial problems—problems that are unlikely to go away. If we are going to deal with the Soviets successfully, we must be aware of their strengths, but we must also perceive their weaknesses. For it is the interplay of these strengths and weaknesses that provides them with the viable options.

Soviet Policy Options

One day I went to a press conference on a regional issue, along with several other members of the House of Representatives. The session was well attended by the media, including television crews.

The younger congressmen vied with each other for the most pithy and quotable statements. The implications, both local and global, were examined in great detail, with profound observations and eloquent insights.

An older member standing next to me said absolutely nothing throughout the conference. When it was over, I felt bad about how we had hogged the microphone and never provided him with a clear opportunity to speak. When I expressed a few mumbled regrets, he put his arm around me and assured me that his silence was self-imposed. "You'll learn someday, son, that you can't get in trouble for what you didn't say."

Predicting future Soviet options is a risky business. There is no wisdom so brilliant, no insight so powerful, no analysis so sage as retrospection. Any political candidate running against an incumbent has the advantage of shaping his campaign on the thesis of what he would have done differently. The would-haves are a piece of cake; it's the will-do's that always come back to haunt you.

The joy of retrospect can be experienced when one reads political commentary or listens to Howard Cosell on "Monday Night Football" (a draw play to the halfback on third and long is "genius" if it works and "too conservative" if it fails).

Theodore H. White's book on the 1960 presidential campaign has an anecdote about Richard K. Donahue. Donahue was one of Jack Kennedy's young "Irish Mafia" assistants, who was referred to in the book as "coruscatingly brilliant." Kennedy later was to say to Donahue that if 10,000 votes had gone the other way he would have been described as "coruscatingly stupid."

The Soviet Union must confront a series of decisions in the 1980s and 1990s quite unlike those of the last three decades. While it will have to face, like the United States, a number of irresistible forces and immovable objects, that is only part of the dilemma.

The crucial difference is this: a thoughtful, non-dogmatic Soviet leader looking at the world around him will come to one very startling conclusion: *Time may well no longer be on the side of the Soviet Union.* That reality has an inexorable momentum. The Soviets are capable of enormous effort and sacrifice, and of steadfast devotion to a charted course (including inflicting brutality upon their own people), because they see themselves as agents of history. Theirs, they argue, is the true manifest destiny, bequeathed to them by Lenin, Marx, and Engels. But what if the tide of history has changed?

It seems to me that the Soviets will have to consider options that seek to deal with these problems, or at least arrest the shift in momentum. Specifically, the Soviet Union must ponder policies that carry increased risks. When time is on your side, the instinct is one of optimistic caution, ever probing, ever advancing, but never doing anything that is so hazardous as to interrupt the tide of history. When time is not on your side, the instinct is to gamble, to undertake actions which can reverse that tide.

Dealing with a powerful beast requires power.

Dealing with a beast that feels increasingly cornered requires power—and brains.

Any political candidate soon learns that the one opponent he doesn't want to debate is the opponent who knows he is going to lose. He has no limits and is capable of irrational and desperate actions.

The next two decades, but especially the 1980s, will be a watershed of U.S.-Soviet relations because the Russians and Americans will come face to face with reality. Both will need to devote significant resources to solve the economic and energy problems that threaten their respective systems. Pressures will build, and the corresponding need for rational decisionmaking will increase.

It should be the policy of the United States to keep the Soviets from probing and advancing. And we should render impossible any move by the Soviets toward nuclear superiority. Both are basic.

Yet it should also be the policy of the United States not to engage in actions that will corner the Russian bear in such a way as to invite frenetic madness. We should assist history in providing the Soviets with a set of diminishing returns. But we should do so in a way that allows room for the process of lowered expectations on their part.

The basic flaw of the Soviet system is its economy. An overly bureaucratic, socialistic structure simply runs counter to the pursuit of individual self-interest. An economy that focuses its best technical minds on military hardware will find itself unable to export quality domestic products, and with an increasing need to import high-technology equipment for non-military uses such as oil exploration and production. An economy that can't provide increased investment to developing countries will become less relevant to those countries the further they get from their war of liberation. And finally, a non-expanding economy that is gun-heavy and butter-shy will take a toll on a constituency—be it Soviet or Polish or Afghan—that has enjoyed increased living standards, no matter how marginal those increases may seem to us.

In order to accommodate the social and international pressures of a stagnant economy, the most obvious escape valve for the Soviets is to cut back on defense spending. That, however, would run counter to every Soviet instinct. Whether imbued with the Marxist–Leninist–inspired "mission of history" or still scarred by the memory of a Mother Russia ravaged during World War II, the Soviets look to their military force as a literal security blanket.

The options open to the Soviets will then be as follows:

Internal Repression at Home. If there are difficult times ahead in the consumer sector, the Soviets will have to tighten the reins among the affected constituencies. Using the excuse of strengthening resolve in the face of growing American aggressiveness, the Soviets will continue to squeeze channels of dissent. This policy has been used before, so it may not be too disruptive. The utter disregard for the Helsinki Accords and the repression of people like Andrei Sakharov and Anatoly Shcharansky are just the more dramatic of the actions taken.

Drive a Wedge Between America and Its Allies. Every effort will be used to keep the Europeans and Japanese from strengthening their military defenses. Adding the European GNP, for example, to that of the United States only exacerbates Soviet arms-spending requirements. Indeed, while Americans always compare U.S. arms outlays to those of the USSR, the level of the NATO allies relative to the Warsaw Pact nations is just as relevant. The Soviet policy will involve the age-old technique of good cop/bad cop applied to the West Europeans and Japanese. By deploying the SS-20, they can play to the European's "a plague on both superpowers" syndrome. There exists a continuing European concern that the United States and the Soviet Union may someday engage in a nuclear exchange over some irrational event—a concern intensified by the loose talk of Reagan administration officials about "limited nuclear war." Europeans are appalled when they consider that they themselves might face obliteration because of some miscalculation or paranoia on the part of either superpower. To Europeans of this persuasion, the more independent their own posture, the greater the chance that the Soviets will spare them. That's the bad-cop approach. At the same time, the Soviets will sweet-talk their European neighbors, proclaiming a fervent desire for peaceful coexistence and insisting that they would be less bellicose were it not for the NATO buildup. This will play to the omnipresent instinct of American allies—raised to an art form by the Japanese—to avoid carrying their share of the mutual defense burden. "America gets its jollies from the Cold War saber-rattling, let them build the sabers," or, "Look, our economy will be better off if we manufacture Toyotas rather than armored personnel carriers. If anything happens, the Americans will defend us anyway."

The American instinct is to build arms; the allied instinct is to avoid such production. These tendencies can be exploited since the allies well know that the smaller the percentage of GNP they devote to defense, the more they can devote to their non-military industrial efforts. And thus the more quickly they can out-compete the United States in the international trade markets. The allies are content to allow this to happen as long as the United States remains relatively mute—and so far it has.

Back to Basics: More Targets of Opportunity. Nothing has worked for the Soviets as well as their skillful "targets of opportunity" policy, in terms of territory gained, influence exerted, and goodwill received. In terms of the few monies spent and the minimal risk incurred, it has been an accountant's dream—the kind of situation for which the term "cost benefit analysis" was invented. In addition, it drained the U.S. Treasury and caused both the allies and the Third World to wonder about America's common sense.

Batista ripened Cuba for Castro. Somoza ripened Nicaragua for the Sandinistas. France ripened Vietnam for Ho Chi Minh. Portugal ripened Mozambique and Angola. El Salvador and Guatemala beckon.

The Soviet strategy is to play to America's blind spot: its tendency to react to Third World events by abandoning its domestic principles. Self-determination, equal justice, and racial equality are powerful American ideas that the Soviets ignore at home. In exploiting targets of opportunity, however, it is the Soviets who talk successfully about racism and suppression. Why? Because the United States has resorted to the politics of expediency when faced with supposed Communist subversion. We look for political, not principled, kindred spirits.

Our unfortunate attitude can be summed up by an unrelated incident.

In the fall of 1966, I was working for the reelection of Congressman Bradford Morse for whom I had interned the summer before. One day he invited me to accompany him to a few social clubs and men's organizations in a swing through Lowell and Lawrence. At one stop we encountered a fellow who was a notorious ne'er-do-well and political hanger-on. He was, in the eyes of a twenty-five-year-old political novice, not the kind of person you would want on your side. Upon leaving the club, I asked one of Morse's assistants why we were tolerating such help. "He may be a son-of-a-bitch," he replied, "but he's our son-of-a-bitch"—which of course repeats the famous statement allegedly made by FDR of the Dominican Republic's Trujillo. The reference is apt, since we have historically viewed right-wing Third World leaders with exactly this attitude.

The Soviets are sorely tempted to exploit existent situations. In addition to the constantly festering Palestinian issue, which helps the Arab states forget about Afghanistan, there are several "ripe" pieces gleaming in the sun.

Most notable is minority rule in South Africa and Namibia. It is such a morally unambiguous situation that our lack of concern severely tarnishes America's claim to be sensitive to racial inequality. American corporations and conservatives can be depended upon to defend the white minority government.

(In early 1981, a Middle Eastern ambassador to the United States paid me a visit. Among other things on his agenda was a strong plea that we use our influence to resolve the issue of Namibian independence so that black Africa could continue its noticeable drift away from the Soviets. In arguing this approach to me, he was preaching to the already convinced. I asked him to forget me and focus his efforts on the Senate conservatives, who might find his advice more credible than mine.)

In addition, the Soviets will concentrate on the regimes in Latin America, Africa, and Asia that are clones of the unlamented Batista and Somoza regimes. Stir these up, get America to overreact, and you've done a good day's work.

These policies will relate to the most fundamental question: the interplay between the United States and the Soviets. Let us now focus on that bilateral relationship.

In recent years the Soviets were the initiating agent, being committed to a 4 percent real growth military buildup. That course, if unmatched by the United States, would have eventually resulted in an imbalance, which in turn would reap enormous dividends without a shot being fired. But Carter began to move ahead on the Cruise missile and the Trident submarine systems, which worried the Soviets. He canceled the B-1 and the neutron bomb. In addition, the Stealth technology bomber was being readied for a decision. Carter took a defense budget that in the post-Vietnam period had experienced a substantial net decline in real terms and began a 3 percent real dollar increase. President Reagan's first budget proposed 6 and 11 percent real growth increases in 1982 and 1983.

Given America's significantly larger GNP ($2.6 trillion as compared to the Soviet Union's $1.4 trillion), the situation closely parallels that of World War II. The United States began far behind the Axis powers in military might, but a vast industrial capacity enabled it eventually to overcome its adversaries. An aroused America increasing its dollar deployment into defense is certain to offset any Soviet advantage.

Thus, the Soviets cannot win an arms race. But neither can they lose one. Earlier in this chapter I referred to the issue of survival. It is relevant here in the context of a current "bleed-them-to-death" theory.

This theory suggests that the Soviet system is about to be badly strained (and I agree with that). It is therefore in the American interest to force the Soviets into an arms race, declaring that our intent is nuclear superiority, so as to further burden the Soviet system and cause its internal collapse. Depending on whom you talk to, this theory may or may not call for keeping stoked the fires in Cambodia, Angola, Ethiopia. It is advanced by those who seek "victory" over the Soviets, but fails to be realistic for three very good reasons.

First, an arms race "victory" would occur only after several years of massive U.S. military budgets. Such a commitment would exact enormous costs on *our* system, given the twin problems of inflation and a federal budget deficit.

Second, the Soviets, because they are a totalitarian regime, can simply muscle a greater percentage of their GNP for defense, thus offsetting our advantage. Soviet citizens can endure five meatless days a week in order to accommodate arms spending—their American counterparts are unlikely to cope with three meatless days a week. Is America prepared for gasoline rationing over the long haul in order to achieve nuclear superiority? Whether Russians were ready or not for such a regime would be almost irrelevant. Try persuading our senior citizens to do with less Social Security for ten years; try telling our college students that government educational loans are not going to be available so we can achieve nuclear superiority. There is every reason to believe that Americans could meet the Soviet challenge, if not doing so would jeopardize their survival. There is also every reason to believe that Americans are not prepared to respond to a theory of how to "get" the Soviets when there is a clear lack of consensus as to the viability of the theory and when the cost would be serious and sustained sacrifice.

Third, the Soviets won't lose because they cannot lose. We would present them with a situation that would trigger their survival response mechanism. That is a far more powerful instinct than Soviet aggressiveness. And we should not gloss over the distinction. Faced with actions required for survival, any nation is prepared for sacrifice. We certainly would be. Why do we assume that the Russians are any different, remembering the horrors they endured during World War II? Push them into a corner, either physically or politically, and we'd better be prepared for a fight. Put the lives of my children at risk and, I, despite my civilized veneer, would be prepared to inflict mayhem upon the intruder.

Even beyond the fact that the Soviets would be prepared to match rubles for dollars in an arms race, suppose we did achieve nuclear superiority, would we be prepared to use it? We didn't do so when we had it in the decades after World War II.

And what if the Soviets could not keep up with us? Would the world be better off if there existed a nuclear superpower with nothing to lose? Imagine how we'd react. When Butch Cassidy and the Sundance Kid came out at the end of the film with guns blazing to "take the bastards with us," it honored a deeply rooted American tradition: Never give up. If the enemy is going to win, inflict as much cost upon him as possible. The same mentality exists in all peoples, including the Soviets.

American Policy Options

An American policy must respond to the realities of the Soviet challenge and the Soviet political structure.

What those realities are, of course, is subject to intense debate. Sometimes that debate is between extremes, but usually it's between reasonable people. Let me illustrate this with an experience I had in the spring of 1980.

The Senate has a Wednesday morning prayer breakfast. It is non-partisan, non-ideological, and non-sectarian. The meetings last for one hour, evenly divided between breakfast and a discussion led by a different senator each week. I am not an overtly religious person. My beliefs in God are intensely personal, and the current politicizing of religion repels me. The prayer breakfast, however, is a warm and comfortable experience. Although my attendance is very irregular, the feeling of fellowship is important to me. It is an intensely personal situation, and the most humanizing event that occurs in the Senate on a regular basis.

After one meeting, I was walking out with Peter Domenici, Republican senator from New Mexico, and someone I feel close to. Pete is a conservative, and considered very thoughtful by members of both parties. We were discussing our families and the subject turned to the Soviets. He remarked that he worries about his eight children living under Soviet domination if we don't get serious about defense. That statement has stayed with me. Pete looks at his children and sees the threat of Soviet domination. I look at my children and see the threat of nuclear holocaust brought on by the madness of either side. I spend as much time worrying about the narrow-minded belligerence of hardline Americans as I do about the narrow-minded belligerence of hardline Soviets.

An American defense posture that wants to avoid the extremes at both ends of the political spectrum cannot ignore the deep concerns of thoughtful moderates and conservatives like Domenici. To ignore these concerns is to force them into the arms of the Dr. Strangeloves and Darth Vaders in the halls of power.

I believe that these concerns could be met if there was an assurance of never losing parity ("rough equivalence") *vis-à-vis* the Soviets: "We must never be second to anyone." Thus, we as a nation must—as Senators Moynihan, Nunn, and Domenici have said—come to grips with the actuality of the Soviet military buildup.

That's the easy part. The hard part is figuring out how much is enough. How much military spending is necessary to counter the Soviet threat? The buildup is measured in both quantitative and qualitative terms.

Quantitative Buildup. Arguing defense needs in percentage terms is overly simplistic. But that is how the debate has emerged, and for better or worse we are locked into that frame of reference. At the London NATO Conference in 1977, President Carter and the other allied leaders agreed to a buildup of 3 percent real growth in defense spending. When Senator Tower, chairman of the Armed Services Committee, speaks of a buildup, he refers to figures up to 13 percent. President Reagan speaks in terms of a 6 to 11 percent real growth over the next two years. If the range of national discussion varies between 3 and 13 percent, how does one decide?

We must ask what our objectives are. Are they rough equivalence or superiority? If rough equivalence, we will focus on the 3–5 percent range, which parallels the Soviet spread, even without accounting for the advantage we enjoy by being allied with the NATO countries as opposed to the Warsaw Pact nations. If it's superiority we want, then we will concentrate on the 9–13 percent range.

For reasons discussed earlier, I believe that attempting to achieve superiority is madness. It violates everything we know about human behavior and survival response mechanisms. Put simply, if we do it, then they will have to, and the spiral escalates. Since we seek no aggressive or territorial objective, being ahead is meaning-less.

Beyond the military criteria, there is a very real consideration about cost that never seems to bother those who pride themselves on being fiscal conservatives. Although the range is from as wide as 3 to 13 percent, let us examine the difference between 5 and 9 percent for the purposes of discussion—5 percent representing high-side "rough equivalence," and 9 percent representing low-side "superiority."

The difference between 5 percent and 9 percent over ten years is $437 billion (that between 3 percent and 13 percent is $1.17 trillion). Are these massive dollars of no concern in a decade when people are elected to the White House and Congress on a platform of fighting inflation, balancing the budget, and controlling spending? Indeed, the Reagan increases in military spending are at a rate double that of the Vietnam-era budgets.

The nuclear superiority argument fails on a number of strategic grounds and violates any sense of fiscal responsibility. The further we inch up beyond the 3 percent range, the more critical will be the economic consequences. Those consequences provide their own brand of national security weakness by diverting resources from other critical needs (a point that will be examined in detail in Chapter 5.)

Thus, terms like "nuclear superiority," "margin of safety," and "second to none" have meanings and nuances that require the cold question, How much?

Qualitative Buildup. Basic to the question of how much is the question of what it is for. Spending money on defense is valuable only if the right needs are being met. Yet invariably we prepare to ensure victory in the last war we fought, not the next one.

The American military tends to want more and better of the same thing it already has. The Air Force desires the B-1 and a Stealth technology bomber. It would be nice to have them both, but what happens if pushing for the B-1 now results in fewer or no Stealth-type bombers later? And is that the optimum package?

As for the Navy, there is no question that a shipbuilding pro-gram of some intensity is required; but how do we decide what kinds of ships? In recent years the Navy has opted for nuclear-powered aircraft carriers. They are big, powerful, and highly visible targets in an era when anti-ship missile development has outstripped the defensive capabilities of these vessels. What happens if pushing for the $3.3 billion for each copy of a nuclear carrier results in the construction of fewer small, fast, and maneuverable ships?

The issue also arises in connection with the MX missile. Various options have been devised for siting the missiles in such a way as to make them less vulnerable to a first strike by the Soviets. Some have suggested we should build more than twenty vertical shelters per missile so as to hide the true location of the particular missile (at a cost of $36 billion in 1980 dollars). Others believe we should simply place them on planes and shuttle them from airport to airport (at a cost of $37 billion in 1980 dollars). Or we could put together an elaborate network of roads in the Utah-Nevada area and ply the missiles between shelters on those roads (at a cost of $37 billion in 1980 dollars). Finally, we deploy the MX on small electronic submarines in costal waters (at a cost of $32 billion in 1980 dollars). However that debate is resolved, what happens if the pursuit of various unproven concepts for siting the MX missile results in fewer dollars being available for conventional weaponry, such as tanks, armored personnel carriers, anti-tank weapons, in which we are currently lower than the Warsaw Pact nations?

Complicating all this is the problem of lobbyists. The weapons system most likely to pass the Congress is the one with a constituency. More and bigger of the same can plug into the existing political power of the manufacturers. Thus, congressional decisions often reflect the opportunity for pork barrel rather than defense capability.

What we need, then, is intelligent decisionmaking on quality. In my view, the items should include (in order of priority) first, conventional weapons parity; second, a mobile, lean, small vessel–based sea capability; third, the Cruise missile; fourth, an effective penetration bomber such as the Stealth; fifth, the upgrading with the Trident of our sea-leg portion of the nuclear triad; and sixth, the paced development of the MX missile, while reserving a decision on siting and *deployment* until a viable basing proposal is designed.

I would omit from the list: the neutron bomb, as being simply too low a priority, and too controversial among our allies; the B-1 bomber, as unnecessary in the world of Cruise missiles and Stealth bombers; any more nuclear-powered aircraft carriers, as too costly and vulnerable; and any latter-day ABM system, as being inherently destabilizing to the nuclear balance.

These questions as to the quantity and quality of U.S. arms spending are critical. Yet, in focusing on them exclusively we run a very real risk of setting aside the parallel issue of arms control.

For if the objective is the physical security of our people (as suggested earlier), the only viable approach in today's world is to counter the Soviet threat: first, by meeting it head on with the procurement policies listed above; and second, by constraining it through arms control. It is not an either/or situation. Both are needed. Either one by itself is folly.

Arms Control

SALT: Instincts and Characteristics. When I entered the Senate, the most critical issue on the agenda was the SALT II Treaty. After seven years of negotiation by three administrations, the Strategic Arms Limitations Treaty had been signed and it needed to be brought before the Senate for its "advice and consent." Although I was philosophically inclined toward an arms control treaty, this vote was a weighty responsibility, and I wanted to be as analytical as possible.

In addition to studying the technical details of the treaty, I decided to use a technique I had found helpful as a congressman. I put together an advisory committee of some twenty-five people of widely divergent views, representing the best minds on arms control and Sovietology found in Massachusetts. Since the Boston area is home to many universities, defense firms, and high-technology companies, the talent available is imposing.

The committee met three times for three hours each, with these unquestioned experts having at one another. Included were people like Albert Carnesale of Harvard, William Griffith of M.I.T., Samuel Huntington, George Kistiakowsky, Joseph Nye, Paul Doty, and Richard Pipes (all of Harvard), Scott Thompson of Tufts, Kotsas Tsipis of M.I.T., Ernest May of Harvard, Harold Rosenbaum, and others who, if less known, were equally compelling. These nine hours were the single greatest intellectual experience of my political career. The quality of the minds attracted to this, the *ultimate* issue, was awesome.

The debates centered on Soviet history, the technology of ICBM's, the theories on counterforce and countervalue targeting, first strike capability, verification, and so on. Most of the time I was smart enough not to comment. Eventually, however, I began to understand that the divergent opinions, often intensely held, were a function not only of technological assessment but also of individual views about basic Soviet intentions. Those views reflected assumptions based on the Soviet experience, of course; but what struck me was the clear difference in the assumptions about the nature of man.

The technical questions on SALT are easier to resolve than the subjective arguments as to Soviet intentions. Equally, the harangue as to American intentions will rage on in the Kremlin. At some point, however, the debate must end and a decision be made.

I concluded that SALT II was in the American interest. I believe strongly that, on its merits, SALT II would have passed the Senate if the 3 to 5 percent commitment on defense spending had been agreed to, *and* if the Senate had not been spooked by political fears.

One senator known for his hawkish views told Senator John Culver of Iowa, a member of the Armed Services Committee, that he would support SALT II because it was worthwhile, but would have to make preliminary growling and grousing sounds to placate his conservative constituency. By the time he finished growling and grousing, he was locked into a position of opposition to the treaty, and so declared his intentions. Another senator was not considered a potential supporter because he had voted for the Panama Canal Treaties and could not afford a second politically damaging vote in his 1980 reelection bid; on the merits, he had no strong feelings one way or another. When I indicated my disrespect (to put it mildly) for this attitude, a senior colleague remarked that the senator in question "doesn't mind World War III just as long as he's a senator when it happens."

SALT II never had a chance, because the middle collapsed. In the 1979–80 Senate there were about fifty senators who would have voted for a SALT II Treaty that was strategically sound and independently verifiable. There were about thirty senators who would not have voted for a SALT Treaty no matter what—"You can't trust the Russians," they claim. (Any SALT Treaty based on complete trust of the Soviets is by definition foolhardy. The treaty must be independently verifiable.) Then there were about twenty senators who were not passionately involved on the merits either way and whose vote would be a function of the political climate. For the reasons discussed earlier, that climate was hostile, and there was no way that seventeen of the twenty would have voted for the treaty to provide the necessary two-thirds favorable margin.

Is There Life After SALT? A world without SALT is very unsettling, to say the least. Leaving aside the issue of increased suspicion about intent, the sheer arithmetic in such a world speaks for itself.

For example: Under SALT II, the Soviets would be allowed one new missile system; without the treaty there is no limit. They can, and most likely will, upgrade and modernize all their ICBM forces. (The United States would have been limited to one new missile as well, the MX most likely, but that's all we were going to develop anyway.) With SALT II, the Soviets were permitted 10 warheads in each of their 318 heavy SS-18 ICBM's; without SALT II, they can deploy up to 35. This 25 warhead-per-missile increase would give the Soviets some 7,950 warheads *more*. Thus America would have 7,950 more targets for which a nuclear warhead had been earmarked. (The United States has recently developed ICBM's based on accuracy and deployment characteristics—solid-fueled, not liquid-fueled—rather than sheer size. Thus the warhead-per-missile limit of ten is meaningless to us since the Minuteman III only carries three warheads and the MX is designed to carry up to ten.)

If the Soviets are able to deploy 7,950 more nuclear warheads on their 318 SS-18's (not to mention other SS-18's that may be produced, or other air-based or sea-based nuclear buildup), they will have a much greater chance to secure what is called "a first strike counter-force capability." First strike counterforce capability simply means that the Soviets may be able to target effectively all our ICBM sites and other strategic installations. This is the reason so much effort is being spent on the siting of the MX missile. If the Soviets believe they have a first strike capability, the world has become destabilized.

Since we have both the air-breathing and sea-based legs of our nuclear triad, a first strike capability against our land-based missiles is not, by itself, determinative. It is, however, sufficiently threatening to cause a political uproar and bring about requests for more defense spending on our strategic capability, including demands for an anti-ballistic missile system. And who will make this argument? The same people who killed SALT II in the first place.

Finally, most Americans when polled do not mention the SALT process among their major anxieties. Inflation, energy, too much government, the economy, other defense issues, invariably run ahead of arms control in public concerns.

The failure of SALT, however, renders these other matters irrelevant. We have lived in a nuclear age so long that we have become immune to the dimensions of that reality. I was four years old when Hiroshima and Nagasaki were bombed. During the Cuban missile crisis, Americans were forced to think the unthinkable. After the crisis was resolved, we stopped thinking the unthinkable.

That didn't make it go away.

By January of 1981, the United States had 9,700 nuclear warheads, ranging from 40 to 9,000 kilotons of TNT (9,000 kilotons represents 450 times the force unleashed on Hiroshima). The Soviets have 6,600 nuclear warheads, ranging from 500 to 24,000 kilotons.

To get a sense of this, multiply the Hiroshima explosion force by 10, and apply it 5,000 times in our country. (I assume that some Soviet warheads would be targeted to Europe, Japan, and China.) Now apply the same brutal mathematics to Russia. An all-out thermonuclear exchange is unwinnable.

Look out your front window and imagine the condition of your neighborhood and your city and your county and your state if a nuclear weapon were dropped on it. Look at a child and feel the injustice of its life being obliterated because the United States and the Soviets could not resolve their differences. Arms control is not simply another issue. It is a critical component of *the issue,* namely, our survival.

We must renew the SALT process, and not just for a SALT II-type agreement. That by itself is not arms reduction, by any means—it still allows each side 1,200 MIRVed ballistic missiles. The key is a SALT II agreement that, above all, leads to SALT III. And then SALT IV, and SALT V. A gradual but steady chopping away at the nuclear arsenal of both superpowers. Each missile left unbuilt is a missile unavailable for fantasies about the effectiveness of a first-strike attack.

Beyond the effect on the United States and the Soviet Union, there is the very real concern about nuclear proliferation among other nations. The 1981 Israeli attack on the Iraqi nuclear reactor raised the issue of a world mesmerized by fear of nuclear attack. Will Iraq ever use such a weapon? Will Israel? Will Libya? Will India? Will Pakistan? How long can we expect these weapons to exist without being used? Not forever. And, in my saddened opinion, not even to the end of this century. Nuclear proliferation must be stopped. And it can only be stopped if the superpowers show the way to nuclear sanity.

The SALT process is the ultimate test of leadership. No American President can be judged successful by history if his tenure doesn't leave the country and the world safer from the threat of nuclear devastation. The same test applies to any Soviet Premier.

When a Reagan administration official came before the Senate Foreign Relations Committee and declared that arms control had been "oversold," he chilled many of us. Oversold? What is the alternative? An arms race, of course. The Reaganites will term it "containment," "a margin of safety," or "second to none," or some such. But it's an arms race nonetheless.

An arms race carries with it the dangers of miscalculation. Events cannot *always* be controlled—and it only takes one mistake to bring about the decimation of mankind.

In sum, United States policy toward the Soviet Union should be grounded upon the following guidelines:

1. Be very plain that we are prepared to meet any Soviet arms buildup; that we will respond to their aggressive instinct.

2. Be equally plain that we seek rough equivalence, not nuclear superiority; that we will not seek to trigger their survival response mechanism. Our goal is serious, determined negotiations to achieve arms control.

3. Hold our allies' feet to the fire, especially the Japanese, in demanding that they share the military burden. They should not be allowed all the economic advantages of non-involvement and all the military advantages of American protection.

4. Apply to overseas situations internal American principles— such as racial equality, equal justice, and self-determination—to forestall Soviet targets of opportunity in the Third World. In other words, let's stop acting like the Tories who opposed our own fight for independence. Never forget that George Washington, Benjamin Franklin, Samuel Adams, and Thomas Jefferson were revolutionaries.

5. Offer the Soviets a commitment to work toward solutions to our common problems, such as the eventual depletion of oil reserves, which threaten both of us. But this era of cooperation should not be used by the Soviets as a pause that enables them to proceed with a buildup. The collaboration should be coupled with a Soviet realization that they have no mission in history to "bury" us.

6. Provide an environment that enables the Soviets to adjust to the fact that history is no longer on their side, but without being overly threatening to them. It's going to be a politically difficult transition for the Soviet Union, and we should not make it harder than necessary.

The U.S.-Soviet relationship in the 1980s provides an opportunity for realism to prevail over dogma and mutual suspicion. At the rate we are going, both countries will be armed to the teeth while their economic and energy problems still go unresolved. Mired in fear of the other's aggressiveness, each will seek ever more security in ever more arms—and cause the other to respond in like fashion.

Can it be different? Only if there are demonstrations of leadership on both sides. A leadership founded upon mutual self-interest, upon an understanding that we jointly control the survival of mankind.

Once the armies are unleashed, once the missiles are launched, we have all lost. There will be no winners in the next war.

When will we all take it seriously—when the sirens begin to wail? When we reach the top of the waterfall? Will we finally be ready to think rationally, to reject the dogma? Will we plead to God to stop the unstoppable so that we can try to change things?

By then it will all be gone—in one intense blast of technology, devised by a species whose science evolved too fast for its instinct to keep up.

The world cannot wait to decide to put rational defense policy and arms control on the top of its agenda until just before it goes over the waterfall.

4/The Economic Pie: The Third Reality

The third major reality of America's future is the nation's economy —the most bounteous in the history of man.

The great political tugs and pulls of the past thirty-five years have concerned the distribution of the golden eggs. In the 1980s and 1990s, we must focus on the health of the goose.

As in dealing with the energy crisis and fashioning a realistic defense policy *vis-à-vis* the Soviets, managing the economy is essential to our national survival.

The economy is like your health: when it's going well, you never think about it. When you begin to lose it, suddenly it becomes a matter of enormous urgency. During the 1960s, when the economy was booming, my schoolmates would discuss potential jobs in terms of their "relevance." With so many jobs available, you could apply your own criteria.

During the 1970s, the economy occasionally turned sour and the word "relevance" was heard less and less. The question "Did you get a relevant job?" gave way to "Did you get a job?" In the 1980s, we face the issues of stagflation, obsolete industrial infrastructure, and declining productivity. The word "relevance" is not heard in the land.

The Republicans traditionally worry about costs, incentives, and productivity—often to the exclusion of such concerns as pollution, work safety, and workers' rights. The Democrats traditionally worry about pollution, work safety, and workers' rights—often to the exclusion of costs, incentives, and productivity.

This adversary structure has a certain balance, of course; but for the Democrats today, and especially for liberal Democrats, it makes no sense whatsoever. If the economy doesn't perform, who gets hurt? Mostly the working people, the Democrats' natural constituency.

Growing up in Lowell, I learned firsthand about decline. It is pervasive; it eats away at everyone and everything. The traditional focus of the Democratic-controlled Lowell government was the distribution of the city's ever-diminishing resources. Various factions vied over control of the governmental structure, as Lowell continued its steady deterioration. The "enemy" to the city fathers was those s.o.b.'s at the Lowell Chamber of Commerce. The municipal government and the private sector went at each other while the city suffered. Indeed, successful candidates for the city council often attacked the chamber and its "greed."

Living in Lowell during the late 1970s and 1980s, I learned firsthand about resurgence. It, too, is pervasive. It pumps up everyone and everything.

Lowell is a workingman's town, with only 10 percent Republican registration among its voters. The revival of the city thus benefits working-class Democrats. If a Democratic public official contributes to the resurgence, he helps fellow Democrats. As we saw earlier, Lowell's rebirth is mostly a result of private-sector investment. The government acted as catalyst, certainly, but private-sector confidence in the economic viability of the community was the main factor. Why should that combination be alien to a Democrat—or to a liberal? By working with the private sector, by spending time cooperating with businessmen and bankers, a Democratic public official is serving this blue-collar constituency. It certainly beats worrying about workman's unemployment compensation and the other devices resorted to when all else fails.

In sharp contrast to earlier decades, the public and private sectors in Lowell are now engaged in an ardent embrace. The liaison has produced the best of both worlds: the private sector is making a profit and the public sector is enjoying the political security of a generally happy constituency. In the process, the city is becoming known throughout the state and nationally as a prototype of urban renaissance. Watching Democratic officeholders and Republican bankers and businessmen bounce from one ground-breaking and ribbon-cutting to another is fascinating.

This example is relevant beyond Lowell, because our national economy isn't humming along any more.

From 1947 to 1967, U.S. productivity growth averaged 3.1 percent, and liberalism flourished. From 1967 to 1977, productivity averaged only a 1.9 percent increase, and liberalism was slipping. In 1979 and 1980, productivity actually declined, and liberalism was clobbered.

The phenomenon isn't as simple as all this, of course, but the lesson should be obvious: Liberalism, the vehicle that carries generosity and compassion into the public arena, needs a healthy economy. A stagnant economy is, by definition, illiberal. If the economy is expanding, we can open our hearts to the aspirations of others, since the growth can accommodate their demands. If the economy stagnates, or declines, those aspirations can be met only at the expense of other segments of society. All of us end up fighting for the same share of the pie. The dominant force of the 1980 election was the stagflation-induced reversal of the direction of middle-class anger. Traditionally aimed at the privileged, it was now focused downward toward the poor—giving the Republicans a great advantage. Thus, since illiberalism hurts the traditional Democratic constituency (not to mention Democratic officeholders), it is the liberals who should care the most about the state of our economy.

I will return to Massachusetts to make a second point. The state's economy at the turn of the century relied upon shoes and textiles. The old mill cities absorbed hundreds of thousands of immigrants who came to work in those industries. They sought a better life and were willing to work hard. As the twentieth century moved along, however, the owners of many of these industries decided to move their operations to the South—close to both raw materials and cheap labor.

Massachusetts suffered all the problems of a depressed economy. Then, during the post–World War II era, when the decay was beginning to encrust, something new broke through—high technology. The concepts and ideas of high technology sprang up in Massachusetts because of its traditional excellence in higher education generally, but more particularly because of several outstanding technically oriented educational institutions. (The Massachusetts Institute of Technology is the most significant university in the area of scientific research and development.) Spinning off from this university base, scores of high-technology firms took root in our state. Small at first, these companies located along Route 128, and started to grow. Digital Equipment Corporation was founded by Kenneth Olsen, an M.I.T. engineer, and two others in 1957. By September 1980, Digital Equipment had 55,000 employees, 20,000 of them in Massachusetts. Wang Laboratories was begun by Dr. An Wang, who received his doctorate in applied physics from Harvard, with 1 part-time associate in 1951; at the end of 1980, the company employed 7,800 in Massachusetts, 13,000 worldwide. Raytheon, founded by three Tufts engineers in the 1920s, is the largest industrial employer in the state. Raytheon has 26,000 people in Massachusetts, 76,500 worldwide. Computervision went from 10 employees in 1969 to 2,966 in 1980, with most of that increase in the last two years. Data General grew from 4 full-time people and 1 part-time in 1968 to 5,000 in Massachusetts in 1980, almost 15,000 worldwide. The list goes on—Compugraphic, GTE Sylvania, Augat, Applicon, Prime Computer, GCA.

All are high technology, and all have prospered. Rather than a dearth of employment, Massachusetts started to worry about finding enough workers. Instead of being, as formerly, 3 or 4 percent above the national unemployment rate, Massachusetts has ranked first or second among industrial states in lowest unemployment. These companies liked the state, and the state liked them. After decades of perceptible decline—and its attendant negative psychological effects—this was a welcome change in fortunes.

There is one cloud in the Massachusetts economic sky, however. In the wild transition from the traditional industries to the glamorous high-tech firms, the state has assumed an air of blind faith in the future. This faith ignores the upcoming challenge now being mounted by Japan, Inc. Since its energy-intensive industries are increasingly vulnerable to energy shortages, Japan has targeted the high-technology sector for a major onslaught. If our high-tech industries were to be phased out for any reason, where would Massachusetts rebound next?

There is no obvious next recourse. Having neither extractive minerals nor timber, no oil, gas, coal, oil shale or tar sands, the state needs these high-tech firms to keep the economy going. Vigilance is important because there is no reliable industry to fall back on. Fishing, tourism, education, all contribute to the health of Massachusetts; but the removal of high technology from the state would cause a depression. Massachusetts must keep that industry viable, not only for the sake of the businessmen involved but also for the people who work in those plants.

In many respects, America as a whole is in a similar position. Our unsurpassed natural resources provide a powerful base. We have the world's best farmland and more oil and gas reserves than any other industrialized Western nation; our supplies of coal and timber, our fishing and mineral resources, all provide strength. But we desperately need to be more than a country exporting raw materials. We must not be reduced to the status of a glorified banana republic diminishing its raw materials, while importing man-made goods. If we do, our standard of living will plummet accordingly and the resultant political tensions will be extreme.

The future of America, like the future of Massachusetts, depends on its capacity to produce quality manufactured products that can compete in the world market. We need to secure an industrial base geared for the long haul. Unfortunately, we won't worry enough about this base until it starts to crumble.

We must give much more consideration to what it will take to motivate and strengthen that base. For example, by way of allocation, we must commit fewer of our resources to consumption and more to investment in plant and equipment, in technological innovation, in infrastructure and in human capital. A concern for the condition of our nation's industry constitutes the third reality—the need to keep our economic pie growing. It is an issue that receives the most attention these days, and yet most of that attention has been on a very superficial level.

But, first, I want to digress for a moment to deal with the political implications involved—especially for Democrats.

When I was elected to Congress in the Fifth District of Massachusetts, I was both a liberal and the first Democratic congressman in eighty years. I decided to allocate a major part of my staff salaries for an economic development unit to work on the revitalization of Lowell and Lawrence, and on the industrial infrastructure of the district. Both cities were experiencing economic strain and the national economic decline was taking its toll on local industry.

Certainly my reasoning was partly political. The people I would deal with were instinctively conservative—and instinctively Republican. By working with them in a professional and credible manner, I could blunt the potential fund-raising power of the former Republican incumbent who was expected to try to regain the congressional seat.

I soon learned that the economic development staff could make a serious contribution, and one that did not violate my liberal tenets. We were, I believe, increasingly proficient, and found the effort intellectually fascinating. By the end of my four years in the House, the product of this staff would be our major achievement in office.

We became involved with revitalization efforts in the two older cities, efforts that gave promise of significant success. Both Lowell and Lawrence today reflect the results of that commitment of our resources. We helped industry remain in the district and expand. Much of what we did was to demonstrate interest, but much was substantive, including legislation that Congress passed. As it turned out, the previous incumbent, Paul Cronin, decided to remain in the private sector, but these efforts were not without return for me politically. When I ran for the Senate in 1978, although my workers were primarily young liberal Democrats, the bulk of my financial support came from the business community—mostly conservative Republicans with whom I had worked in the Fifth Congressional District. They had learned to respect our capacity to be concerned with and knowledgeable about their particular problems. Despite clear differences of views on social issues, close personal ties had developed, and these men and women came through in my time of need. Today, in Massachusetts, several congressmen use the economic development staff approach productively.

I believe that if a businessman is presented with an environment that allows him to grow, he is able to share this growth with his employees and the community at large. The nature of being in business—pursuing your own self-interest—doesn't mean that you are socially irresponsible. The challenge to the Democratic Party is to show that the enlightened self-interest of the business community overlaps in large part with the enlightened self-interest of government. Working together for their many common goals makes much more sense than battling constantly and exaggerating differences.

This arrangement has many characteristics similar to the "Only Nixon could have gone to China" theory of politics (i.e., only the left can do what the right wants, and only the right can do what the left wants). As a certified liberal Democrat, my maneuverability in economic development is considerable. When I introduce a banking bill, for example, I have a much greater chance of influencing other Democrats to analyze the legislation on its merits than if it were sponsored by a conservative Republican. Inasmuch as valid legislation in these areas would be supported by most Republicans anyway, the coalition is potentially powerful. In addition, a liberal Democrat can devote a much greater share of his time and influence to economic development issues than a conservative Republican— especially in a state like Massachusetts—because his left flank is politically more secure. Finally, a liberal Democrat can bring his natural sensitivity to the human implications of economic development, and as a full participant in the economic development process, ensure that the impact on people, especially poorer people, is not negative.

All this suggests that the marriage of divergent ideologies and politics can be quite natural in the area of economic development. I believe it is a liaison that will become increasingly common throughout the country. (A significant number of the class of 1974 "Watergate Democrats" feel the same way.)

The marriage, however, is not without its follies. My chief fundraiser is Nick Rizzo, an Andover, Massachusetts, businessman. Rizzo's own politics are, in his words, "to the right of Attila the Hun." At least a hundred times we have had the following conversation:

RIZZO: I spent an hour with businessman X and told him about the economic development work you're doing, and finally convinced him that you're not a liberal.

TSONGAS: But I *am* a liberal.

RIZZO: No, you're not.

TSONGAS: But how do you explain my views on [issues a, b, c, d,
          e, f, g, etc.]?
RIZZO: I don't. I don't even want to know about them.

This has led to an unending series of Laurel and Hardy episodes.
For example, in 1979, I organized a dinner to express my appreciation to twenty longtime contributors and supporters. Almost to a
man they were conservatives; most were Republicans.

When we sat down to eat and talk, the leading businessman of
the group—a great benefactor of mine—started off the conversation
as follows:

BUSINESSMAN: Paul, what the hell is this gay rights bill you're
             supporting? (At this point, Rizzo blanched)
TSONGAS: Charlie, if we talk about this, I'll get mad at you.
             You'll get mad at me. I won't change your mind.
             You won't change my mind. And besides, a very
             good dinner will taste awful.
BUSINESSMAN (laughing): All right, we'll talk about something
             else.

The tolerance of my social liberalism by the Massachusetts business community is a function of my acceptance of their critical role
in our collective well-being. I recognize and support their motive
for profit, and thus have a greater opportunity to channel it in
socially beneficial directions. In addition, by working in economic
development and (I hope) being good at it, I can lend credibility to
the social views that I hold. The sense of coming together, of feeling
out each other's perspectives, is not threatening to either side.

The Public-Private Mix in America

The United States is neither a pure free enterprise system nor a pure
welfare state. It is a combination of both, and it is capitalist-based.

A pure free enterprise system is designed to maximize the incentive mechanism of the individual pursuing his self-interest. It also
is indifferent to the obligation of society to protect its disadvantaged. As President Nyerere would say, it lacks "justice."

In theory, a pure welfare system maximizes the distribution of income and "justice." In reality, it minimizes the incentive of the individual to achieve in the face of an amorphous bureaucracy.

The motivating force of each system in its pure form is objectionable. The one gives us the slave trade, robber barons, child labor, black lung disease, unsafe working conditions; the other stagnation, an unresponsive bureaucracy, and a psychological dependence on the state.

Although in some sense it is "justice" that can claim moral superiority for our society, it is actually the nurturing of incentive that is the essential condition for achieving justice. The reason is that if we maximize "justice" we destroy the conditions for economic growth. In more specific terms, if you maximize all your "just" social programs, the costs would be so burdensome as to cripple the economy, leading to sharply reduced governmental revenues, and the collapse of these very programs as a result.

Most people in America and abroad have come to understand the need for balance. The objective is an economic environment where "incentive" and "justice" are at acceptable levels relative to one another. But in the debate here over what constitutes an acceptable mix, we have been shortsighted. In arguing for today's "fair share," many Americans need to stop and think more about tomorrow. Americans have a deep-seated desire for a better future, one with the promise of more "justice" for their children. The only hope for this brighter future, however, lies in restoring the goose to health —this is essential for a fair distribution of golden eggs for our children.

A healthy economy, one that can provide for the growing needs of Americans, must be ensured. America has to commit itself to a pragmatic economic recovery program. But does concern for economic growth dictate total reliance on the private sector? It was this simple, appealing assertion in 1980 that helped generate a Republican landslide.

Burdened by the governmental interventionism of the Democratic philosophy, the country ran headlong into the arms of those extolling the joys of "unleashed" free enterprise, as if the country were unaware of how inadequate "unleashed" free enterprise is for so many of the wants of our nation. The conservative mandate prescribes less government—less regulation, taxation, spending—

and promises expanded output and a rising standard of living. That formula will surely tickle the Japanese, Swiss, and West Germans. The success of our most competitive trading partners and the complexity of today's world economy suggest that an aggressive business community, an aware labor sector, *and an activist public sector* together tackling problems is our nation's only chance for economic success.

An Economic Program

The economic revitalization of America requires a commitment to the long term. The problems we face were accumulated over a period of years—and there is no overnight solution. The suggestions that follow attempt to recognize and turn around the existing dilemmas. As of this writing, many have a serious support base.

Improve Incentives to Save. The United States has become a society living on its financial tippy-toes. The penny-saved-penny-earned philosophy is now considered both quaint and naïve. Savings, whether private or public, have been the only source of capital for a whole host of economic activities, and today that source is drying up rapidly. The abundance of capital has been an essential part of the growth of America. But today, the U.S. personal savings rate hovers around 5 percent, in sharp contrast to the rates of our major international competitors, West Germany (12%) and Japan (20%). If we and they continue present practices, it is easy to see who will be left by the wayside when it comes to capital availability.

Why do we refuse to save? Part of the reason clearly is cultural. Mass media advertising equates happiness with instant gratification and eventually we tend to believe it. But there are structural reasons as well. Income on savings is taxed—thus providing a powerful disincentive to save, which adds to the disincentive already caused by the fact that interest paid on traditional saving accounts is significantly less than the rate of inflation. On the other hand, interest paid on loans is tax-deductible—thus creating a powerful incentive not to save, but rather to borrow. The situation is exactly backwards. The "wise" money manager today, looking at the sheer arithmetic of it all, has to conclude that the advantage is with the borrower, not the saver. And as this reality has been understood by more and more people, savings have flowed away from banks and other depositories. My own financial decisionmaking attests to this situation. In order to begin saving for our young children's education, we opened a savings account for them. Those accounts are virtually empty because it was soon obvious that the funds were guaranteed to depreciate in value over time. Instead, we are investing in home improvements and allowing the equity thus gained to be their "savings accounts." That way the return on investment will at least be positive. Other people are now investing in gold coins, stamps, and oriental rugs. Maybe this will protect the individual. But how much potential productive capital is being locked up in this way?

What should we do to change this national economic response? Simply reverse the incentives and disincentives: Every American should be extended the opportunity to form a tax-deferred, individual retirement account, so long as the funds are invested in productive endeavors. The annual deposit limits for such accounts must be greatly increased. In this way, individuals investing for the long term will be rewarded (if funds are removed before retirement, taxes are levied accordingly). Similarly, a reasonable reduction in the capital gains rate makes sense, as long as the capital gains stem from productive endeavors.

It makes no sense for us, mired in stagflation, to reward borrowing to buy non-necessities like hair dryers, oversized television sets, and power boats, while small businessmen cannot secure loans to run their operations. We must eliminate the tax deduction for consumer loans. Our European competitors and Japan tax consumption. While Americans may deem such action extreme, to continue to subsidize consumption is simply absurd.

Autos and homes merit special attention. Autos should continue to receive an interest tax deduction, for it is imperative that Americans purchase more fuel-efficient cars. Home ownership provides much-needed community roots in our highly mobile society. But how much of a deduction is necessary for this objective? (Country rock star Kenny Rogers recently purchased a home in Beverly Hills for $14 million.) Does permitting tax deductions for interest payments on million-dollar homes increase homeownership in America? I think not. Moreover, many Americans are purchasing third and fourth homes as investments. Today, investment in appreciating housing simply pays better than investment in reindustrialization. To afford the carrots to stimulate productive investments described in this chapter and to reduce the attractions of unproductive investments, we need to wield some sticks. I believe a maximum interest deduction and the limiting of deductions to two homes per household would channel substantial funds into productive endeavors. Moreover, such limits on interest deductibility for homes would reduce pressures on housing prices, making them more accessible to first home buyers.

Improve Incentives to Invest. The savings rate advantage enjoyed by our international competitors is accompanied by their lead in reinvestment in plant and equipment. Physical plant and equipment is renewed at a rate of 14.4 percent in the United States, 18.4 percent in West Germany, and 23.1 percent in Japan. (These figures account for private sector investment only. Public sector investment as a percentage of GNP is 2.9% in the United States, 3.8% in West Germany, and 9.3% in Japan. It is particularly ironic that reduced levels of such investment spending have been proposed by an administration that is arguing for more investment. Such a decline in government spending, earmarked for investments, must sound odd in Japan.) Obviously, given current trends, there is no way our economy is going to be sustained. Old steel mills in Indiana will not compete with new steel mills in Japan.

The problem is very simple: Investment in industry is not profitable enough today because of inflation. That is, the cost of replacement is rising at a rate well beyond the rate of allowed depreciation of that equipment. This policy, of course, contains the seeds of guaranteed obsolescence.

The solution is to increase the financial attractiveness of investment. For Democrats, this can be hard to accept, since we have traditionally viewed investing as a rich man's endeavor; and we have always been hard-pressed to sympathize with the need to provide business with greater advantages. Yet that is what must happen. We must make the chief executive officers of thousands of

American corporations decide that a reinvestment in plant or equipment is sound policy.

How do we do that? By utilizing a number of tax incentives. First, we should provide for accelerated depreciation to speed up the corporations' receipt of tax write-offs for their investments, thus minimizing inflationary impact. I prefer the 2-4-7-10 approach. This scheme combines all equipment categories into four classes, and results in substantially reduced tax lines for most assets. The original accelerated depreciation bill, 10-5-3 (10 years for buildings, 5 years for equipment, and 3 years for vehicles) tilts benefits too strongly toward construction of new buildings. The Frostbelt-to-Sunbelt implications of this last point are obvious. Rehabilitating an existent plant should be equally rewarded. Second, we should increase the investment tax credit and make this credit refundable. Firms that fail to earn a profit should also have incentives to modernize. For our declining industries in particular, a refundable investment tax credit is an excellent means to motivate reinvestment. And third, we should provide tax reforms aimed at allowing small business to retain and attract necessary capital. Small business enterprises typically have poor access to equity capital and must pay above the prime rate for funds. Yet it is that sector of industry which is the most productive when it comes to innovation and new jobs.

Almost as important is the question of what should not be done.

Suppose a tax plan is introduced by two Democrats. It is attacked as unworkable by the following all-star line-up of leading conservative economists and Republican leaders: economists such as Paul Volcker, Arthur Burns, Herbert Stein, Henry Kaufman, and Alan Greenspan; Republican leaders such as Vice President George Bush, Senate Finance Committee Chairman Robert Dole, and House Ways and Means Committee Ranking Member Barber Conable. Now, clearly, the Republican attitude would be one of strong opposition, given such an array of distinguished dissenters. Faced with such opposition today, the two Democrats would be obliterated.

But what happens if you have the same line-up of opposition and the bill's sponsors are Republicans—and their names are Jack Kemp and William Roth? Is the bill any less suspect? No.

Nevertheless, in the battle for control of the Republican Party, ideological purity has superseded pragmatism. President Reagan is adamant in his commitment to a great "supply-side" experiment, and a trembling Congress delivered it to him in late July 1981. The Administration's official faith in supply-side prescriptions runs counter to the contentions of many other analysts, both liberals and conservatives, who talk about forgoing consumption today for renewed prosperity tomorrow. Republican dogma, as the alleged antidote to our deep economic problems, may be politically good for Democrats but very bad for America.

It is Kemp-Roth, according to supply-side scripture, that promises a born-again American economy. The Kemp-Roth bill calls for a 25 percent across-the-board tax cut. But with a federal budget out of balance, one has to question why there must be a tax cut at all since the federal government would need to borrow the money to provide the tax reduction. That is a sleight-of-hand by any account.

Kemp-Roth offers billions of dollars, skewed to help the well-to-do most, on the theory that they will use it wisely—save some and invest some. It is trickle-down economics at its purest.

But that is not how people react to suddenly available money. A lot of the money just gets spent. And in a time of double-digit inflation, such a stimulative plan is even more inflationary. The proponents of Kemp-Roth argue the parallel of the "Kennedy" tax cut of 1964, and its beneficial effects. To an extent the parallel holds true. The difference is that 1964 is not the 1980s. The inflation rate at the time of the Kennedy tax reduction was 1.3 percent. A massive tax cut stokes the inflation fires to a fare-thee-well. And adding to inflation with federally borrowed dollars is more than ironic. The Democratic alternative of the late 1970s was the Carter administration's notion of a $50 tax cut for everyone. This was abandoned when the potential inflationary impact became obvious. The decision to stick with Kemp-Roth despite its almost assured inflationary impact will haunt the Reagan administration—and the country —for a long time. It is the equivalent of LBJ's war-in-Vietnam-cum-war-on-poverty inflationary spiral of the 1960s. (I won't dwell here on the issue of economic equity raised by Kemp-Roth being tailored for the wealthy. It is very troubling and will be addressed later, but I feel that Kemp-Roth fails even if you discount the inequity of the approach and are solely concerned with productivity.)

Finally, it must be understood that every dollar earmarked to the scattershot Kemp-Roth bill is a dollar not available for the targeted business tax provisions referred to earlier.

Provide Incentives to Target Investment. Stimulating the economy to provide for restructuring and increased productivity is the first order of business. If this is successful, industrial investing will recommence. It is also critical that the government provide channeling mechanisms to ensure that economic growth be consistent with other national objectives.

Two such objectives are urban revitalization and energy independence. If possible, economic growth should occur in areas of poverty and high unemployment to stimulate urban renaissance, and near mass transit systems to lessen the dependence on gasoline. The country needs new plants, but it would also be better served if they were located in the Bronx, not Fairfield County; in Roxbury, not Route 128; in Detroit, not Bloomfield Hills. This can be accomplished in various ways, such as the Republican-sponsored enterprise zones and the Democratic-sponsored UDAG (urban development action grants). (The UDAG program uses the remarkably Republican notion of leveraging private sector investment with public funds. It has been enormously successful in doing just that. Why it is such a prime target for the Reagan budget cutters is beyond me.) Our under-utilized cities and their people represent an important infrastructure investment. It should be government policy to correct that under-utilization so as to maximize "justice" and minimize the drain of urban decay on the Treasury.

The Three R's—Regulation, Red Tape, and Responsibility. Breathes there a soul so dead who never to himself hath said, Let there be less red tape? Next to the Ayatollah, there is no villain in America quite like red tape. And it's not all irrational.

Senator Charles Mathias tells the story of a food processor who was visited by Food and Drug Administration agents. They surveyed his new facility and decreed that the plant had to be washed down five times a day to heighten cleanliness. The processor thought the regulation was absurd but felt helpless to complain, so he complied. Two weeks later, Occupational Safety and Health Administration representatives promptly cited him for unsafe working conditions due to slippery floors. At that point he did complain, and became a lifelong advocate of less regulation. More importantly from a political perspective, he will probably never again be willing to be persuaded that government protects people.

I have heard countless similar stories. In Groton, Massachusetts, I have two young, very loyal and liberal supporters who run a small manufacturing plant. They have been outspoken about the constant stream of paperwork with which they have to deal. "Look, Paul," Carl Genner has often said, "we just don't have the staff necessary to fill out all these forms and it's jeopardizing our livelihood."

The syndrome here is understandable. The regulatory bureaucrat knows that Congress passed a law to curb an abuse. His job, his very raison d'être, is not to permit that abuse. The only time he'll be hauled on the carpet or mentioned by Jack Anderson or publicized on *60 Minutes* is if an abuse occurs. So in covering his flank, he makes sure that he follows the rules strictly. Thus we get over-regulation and excessive bureaucracy.

Inevitably, the nation is focused on the bureaucracy, not on the original abuse that spawned the bureaucracy. With red tape as the enemy, the consensus is to "get government off our backs." Further, the people elect those candidates who appeal to the general disgust over excessive regulation—and that appeal is couched in terms of no regulation.

Without some oversight, we end up with unfettered entrepreneurs. Even if most act responsibly, inevitably some won't. Without a system of self-policing in the private sector, abuses will occur, since sensitivity to issues like worker safety and environmental degradation may be costly. People will be hurt, angry, and into that battle will ride the "protectors." And how do you protect? By laws, of course. And who enforces the laws? Why, bureaucrats, of course. And so the unending cycle of abuse-anger-laws-regulations-bureaucracy continues ad infinitum.

So do you blame the liberals who refuse to admit to over-regulation, or the free enterprisers who accept abuse as simply "the way it is"? The answer, obviously, is both.

I am not here addressing regulation that seeks to protect particular interests rather than curb abuses. Many of the regulations on the books are protective devices and are ironically supported by free enterprise advocates. For example, in 1981, the Senate attempted to remove the regulation that barred retailers from levying a surcharge on items purchased on credit. This removal would allow different prices for cash buyers and credit buyers, so that "savers" would not subsidize "borrowers." The repeal was supported by consumer groups, the elderly, the Federal Reserve Bank, and the conservative Heritage Foundation. It was opposed by only one group—the credit card industry. The battle to deregulate was led by Democratic Senators William Proxmire and John Glenn; the opposition was led by conservative Republican senators. The repeal died 56–41, with the Republicans voting 2 to 1 against deregulation.

This is not "regulation" in the sense referred to here. It is just one more instance of special-interest legislation, promoted by the same people who rant endlessly about less government interference. Special-interest regulations are bureaucratic and hurt productivity, but when push comes to shove, free enterprise politicians easily abandon their rhetoric and serve their friends. This is simply power politics; its hypocrisy doesn't make it any less real. It is distinguished from the regulations passed to curb abuse that are the focus of this chapter.

Now let us see how regulation precipitated by abuse endures in the real world.

In 1974, the Congress passed a law calling on banks to provide detailed financial information to the home buyer some twelve days prior to the real estate transaction. It was intended to give the purchaser adequate time to digest fully the terms of the sale, so that he or she would be an educated consumer. The Real Estate Settlement Procedures Act was a reasonable proposition. The problems were that (1) it required an incredible amount of paperwork; (2) it was impossible to comply with, since, as any lawyer knows, many details of real estate transactions are not resolved until the last minute; and (3) the effect was beneficial for a minuscule number of buyers—almost no one was dissuaded from acquiring a home on the basis of the information. It frustrated thousands upon thousands of lawyers and bankers, and added costs to hundreds of thousands of consumers.

Did the positive impact on the handful justify the negative impact on everyone else and the resultant decline of national productivity? I think not, and neither did the Congress, which repealed the law in 1976 by a vote of 379 to 21 in the House, and by voice vote in the Senate.

The point of this example is the backlash it creates, not just among the reactionary and the callous but also among the reasonable. And that's how elections are won and lost. It is obviously in the political interest of liberals to guard against regulatory excesses, since they are the ones who will pay the political price in the long run.

During the 1970s, there were several attempts to pass a bill to regulate strip mining. For decades, coal mine operators had raped the land, with resultant abuse of both environment and people. Mud slides and flooding caused by strip-mining practices killed scores of people and destroyed the homes of thousands.

When Congress moved to address the issue, many mine operators cried "bureaucracy." For a while, they succeeded in staving off a bill (President Ford vetoed one in 1975). But eventually the momentum of anger and bitterness caused by the flagrant abuse of the offending operators was to prove irresistible, and the bill became law in 1977.

Did the positive impact on the land and people involved justify the added costs and resultant decline of national productivity caused by bureaucratic oversight? I think it did.

A similar example is the issue of the "midnight dumpers" who unload hazardous wastes at random to avoid the costs of responsible and safe disposal. Needless to say, no society is prepared to endure the damage to human beings caused by such outrages.

The point of these examples is that they also create a backlash, and not just among liberals and bleeding hearts. Here it is obviously in the political interest of the free enterprisers to safeguard against such excesses, since they are the ones who will pay the political price in the long run.

The political future belongs to that group which knows its limits, and which knows when not to press its advantages for the optimum situation.

Provide for the Long-term Health of the Goose. Savings, reinvestment, and regulatory sanity are short-and mid-term necessities. They do not, however, guarantee long-term health.

The future of the goose can be ensured only by the willingness to invest in those ideas and technologies that are of long-term value, without short- or mid-term return.

Japan is cited as a classic example of an economy that works. The Japanese are capable of remarkable collective decisionmaking. They realize that the key to the future industrial base lies in knowledge. Ideas, concepts, innovation—these are the future. And they do not come by chance; they require funding, risk-taking, patience, and tolerance.

A society that is enchanted by Golden Fleece awards, that accepts the Reagan cuts in basic research grants to universities and National Science Foundation monies, is consuming the corn required for the next year's planting. Such a self-destructive process plays into the hands of our international trade competitors.

Economic growth is a function of the creative mind. These minds exist in America, but the question is how well they will be used. That intellectual capacity must be viewed as our greatest industrial resource. Other countries treat theirs with honor and respect; we should do no less. The employment of tomorrow rests on today's application of intellect.

To conserve our intellectual resources, three primary programs (and one related program) should be implemented:

1. Tax credits for business funding of university research and development.

2. Major increases in government-sponsored basic research (National Science Foundation, National Institutes of Health).

3. Tax credits for increases in industrial research and development.

The objective is to provide an increased percentage of GNP related to research and development. During the 1960s, that percentage hovered around 3 percent; during the 1970s, it fell by almost a third. This is in contrast to the Japanese and the West Germans, each of whose research and development expenditures as a percentage of GNP have been expanding over this period. The implications are obvious. In addition to the quantity of research, there should be a commitment to its quality. There must be solid support for quality work, and the government should not be picayune when monitoring basic research grants. If we allow politicians to hamper the effectiveness of these grants by ridicule, the result will be low-risk, low-gain ideas. Scientists who need political approval will cost us dearly over the long term. The past is replete with examples of basic research that appeared absurd at the time and then proved historic in its application. This is not to argue against common sense, but for running room. The scientific community should be given the benefit of the doubt. A NSF or NIH official who must decide who gets grants and who doesn't, and who is paranoid about public ridicule and undefended by his superiors, contributes to a sterile environment in which only safe projects are funded and brilliant concepts cannot take root.

The related program referred to earlier is that of student loans. It is in the long-term interest of society for its best minds to percolate to the top. To the extent that the process is handicapped by students unable to afford an education, we will realize less than the best foundation for industrial development. Student loans should be viewed as a program for economic development as well as social development, and should be vigorously supported by those concerned about a strong economy. Parents' income should never preclude a student from access to a school loan. Once the repayment period begins, it probably makes sense to prorate the interest subsidy awarded students as a function of their parents' income. But access to school loans is a clear example where the needs of "incentive" and "justice" are in happy congruence. The careful nurturing of the country's intellect, from the Head Start program to graduate school fellowships, is in everyone's interest, and should not be ignored. We do so at our long-term peril because no other major nation is making the same mistake.

The Role of Labor and Management. The next decades will require a reassessment on the part of both labor and management. Such a reassessment should not be very threatening since both are scarcely enjoying halcyon days at present.

Most American industrial executives spend a great deal of time on issues like productivity, quality control, and absenteeism. Most American labor union leaders, on the other hand, worry about the continued, and seemingly inexorable, decline in union membership. (Union members represented 33.2% of non-farm employment in 1955, 23.6% in 1978.)

In past years, when the survival or success of a particular industry was not in question, both labor and management could train their guns on each other in a traditional adversarial struggle. That fight over the sharing of income was very important in providing "justice" to the worker. But in today's atmosphere such a struggle can be counterproductive to the interests of both labor and management.

In the future, it will be necessary in some industries for labor to realize that the "enemy" is not management; the enemy is the set of circumstances that threatens the viability of the industry—and the jobs involved.

Thus in our troubled, and about-to-be-troubled, industries, labor must think about the longer term, not simply the years covered by a contract. During the decline of Chrysler, several factors contributed to the woes of that company. One of them was quality control. The cars rolling off the various Chrysler assembly lines were often not put together as well as a Toyota or Datsun. Yet when management pushed for quality control measures, it was perceived as something they were extracting from the workers rather than being in the interests of both. So when Americans turned away from Chrysler cars, in part because of inadequate quality control, labor and management called for import quotas.

As an aspect of the Chrysler reorganization, it was finally understood by both labor and management that quality control was essential for the company to have any chance of survival. Beginning in late 1979, quality control improved dramatically at Chrysler, with cooperation from the UAW, whose lenders and members clearly understood their stake in this "management" issue and responded accordingly.

We need labor unions that care about the condition of the goose.

Along with issues like pay rates, health benefits, and work safety, their agenda should include such matters as quality control, productivity, and absenteeism.

Organized labor began as a movement to protect workers from abuse and to give workers their rightful share of economic benefits. The unions were critically needed and have served America well. Now they have entered a new era.

Today, many unions see more than just declining membership: they recognize the increased public hostility to what is perceived as union grasping. These examples may be exceptional, but they are well publicized and erode citizen support. In Massachusetts, the Carmen's Union of the Massachusetts Bay Transit Authority (MBTA) was very successful in its bargaining with a long line of governors. The union was legendary in getting the most benefits for its members; its leaders were tough, effective, and very thorough. In late 1979, however, when the MBTA ran out of money, the union's house of cards collapsed. Newspaper exposés about members' salaries and work rules so poisoned the attitude of the public that when the financial crunch came, the union found itself isolated. A previously supportive state legislature voted to strip away benefits that the union had gained over the years. Without public backing, then, most unions will find the future hostile.

I believe that unionism is a tradition in this country whose values must be maintained. The only way it can reverse its current decline is to present a new face to America: tougher, leaner, more flexible, more innovative; concerned about efficiency and productivity, and intolerant of featherbedding. Management in particular and the public in general have to regard unions as fighting for economic equity, not for unreasonable work rules. They have to see unions as partners in the long-term survival of an industry, not as an obstacle to that future.

Some unions have begun to adopt this attitude already; for others, it will be a seismic shift. Indeed, there are brotherhoods that will find the idea of partnership offensive to everything they have believed in. There will be much suspicion and past bitterness to bridge—but it must be done.

Steel mills, automobile assembly plants, electronic component facilities, all should have workers who think constantly about their

Japanese, West German, and Swiss counterparts. These are the "enemy" in the long run.

The mission, then, is the kind of partnership necessary to hold off the enemy, not only for today but also for the future. This sort of cooperation will aid industry and gain public respect. Such respect and goodwill is the labor movement's truest shield against attacks on unionism.

If this "new unionism" is to become a focus of the labor movement, management in turn must provide an atmosphere conducive to it. Corporate officials cannot expect to receive the benefits of union progressivism and offer nothing in return. The "new unionism" is in management's interest because it basically fosters the viability of the company.

Management must share part of its power. If unions are to be held responsible, they must be assumed to be responsible. Union leaders should not be viewed as the enemy; they should be brought into the inner circles of information-sharing and decision-making.

A union leader who abandons the traditional adversary relationship with management is vulnerable—he runs the real risk of being ousted by a rival who will accuse him of "giving in" to the corporate interests. His willingness to be cooperative has to be reinforced if it is to succeed. For each such step taken by the union leader, there must be a corresponding return in power and partnership.

In Europe, there is increasing evidence of this arrangement. Management in America should do no less. Electing a union official to a board of directors would be the first step in the realization of a genuine partnership. In addition, in at least one important respect, management must take a leaf from the Japanese. One of the advantages the Japanese enjoy is their willingness to consider the long term, and they often cite American preoccupation with short-term profit-making as a structural defect. (Japanese firms, on average, invest 6 percent of total sales in R & D expenditures, whereas U.S. firms average only 1 percent.) Bound by immediate considerations of dividends and annual reports, and the likelihood that he will hold his current position for only a few years, the American corporate decision-maker is less prone to support long-term projects whose profitability can only be realized in decades, not years. The negative effects of such shortsightedness are obvious.

Japanese companies have been able to import their management techniques to their American operations. They seem to have created a relationship with workers which is conducive to greater productivity and work quality. By contrast, the traditional adversary relationship between American management and labor has often been counterproductive.

Governmental Activism. The doctrine of the Reagan administration is less governmental influence in the marketplace. That, of course, is not a new idea. The question is whether the concept is appropriate to the last two decades of the twentieth century.

In the next few years we will witness a number of additional industries in serious trouble, with an enormous loss of employment no matter what policies are applied to them. The auto industry, for example, is projected to lose 500,000 jobs under what the Department of Transportation referred to as the "best-case scenario."

At the other end of the spectrum, small businesses are finding it difficult to secure adequate capital because large institutional lenders are reluctant to become involved in the high risk of young, innovative companies. The fact that small companies provide the greatest opportunities for new jobs, new products, and technological innovation is less important to these lenders than the perceived risk.

What is the proper response of government?

The traditional Democrat will protect the jobs and security of the workers no matter what the cost. To that end, he will support such measures as quotas and tariff barriers, unemployment benefits, and trade adjustment assistance. This approach reverses the cliché about the best defense being a good offense. Lacking a good offense, he searches for the best defense.

The traditional Republican view, raised to an art form by Budget Director David Stockman, is that free enterprise is based on winners and losers and government should keep out. The losers' equipment will be sold; employees can move elsewhere and find new jobs with the winners. This theory, of course, is most effective in econometric models that ignore human needs. In the real world it's hard to find a captain of industry who disagrees with this approach —for every industry, that is, but his own. Usually the louder the cry for less government, the more certain it is that the particular company has already been helped. The oil industry, for example, successfully lobbied Congress for import quotas when foreign oil was cheaper. The tobacco business secured its subsidies, as did a number of other agriculturally based industries. Broadcasters fight to prevent the spread of cable television or unlimited access to public airwaves.

This double standard is something that shocks a newly arrived member of Congress, but it is so all-pervasive it soon becomes as much a part of the landscape as the Washington Monument.

I once spoke at a small Washington dinner party for visiting businessmen from around the country. The person sitting next to me was a publisher who bent my ear incessantly about "damn governmental meddling." He criticized the Congress for giving in to the requests of industries that were obtaining help from government while espousing free enterprise rhetoric. We ought to stand up to them, he insisted, and make them live by their rhetoric. The intensity of his feelings and his unabated expression of them did not allow me very much time to respond. After the dinner was over and we were all walking out, he came over to me and said: "By the way, Carter is proposing a decrease in the subsidy for fourth-class mail. That would really hurt my business. I hope you will oppose him on that." What shocked me most was the fact that I was not shocked.

Neither the traditional Democratic nor the theoretically Republican approach is relevant to the circumstances of the 1980s. The answer is to reconstruct industry, not try to prop it up artificially. For my part, I would decrease trade adjustment assistance (which provided workers with a merely superficial sense of security, based on an unreal and unsupportable status quo) and use that money to provide more tax credits for revitalization. The same analysis would lead one to abandon the CETA program. That program was meant to be developmental, but in its application it became a social welfare mechanism. I would take CETA funds and use them in the Urban Development Action Grant (UDAG) program. The only long-term policy that can be justified is one that leads an industry or a workforce into true competitiveness.

In the meantime, while the revitalization is taking place, it is important to keep shaky but potentially viable industries from

going under. And in that special circumstance, governmental assistance is necessary. Some have argued for a reconstruction finance
corporation to provide this service. The agency would attempt to
pick winners and assist them, and to identify losers and expedite
their phase-out. The concept is theoretically valid, but what happens if the decisions of the agency reflect the political clout of the
questionable industry rather than its potential for future viability
and competitiveness? To be effective, such an agency would need
to organize itself on an independent basis like that enjoyed by the
Federal Reserve Bank, place a limit on the capital it can provide,
and ordain that the standard for its assistance be the potential for
future, unassisted viability. The agency should be a rehabilitation
center for the temporarily weak, not a nursing home for the termi-
nally ill.

Beyond such a device, the question of "how much government"
remains. Should the earlier proposals for savings, reinvestment,
research and development and regulatory balance, be categorized
as governmental interference, or less government? It really doesn't
matter. The question should be, do they work? If they do, then the
ideological debate is irrelevant.

Let me offer one more example from Japan. The Japanese recognized early on the industrial potential of robots. The private sector
was hesitant to invest for a myriad of reasons, including the risk of
an uncertain market. The government stepped in, provided guarantees, then rented the robots to industry with a warranty on performance. The venture was risky, interventionist, activist, paternalistic
—and wildly successful. Today, Japan is the only nation in the
world with a thriving robotics industry.

This is not to argue for cloning the model; it is to suggest, rather,
that many Japanese industries have the advantage of robots and we
better have an answer if we hope to be competitive in these industries.

Government and industry must be in harness. To argue for less
government is to presume that economic problems are the fault of
government alone, and to overlook the growing consensus that
American management techniques are in need of an overhaul. To
argue for less governmental investment is to avoid the question
about who will build the roads and bridges and other parts of the

infrastructure that the private sector requires. To argue for more governmental protection is to direct capital away from young, growing companies to older, traditional enterprises. It is to postpone the critical realization that long-term competitiveness is our only hope.

What we need is less rhetoric and more common sense. Fewer pendulum swings and more steady courses. Less antipathy between the public and private sectors and more cooperation.

In a word, realism.

5/Resource Allocation: The Fourth Reality

I have been focusing on the first tier of realities—energy, defense, and the economy. Later, I want to discuss a second tier—Third World, international trade, and environmental overload.

But before going on, I wish to emphasize that energy, defense, and the economy are not separate matters. They are inexorably connected because the resources required to address them are not unlimited. This link becomes critical if one assumes, as I do, that all these issues must be addressed and resolved.

Dealing with the defense issue by itself is very different from addressing it as part of a troika of crucial issues. It is different because it requires the introduction of a new reality—resource allocation.

All three issues require that two resources be allocated: capital and technical expertise. These resources are not to be found on trees or street corners; they are limited in any society.

Unfortunately, there is a tendency in the United States to avoid confronting these issues as part of a complete puzzle. There is an abysmal lack of perspective. At present, we suffer from a kind of institutional myopia, wherein each special-interest group focuses on its own set of concerns as a priority before other needs. To make matters worse, these groups perceive the notion of adopting a wider perspective as somehow an attack upon the validity of their own concerns. The task is to persuade each group to step back and begin to understand the basic realities of resource allocation—and why we cannot ultimately resolve any of these issues if they are not all resolved.

In grade school, many of us were asked to construct three rectangles with ten straws. If we tried to arrange them separately, each rectangle would contain four straws, leaving only two and one-half rectangles built. Eventually we would learn to resolve the problem by having the rectangles share connecting walls.

Energy, defense, and the economy are three such rectangles. The straws (money and technical expertise) are limited. To the extent that each rectangle-builder ignores the needs of others, the end result is inadequate, even though any one part may appear to be in place.

So it does no good, for example, to structure a defense posture and an energy posture if the economy has gone to hell. It should be obvious that if our economy falters, in the long term there simply won't be an adequate industrial capability for defense and energy policies.

One day in 1980, when I was presiding over the Senate, an especially ferocious hawk paced back and forth near his desk pleading for a huge arms increase. His voice rang out across the chamber about the need to secure "our" oil in the Persian Gulf. He called for the purchase of just about every military item conceived by man.

I wanted to relinquish the presiding officer's chair and enter into the debate to pose one question: Instead of spending billions solely on arms to defend "our" oil, why not allot some of those billions to conservation and renewable sources of energy so we don't need *their* oil? By the time I found a replacement to preside, the superhawk had left the chamber. It was probably just as well. He would have thought my question ludicrous, and no doubt would have become even more apoplectic. That senator wants all the straws for *his* rectangle. The idea of maintaining slightly fewer MX missiles in order to share resources with our domestic industrial plant or a viable array of low-head hydroelectric sites would have seemed somehow unpatriotic.

I have mentioned that the difference between 3 percent real growth in defense spending and 13 percent real growth in defense spending is $1.17 trillion over ten years, and that the more modest differential (that of 5 percent vs. 9 percent) is $437.1 billion.

Now, when someone proclaims that he wants superiority over the Russians (9 to 13 percent), not just equivalence (3 to 5 percent), chances are he will be applauded wildly. Right on. Stick it to them.

It feels better to be "superior," so why not? Leaving aside the argument made earlier that superiority is an elusive beast, there is a valid reason why not. The difference of $437 billion is an enormous amount of money.

What does $437 billion represent in real alternatives? We could draw up a few proposals:

1. *Energy.* Equip every home in America with a solar-power hot water heater (less dependence on OPEC): cost—$174.6 billion.
2. *Capital Formation.* Enact the so-called 2-4-7-10 accelerated depreciation proposal for ten years, providing funds for capital investment: cost—$157.2 billion.
3. *Industrial Research.* Pass the 25 percent tax credit for business-sponsored research and development for ten years: cost—$7.0 billion.
4. *Basic Research.* Double the budgets of the National Science Foundation and the National Institutes of Health each year for ten years: cost—$43.5 billion.
5. *Education.* Fully fund one million college students for four years: cost—$22.5 billion.
6. *Quality of Life.* Double the budget of the National Endowment for the Humanities for each of the years in the 1980s: cost—$1.41 billion.
7. *Tax Cuts.* There would be $30.0 billion left over with which to give each family a tax rebate of $585.

Now let's re-create the same hawkish speech and the same audience:

The businessman knows that the senator's call for superiority over equivalence means he won't get the accelerated depreciation allowances he desperately needs to modernize his equipment.

The parent knows that her talented daughter may not be able to obtain a loan to continue college and must drop out of school.

The scientist knows his basic research might not get funded.

The homeowner knows that he will have to forgo a solar hot water heater.

The mayor knows that the art museum that gives the city a deep sense of pride may close due to lack of financial support.

And every citizen knows that there will be no rebate of $585.

A very different perspective.

The same dilemma of resource allocation comes up between subsets of the same issue: synthetic fuels versus conservation and renewables. Kemp-Roth across-the-board tax cuts versus tax cuts for investment in capital goods, equipment, and plants. Nuclear-powered aircraft carriers versus small, mobile warships.

The straws are limited. As a reality, that is not easy to accept. We want to believe that God gave us endless straws.

In November of 1980, I spoke to the Boston Chamber of Commerce about economic issues. I recommended various kinds of tax incentives for business investment to stimulate reindustrialization and international trade. I pointed out that if we passed all these measures, it meant that the Kemp-Roth bill, which was inflationary anyway, should not be enacted as well.

"That's your opinion" was the hostile response of one questioner.

One week before, I had talked in Washington to the Atomic Industrial Forum and called for financial support of conservation and renewable sources of energy in order to achieve a balance with the funding of nuclear energy. The applause from the audience would have disturbed no one who might have dozed off.

The solutions to energy, defense, and economic issues are by nature vast. The sheer capital requirements are awesome. To give just one example, in 1977 our energy-related investments represented 43 percent of all funds allotted to plant and equipment. If we add to that massive funding need the requirements for defense and reinvestment in capital equipment for industry, the impossibility of achieving all this becomes obvious.

We are forced to choose. In a time of high inflation and chronically unbalanced federal budgets, we cannot have everything. When the public mood is to cut back on basic human services and other domestic needs, to attempt all these investments at once would diminish the quality of American life to a point of widespread social unrest.

Energy, defense, and the economy are, in my opinion, the three highest priority items on the national agenda. They are survival issues, or in terms of this book, "waterfall" issues. Their solutions must be pursued with determination and a sense of mission. The pursuit should not be blinkered, however. We need leadership in providing a perspective—and that includes leadership in the private sector.

Business leaders must realize that accelerated depreciation allowances for capital reinvestment coupled with tax cuts for research and development are more critical than Kemp-Roth tax decreases. Military leaders must realize that keeping America strong means having a viable economy, and thus making the choice of a Stealth bomber force over a B-1 bomber. Lobbyists for the synthetic fuels and nuclear industries must accept responsibility for sharing some of their funding with the less powerful conservation and renewable resource industries. And all such leaders must sense that there comes a point where their absorption of funds means that our elderly are not housed and our poor are not fed. If America is thus weakened, we are all diminished.

The keys to resource allocation are a sense of priorities and a sense of limitations. People must be sensitive enough to stop pushing for their cause when that pushing exceeds what is reasonable from a national perspective. In today's selfish political arena, the pushing stops only at the boundary of political power, not at the point of reason.

Beyond the matter of limited capital resources and the necessity to allocate them wisely, there is the question of human resources.

The future of America lies inside the heads of its talented people. In the areas of energy, defense, and the economy, technical and management skills are the most critical. The John and Jane Does who come out of Cal Tech, Georgia Tech, M.I.T., and Purdue are essential straws in our rectangle-building; they are also few in number.

Although there is much debate over the extent that these three areas compete for human resource skills, it is becoming increasingly obvious that the loser will be the domestic private sector. As military and energy spending expand, they will drain talented technical workers away from domestic pursuits. An engineer concerned with the design of an armored tank will not be available to plan a

fuel-efficient automobile; a scientist seeking breakthroughs in neutron bomb development will not be developing new microprocess-
ing techniques for computers.

Given the already low percentage of GNP and technical talent
allocated to defense by our European and Asian competitors, how
can we compete over the long term in manufactured goods? Are we
to be a muscle-bound superpower whose vital internal economic
organs atrophy? Do our generals and admirals and oil company
executives worry about how their counterparts in private industry
are going to produce the weapons and capital necessary for their
battles? Do they realize that their survival is in serious doubt if the
domestic economy becomes non-competitive?

Who is to raise these issues? How does a society step back from
the short term to look at the long term? It does so by understanding
that a lack of perspective jeopardizes its survival.

Think of the Japanese industrialist intent upon surpassing America's advantage in high technology. He has seen the prosperity
along Route 128 in Massachusetts, in the Silicon Valley of California, in the complexes around Austin, Atlanta, and Minneapolis. He
wants to avoid the energy-intensive industries that are vulnerable
to crude-oil supply interruption. If he is to be successful, he needs
to channel his capital and technical talent into this area, and
equally, he needs America to direct its capital and its technical
talent away from this area.

That is exactly what is happening today. Let America achieve
nuclear superiority over the Russians, and the Japanese will achieve
micro-chip-processing superiority over the Americans. The Swiss
will have an advantage in digital watches over the Americans. The
Germans will produce better navigational equipment than the
Americans. And the British, French, Taiwanese, Koreans, and Bra-
zilians all will gain in production and prosperity at our expense.
America will become a nation of unemployed workers with foreign-
made products at home and American-made missiles at the ready.

To underscore this point, one need only look at the economic
indicators comparing the United States with Japan and West Germany. In the past decade, the 1970s, the United States each year
allocated between 5 and 8 percent of its GNP on military spending;
the Germans less (3–4 percent), and the Japanese much less (about

1 percent each year). In per capita expenditures, it was $441 per American, $252 per West German, and $47 per Japanese.

So what?

Well, let's look at fixed, non-military investment. In the U.S., such investment in the 1970s increased from 16.9 percent of GNP to 19 percent; in West Germany, it ranged from between 20.6 and 26 percent; in Japan, between 31 and 36 percent. Our best year was worse than the worst year of the West Germans and nowhere near the worst year of the Japanese!

And these figures reflect the 1970s. Imagine what the figures for the 1980s will reveal—and, more important, what they will mean about America's economic prospects.

Even some military leaders are beginning to understand that America cannot be a first-rate military power or a world power in any sense with a second-rate industrial and technological base.

It makes no sense. The leaders of America's private sector must understand the problem. If they make the effort, they will be listened to. Indeed, they will be far more effective in bringing home this argument for wise resource allocation than we liberals and Democrats.

They will, in any case, sooner or later, be wending their way to Washington. The open question is whether they will arrive early enough to avoid coming as latter-day Lockheed/Chrysler supplicants. Since the posture of a bail-out supplicant imposes a heavy burden on the psyche, there is hope that they will rally round before too much longer.

The nation needs their counsel, for the simple reason that they know better, and can bring America into an unprecedented appreciation of, just what resource allocation is all about—namely, economic survival.

6/The Third World: The Fifth Reality

In June of 1964, I was preparing to leave Wolisso, in Ethiopia, after two years of Peace Corps service. I was part of the first contingent of Peace Corps volunteers in that nation, and part of the wave of enthusiasm that responded to the challenge of participation by John F. Kennedy. They were two years that transformed both my country and me.

For America, the changes were traumatic. President Kennedy was assassinated. Race riots were breaking out across the South. And Vietnam was a boil surfacing on the body politic. Soon Lyndon Johnson and Barry Goldwater would do battle to see who would succeed the New Frontier.

For me, it was a period of profound personal change. I learned for the first time in my life how diverse our world really is. For someone who had never been more than five hundred miles away from Lowell, Massachusetts, the challenge of cross-cultural living was formidable. But I had learned to speak Amharic, the chief language of Ethiopia, to transcend cultural barriers, and to actually "think" as an Ethiopian. (This latter point did not seem very important at the time, but it would prove invaluable when I got to the Congress and had to evaluate Third World issues.)

The students at the school where I taught had arranged for a farewell ceremony. Ten of them had lived in my house, along with Steve Silver, a volunteer from Queens, New York. These students were very poor, most were living away from home, and some had come hundreds of kilometers to Wolisso to be educated. They each owned only a pair of pants and a shirt, and survived on the meager subsistence provided by the government. Almost without exception they were the children of rural African peasants, whose lifestyle had not changed for generations. When I first saw the students, I found it hard to believe that they could deal in twentieth-century concepts. As it turned out, not only would they be able to do the schoolwork in Wolisso, but four of them would later come to the United States on American Field Service scholarships for their last year of high school. All would be at or near the top of their classes in schools ranging from rural Maine to suburban California.

The students' farewell ceremony was the last of several given by the Ethiopians of Wolisso. They presented me with a complete suit of traditional native dress. Knowing the cost of the clothes and the students' poverty, I found this gift extremely moving. I think it is fair to say that a great deal of love passed between the departing Peace Corps volunteers and the Ethiopian students.

As I drove away from Wolisso past the mud huts and tilled fields, I couldn't decide whether I was going home or leaving home. That place and that time had become part of me and was very real. And I was sure that I had become very real to them. I was thoroughly American, but our lives had touched in a truly basic sharing.

Over the years, thousands of volunteers would serve in Ethiopia, and almost all would develop a strong bond with the country and its people. Their affection would be returned by the Ethiopians. The strength of Ethiopian-American relations seemed absolutely rock-solid.

Thirteen years later I returned to that country, as part of a congressional fact-finding tour (along with Representative Don Bonker of Washington and Bryant Salter of the State Department). We arrived in the capital city of Addis Ababa at night. On the trip from the airport to the American Embassy, I was startled by the changes I saw. The country had experienced a revolution that had toppled the aging Emperor Haile Selassie, and the new government was Marxist. But I was still not prepared for what I found. Although it was only ten o'clock at night, the streets were deserted. The Addis Ababa I remembered was always full of activity until late into the evening. Driving through the dark streets, we came to a large square. Lit up by giant spotlights were three huge pictures of Marx, Lenin, and Engels. In a country whose rich history stretched back thousands of years with a tradition of African nationalism, this glorification of three white foreigners seemed absolutely shocking.

I had long since discarded my paranoia about Soviet effectiveness in the Third World. Although the Cubans and Chinese (remember when they were lumped together?) were skilled in dealing with Third World nations, the Soviets were hopelessly rigid and removed. Coming from a society that was reflexively racist, they simply didn't have a feel for the sensitivities of Third World peoples. And since their purpose was ideological rather than humanitarian, their demeanor was usually cold and steely. How could these doctrinaire heroes be so enshrined in the heart of Africa? Yes, the Soviets and Cubans had come to Ethiopia's aid when Somali troops invaded the Ogaden region. Yes, Haile Selassie's regime had become bureaucratic and corrupt, and deserved to be unseated. The ascendancy of opposition leftist elements was not surprising. But Marxism in the African sense of that term was one thing. This apparent rejection of Ethiopian values and total acceptance of Soviet values was quite another matter.

Two days later, Bonker, Salter, and I were to meet with the leader of the ruling military junta, Colonel Mengistu Haile Mariam. The encounter was the most bizarre example of multi-cultural influences I have ever experienced. It was held one evening in one of Haile Selassie's old palaces. The room was austere, high-ceilinged, and cavernous. On one end of it hung a picture of Marx, rendered all the more severe by the fluorescent lighting overhead.

Colonel Mengistu greeted us dressed in his army fatigues. He was of medium height, with hard features that reflected the violence he had both experienced and occasioned. While government television cameras and photographers recorded the event, I mumbled as much Amharic as I could dredge up from memory. We then sat around a coffee table on French Provincial chairs, and were given refreshments on an elegant tea service still bearing the crest of the now-dead emperor. To the side was an exquisite grandfather clock that rang forth with delicate chimes every fifteen minutes. From deep below I heard the guttural roars of the emperor's lions, which Mengistu still kept.

The mixture of European, American, and Soviet intrusions joined with Ethiopian influences, both past and present, to create a totally surrealistic time warp. The meeting lasted for about ninety minutes, with Mengistu speaking through an interpreter. (Mengistu speaks English—he had been given military training in the United States many years before—but he preferred to communicate in Amharic. Haile Selassie had used the same technique on me fifteen years before.) He talked tensely about American support for Haile Selassie during the emperor's last years of corrupt power, when thousands of Ethiopians died of starvation during the drought. The imperial government had refused to acknowledge the problem publicly, content to let its people die rather than be embarrassed internationally by a relief mission. The willingness of the United States to support Haile Selassie despite the human suffering, the corruption, and the exploitation of the peasantry (which I had observed many years before) was a wellspring of bitterness that will last for decades.

He also asked why the United States had refused to deliver arms to Ethiopia in 1977 when Somalia attacked his homeland and moved deep into the Ogaden region. The arms had been contracted for, and the lack of them jeopardized the country's existence. The Somali invasion violated the principle of territorial integrity so fervently embraced by the United Nations and the Organization of African Unity, and so honored publicly by the United States. Yet America was unmoved, and focused instead on the ideology of the Mengistu regime. Faced with the disintegration of his nation, Mengistu turned to the Soviets and Cubans, who responded readily. The relationship between the United States and Ethiopia then became one of accusation and polemics. Eventually, Mengistu ordered us to reduce the size of our diplomatic mission; we reacted by withdrawing our ambassador. After a generation of close ties with America, Ethiopia would in a matter of months become the Soviets' closest ally in Africa. The Soviets had indeed "saved" Ethiopia, and the United States was content to talk about political doctrines.

The meeting had begun haltingly, but was soon marked by more than Mengistu's bitterness. Despite the tough-guy bluster, it was obvious that he felt betrayed by America's rejection of him in his time of need. Mengistu was a soldier, not a political theoretician. He saw Americans as hypocrites who espoused human rights selectively and operated from expediency, not principle. His view of

America was the polar opposite of that held by the students I had taught thirteen years before.

Two other incidents added to the gloom of our trip. I returned to Wolisso but had to obtain security papers to get past military checkpoints—the easy days of free access around the country that I remembered were gone. And the city of Addis Ababa was wracked by violence between Mengistu's forces and rivals for power. On one early morning drive through Addis, we saw several bodies on the street, victims of the previous evening's terrorism.

Our planned departure from Ethiopia the day after the Mengistu meeting was blocked by a Soviet transport plane that was disabled on the airstrip. During these unexpected extra three days, we were left mostly unaccompanied and unscheduled. It gave me a chance to wander around Addis Ababa resurrecting my Amharic and speaking to the people, including several former students who had heard of my visit. Whenever Ethiopians found out I was an American, they went out of their way to be cordial. Instead of the hostility I had expected, the reaction was one of unabashed warmth. Despite months of anti-American rhetoric, the positive feelings toward Americans remained strong. Some things had changed, but others had not.

Yet even from those who were least supportive of Mengistu came the recurring inquiry: Why had America abandoned them? Why had we allowed the Soviets to take on the role of saviors after the Somali invasion?

One of the more articulate put it this way: "Senator, you've got to realize that we are in a struggle for Ethiopia's soul. Some want us to become a Communist state. Others hope to reassert their African nationalism by genuine non-alignment. Your actions cut the ground out from under those of us who want to be free of Soviet control. You're playing into the Soviets' hands by your policies, and making it impossible for us to break away from the Russians."

These comments were all the more compelling in that I knew the speaker was literally risking his life to meet with me. The Soviets were trampling the fierce independence of the Ethiopian people, but the resistance was considerable.

Upon our return to the United States, Bonker and I met with Carter administration officials, including the President, and argued for the dispatch of a top-rate, skilled American ambassador to Ethiopia to compete for influence and give the Soviets a run for their money. Weeks and months passed. Eventually, the State Department sent an envoy with no previous ambassadorial experience whose mission, apparently, was to negotiate compensation claims for the few American companies affected by the change in government. The Soviets must have died laughing. In late 1980, the Ethiopians asked that the envoy be recalled and replaced. We had shot ourselves in the foot again.

A good barometer of Soviet influence in the Third World is the 1980 vote in the United Nations on the Afghanistan issue. Twice, by counts of 104 to 18, and 111 to 22, the Soviets were clobbered. Despite a legacy of skillful exploitation of anti-colonialism in the U.N., they were badly beaten. They had brutally invaded a Third World country and in so doing lost a great deal of credibility among U.N. member-states who had traditionally viewed the Soviets through rose-colored glasses.

Those that voted with the Soviets included the expected East European nations. Beyond them, the roll call of supporting states rang out like a who's who of trouble spots: Vietnam, Cuba, Angola, Mozambique, Ethiopia. These nations had one set of experiences in common: control by a corrupt or colonial regime (Diem, Batista, Salazar, Haile Selassie); a struggle for liberation in which the United States opted for the entrenched, and the Soviets supported the insurgents; victory by the insurgents and a grateful embrace of the Soviets; and a purposeful withdrawal from influence by the United States. Of these five countries, we still don't even recognize three (Vietnam, Cuba, and Angola). One was cut off from American aid by the Congress, subject to presidential waiver (Mozambique), and the other (Ethiopia) has been shunned by two succeeding administrations.

The United States has decided in each case to try to "isolate" these countries. By withdrawing our attentions, goes the theory, we would leave them devastated. They would then throw out the Soviets and beg for forgiveness. Of course, it hasn't worked. It didn't work with China either. Eventually a conservative Republican opened relations with China and everyone was better off—everyone, that is, but the Soviets. Richard Nixon discarded the illusion of Taiwan representing all of China and dealt with the reality of mainland China. In the case of Cuba and Fidel Castro, twenty-two years of trying to isolate him have passed, and he and the Soviets are still there.

Ironically, the brilliant strategists who called for the end of Castro through isolation are immune from criticism. The policy has been a blunder of monumental proportions, serving only the interests of the Soviets, and yet the architects of that policy and its present-day adherents are never questioned. It is one of the few instances in American foreign policy-making where nothing succeeds quite like failure.

Equally interesting in the U.N. roll call on Afghanistan was the list of nations that once had close ties with the Soviets but voted against them: Egypt, Somalia, Guinea, Ghana, and the Sudan. In each case, we did not overreact to the Soviet presence in their country. Without the United States to kick around, the Soviets were left to their own devices, failed, and were cast aside as heavy-handed interventionists.

The conclusion is obvious. The Third World is ours to lose, not theirs to win. The Soviets need Western mistakes in order to succeed. They require an environment poisoned by misguided Western policy before their ideology can thrive. In a neutral environment, they wither rather quickly. (It took 100,000 troops to halt the erosion of Soviet influence among the Afghan people.)

One of the more recent examples of this was the Reagan administration's decision, in June 1981, to be the only nation in the world to vote against the infant-formula code in the UN. By that action President Reagan pleased two parties: the American infant-formula companies and the Soviets.

The question becomes obvious. Why do we insist on acting according to the Soviet game plan? Why do we help them snatch victory from the jaws of defeat? Whose side are we on, anyway?

These disastrous policies reflect conservative thinking in this country. But why would conservatives want to assist the Soviets? The fact is that some American conservatives, including certain members of the Congress, have done more for Soviet foreign policy than any KGB operative. Those congressmen and senators who complain the loudest about Soviet influence are exactly those whose actions promote that influence.

How do you persuade the American people to understand that these misguided leaders aid and abet our most dedicated adversary? How do you make them comprehend that these policies will reduce American influence in the Third World and open it up to Soviet dominance? I don't know. I once fantasized about holding a ceremony on the steps of the Capitol. I would dress someone up like Brezhnev and have him award medals of appreciation to various people representing right-wing members of Congress. He would thank them for their devotion to the advancement of Soviet influence in the Third World. It would have made the front pages of every major newspaper and all three evening news programs. It would have been totally irresponsible, but perhaps it would have forced Americans to think.

A more current example of America's reflexive behavior is Nicaragua, where President Anastasio Somoza and his family had ruled for four decades. Somoza was a prototypical Latin American despot—corrupt, cruel, and insensitive. But he was no fool, and he knew how to deal with America. He presented himself as fervently anti-Communist, and that was all we needed to know and all we wanted to know. It was not, however, what the people of Nicaragua wanted.

In time, Somoza's excesses proved too much. Left-wing insurgents teamed up with disenchanted moderates to oust him. The ideology of the revolution was partly Marxist, and some of the weapons were supplied by the Soviets through Cuba.

When the insurgent Sandinistas took over, there was the usual struggle for power between the extreme and the moderate leftists. Despite the rhetoric, there were early signs leaving room for hope that moderation could survive. The ruling government, for example, continued to allow the publication of *La Prensa*, a respected newspaper that had been critical of Somoza and was not afraid to castigate the ruling junta. In addition, the junta contained elements of the moderate business community.

But the American conservative reaction was typical: The new rulers were Marxists; all Marxists are the same; we had to eliminate them. Isolate them, cried the American right. The Soviets, presumably, could hardly believe their good fortune.

President Carter, who had overcome both the conservatives and the Soviets on the Panama Canal Treaties, decided not to bequeath the Sandinistas to Castro and the Soviets. He sent emissaries to Nicaragua and later recommended a $75 million aid package. The future of Nicaragua was to be contested vigorously. If moderates wanted to stay and work for a free Nicaragua, then America would help.

This gesture, of course, was easy prey back home. Conservatives accused the President of helping Marxists, and the right-wing thunder shook both liberals and moderates. In a conservative year, no one wanted to be accused of helping Marxists, no matter that not doing so would actually help the Soviets. Reality is nothing politically compared to appearances. When the matter came to the Senate for a vote, two responses emerged that tell a great deal about that body.

Senator X, who for obvious reasons shall go unnamed, was a moderate Democrat whose voting record was generally courageous, but not on foreign policy. As the vote on the aid package took place, I talked to him about the complexities of the issue and he nodded in agreement throughout. When I finished, he looked at me and smiled. "This is no time to be responsible," he said, and proceeded to vote against me. He knew I was right, but explaining it back home was hopeless, and he would pay a heavy price politically. He assumed that I, as a fellow politician, would understand that.

If he had voted with me, he would have been accused of helping the Soviets, when in fact he would have been hurting them.

For voting against me, he would be hailed for hurting the Soviets, when in fact he was helping them.

The dilemma would ordinarily have proven too much and the measure would have been defeated. It wasn't, because of Senator Edward Zorinsky.

The Senate has few less likely champions of aid to Nicaragua. Zorinsky is a conservative Democrat from Nebraska. He is a former Republican mayor of Omaha, and the press often speculated that he would become a Republican again if the Republicans took over the Senate. (He didn't.) He joined the Foreign Relations Committee in January of 1979, beating me for the slot by a 14 to 9 vote of the Senate Steering Committee. As the most junior member of the committee, he ended up by default as chairman of the Latin American Subcommittee. He took the task seriously and began to learn about that region. Despite his vote against the Panama Canal Treaties in 1978, he soon realized that the United States was being doctrinaire and ineffectual in Latin America. He studied the Nicaraguan situation intensively, and attended the inauguration ceremonies as part of the official United States delegation. Soon he decided that we should not let Nicaragua go by default, and concluded that the $75 million aid package ought to be supported.

But what about the people of Nebraska? Senator X had concluded he could not explain such a vote in his state. Zorinsky went home to Nebraska and confronted the issue head on. He explained the situation to his constituents, declaring he wasn't about to "cut and run" at "the first sign of a Communist." He was going in there to "fight for America's interests." The people of Nebraska understood, and Zorinsky returned to lead the fight for the aid. He was joined by an unlikely ally on the Republican side, Senator Richard Lugar of Indiana, also a certified conservative. (As a result of this action, extreme right-wingers in the Senate turned on Lugar and worked to scuttle his vice-presidential prospects at the 1980 Republican Convention.)

With Zorinsky and Lugar speaking out for the aid package, it passed the Senate, just barely. The reactionaries were furious. In the 1980 election, every senator who voted for the program was attacked bitterly for aiding Marxists, and several were defeated by conservative challengers.

The conservatives wanted to pull out of Nicaragua, and that would have handed it over to the Soviets. They wanted to apply to Nicaragua the same theory that had failed against Castro all these years. The Senate rejection of this policy only intensified their zeal, which grew with the inauguration of the new administration. By the spring of 1981, conservatives in Washington were telling me that the 1980 election was a mandate to reverse U.S. policies in Latin America. To some that mandate included attempts to "destabilize" Nicaragua, as was done to Chile under Salvador Allende. There was also the push for sending U.S. military personnel to El Salvador despite the opposition of almost all of our Latin American and European allies.

(The policy of using El Salvador as a test of strength for Reagan/ Haig anticommunism was derailed by the continuing fallout from the murder of four American churchwomen by right-wing Salvadoran military personnel. The attempt by Haig and Senate conservatives to imply that the churchwomen had been political activists who might have run a roadblock was so completely contrary to the actual facts of the case as to create a firestorm of protest in the United States. The episode served to weaken the Salvadoran regime.)

We were clearly about to embark on a policy in Latin America that would have honored John Foster Dulles. In doing so, we would provide credibility to the extreme left, and undermine the moderate left and the center. In Havana, Castro would be pleased.

The Soviet interest in the Third World is quite simple—they want control. This is not to belittle the Soviets' belief in their ideology. They do follow the Marxist-Leninist view of the world, but they have moved beyond it. The plight of the world's peasants has become secondary to the desire for expansion of Soviet power.

The Soviets see the Third World as the perfect arena. No one understands capitalistic exploitation as well as those who have lived under colonialism. No one chafes emotionally as much as someone who has endured the racism of Western colonial powers.

For example, every Third World leader in Africa who fought for his freedom did so in spite of, not because of, Western interests. In the struggle for independence, the Soviets were always at the ready with ideology and weaponry. They harvested well.

If the Soviets can gain control of a situation, nothing else matters to them. Not human rights, not racial equality, not economic equity. None of these values is part of the domestic Soviet agenda. As demonstrated in Afghanistan, they are prepared to engage in the same international repression that marks domestic Soviet history. To the inheritors of the Gulag Archipelago, a little repression is no big deal. If today's Ethiopian citizen lives in fear, it doesn't matter just as long as Soviet control persists. Nor does the fact that Fidel Castro never delivered on his promise for free elections, or that the

Angolan and Mozambican economies are having severe difficulties. Individual human rights are secondary to the larger global struggle.

A nation that erects a Berlin Wall, that crushes dissent internally and among its "friends" in Hungary, Czechoslovakia, and Afghanistan, and that denies full participation to the 50 percent of its people who are not Russians, enters the Third World arena with a decided handicap: hypocrisy. If there were no bitterness toward the West, the Soviet record on human rights would be determinative.

The Soviets will be confronted with other handicaps to their Third World policy as the next two decades unfold. They will simply not enjoy the economic base to engage in a massive foreign aid program. They will not possess the sophisticated technology that the Third World needs for development. Nor will they have a viable hard currency to allow for serious trade relationships with Third World nations.

Trade investment and technology will continue to be the prime objective of Third World nations. And where must they go to obtain them? The same place the Soviets go: the West.

These handicaps will lead the Soviets unavoidably back to familiar grounds—dealing in ideology and weaponry. Unable to compete in economic development, and unable to raise human rights issues (colonialism, imperialism, racism) as successfully as before, they will attempt to poison the environment for Western interests. The theory will be as follows: although Third World nations may not like the Soviet Union, if various trouble spots are handled correctly, these countries will turn away from the West, and especially from the United States. The trouble spots include South Africa, Namibia, Nicaragua, El Salvador, Guatemala, South Korea, and the Philippines—and obviously the issue of the Palestinians. Stir these up, rely upon Western right-wing forces to be reactionary, and be ready to realize the benefits.

American interests in the Third World are harder to define. There is a constant struggle between those who see the Third World in East-West terms (as bit players in the Cold War struggle) and those who see the Third World in Third World terms.

In early 1978, Zbigniew Brzezinski spoke to a group of congressmen at the White House as part of an administration briefing on the first year of the Carter presidency. As one of his major accomplishments, he listed the removal of the centrality of the East-West struggle from Third World considerations. It was a major theoretical breakthrough. Although it was not adhered to in many cases (e.g., Angola, Ethiopia, Vietnam), the recognition of the principle was important even if it was done by the Carter official who violated it most frequently. I believe that had Carter been reelected, he would have pursued this policy free from the political worries that hampered him in the first term.

The history of American relations with the Third World is one of consistent inconsistency. Our policy seems to be divided over exactly what we are trying to accomplish.

Cold Warriors aim to enlist Third World countries in the fight against communism. (Witness the attempts of Secretary Haig to enlist Middle Eastern nations in the containment of the Soviets. Needless to say, they balked, given their focus on problems much closer to home.) They tend to judge a Third World leader on a single position—where he stands in the U.S.-Soviet struggle. If he's for us, then we're for him. If he's for them, we're against him. If he's neutral, he's an ingrate and we should forget him. Thus our government never really raised the embarrassing questions in Nicaragua with Somoza about his rampant corruption and exploitation. We tend to forget inquiries about human rights violations in the Philippines and South Korea. We put little pressure on South Africa regarding Namibia and the injustice of minority rule there. The military men of El Salvador and Guatemala are seldom urged to contain the terrorism perpetrated by their own troops.

This Cold War–based policy requires that the United States ignore the values it cherishes at home whenever it engages in international affairs. Racial equality, human rights, self-determination, economic opportunity, freedom from oppression, all are secondary to the issue of expediency. The double standard is quickly perceived by nations looking for our support.

In 1979, a group of white South African members of Parliament came to the United States to garner support for the country's apartheid system. One meeting involved the South Africans and several members of Congress whose feelings about institutionalized racism were openly negative. The group included Congressmen Stephen Solarz of New York, Paul McCloskey of California, Howard Wolpe of Michigan, Senator George McGovern of South Dakota, and myself. The justification of the prevailing system by the South Africans fell on deaf ears. Out of desperation, one MP resorted to his government's old saw about being a bulwark against communism. He must have reasoned that if nothing else worked, loyalty to an anti-Communist position would. I told him we viewed South Africa, not as an ally against communism, but as an open invitation for Soviet adventurism and Communist ideology; they were communism's most valuable tool in Africa. The South Africans were dumbfounded. Needless to say, they are feeling better these days, with both McGovern defeated and a friend in the White House.

In the summer of 1980, Edward Seaga, then a candidate, now Prime Minister of Jamaica, visited the United States in search of help for his candidacy. Senator Richard Stone of Florida gave Seaga a breakfast which several senators attended. Seaga was running against the leftist incumbent, Michael Manley, and most of his audience were conservatives, including Strom Thurmond of South Carolina and Roger Jepsen of Iowa. Seaga attacked Fidel Castro, and claimed that he himself intended to be a bulwark against Cuban communism. When he finished, Senator Joseph Biden of Delaware told Seaga he was making a serious error if he thought we would support him just because he opposed Castro. Americans wanted to know about his record on issues like human rights and economic justice. Biden made it clear that we weren't about to repeat past American blunders. Seaga was taken aback. (I will always remember Biden's blunt response. It was so utterly frank as to leave even me uneasy, but it was a masterful performance in realpolitik.) The point here is not to denigrate Seaga, who is bright and well motivated, but to show that a Third World leader could come to the United States and talk about Fidel Castro as the reason why America should back him. He clearly felt that we as senators cared far more about Castro than about the policies he would institute at home.

Those of us who try to see the Third World in Third World terms do so for two distinct reasons. First, it is morally right in terms of the values we believe in as a nation; and second, it works.

Consistency with American Values. We are a great nation. And we are great because of more than just our natural resources and our military might. We stand as an exemplar for certain basic values. At Lexington and Concord in April 1775, we "fired the shots heard round the world." Those shots represented freedom and the right of self-determination. We began a revolution that emanated from one all-powerful idea—that man had certain "inalienable rights," among them "Life, Liberty, and the Pursuit of Happiness." The reader might spend some time looking back at our Revolution. The willingness of our forefathers to rise up against an oppressive government is too often celebrated by rote rather than by understanding. For a nation that was conceived in insurgency, we are strangely uneasy with it. Americans once were prepared to die for these ideals —and many did. Americans are still ready to die for them. Why, then, do we assume that people of the Third World feel differently about such ideals?

We are a great nation because we have mostly tried to live up to the words in our Declaration of Independence that "all men are created equal." From Abraham Lincoln's Emancipation Proclamation through Lyndon Johnson's "We Shall Overcome" speech to today, America has tried to eradicate racism at home. It's been a difficult struggle and much more needs to be done; but most of us are committed to that end, no matter how fierce the opposition. Why, then, do we assume that Third World people feel any less committed to the end of racism?

We are a great nation because we have embraced the ideal of economic equity. From the New Deal to the Great Society, we have decreed that poverty in a land of plenty is unacceptable. We have understood that economic injustice breeds violence and instability. We have sought to include as many people as possible within the bounds of our affluence, so that all may believe they are a part of this nation. Why, then, do we assume that people living in the Third World in abject poverty will be any less bitter about economic injustice forced upon them by insensitive, wealthy rulers?

These values make us what we are, and are the stuff of our

civilization. They make us the "last, best hope of earth." To be really true to these hallowed principles, we must apply them overseas as well as at home.

Values That Work. Marxism-Leninism as practiced by the Soviets is introduced into the Third World as a powerful ideology. It is, however, no match for the basic human values as practiced by the United States if consistently applied to the Third World.

Take racial equality, which is *the* emotional force in southern Africa. The Soviets have a difficult mission in explaining their domestic racial policies. But if we do not apply pressure for the abolition of apartheid in South Africa, they will have an easier time of it.

Take human rights, which is a rising force throughout the world. How can those who operated the Gulag Archipelago even attempt to identify themselves with freedom-seeking peoples? The Soviets have learned to cloak themselves in American principles overseas, and to position themselves as the friend of the oppressed, while we ignore our principles and end up cast as the ally of the oppressors. This is more than just ironic since it is our belief in human rights that distinguishes us from the Soviets.

American values work. The only question is, who will apply them? They are our values and they are more natural to us. They are ideas whose time has come; we should be confident in their application.

Almost every parent has had the experience of watching his child compete in athletic events. I've seen my daughters ice-skate and play in soccer games, and have been tempted to intervene on their behalf. I never have, for obvious reasons. In trying to analyze my reactions, I've come to understand that the desire to intervene is a function of my not having full confidence in their performance (especially when they compete with boys).

Conservatives take the same approach toward American values, which they feel won't work in the Third World. They believe that these values can be undermined by one Marxist insurgent. How else can one explain the favorable reference to "moderately repressive regimes" by Reagan administration officials? The truth is that basic human values are far more powerful than some of us think. We should be willing to allow them to compete head-to-head with Marxism-Leninism, *for they will win.* These values are as basic to all people as they are to us; because they are determinative in America, I believe they will be determinative in the Third World. They are strong because they control the "hearts and minds" of people. And we have learned in Vietnam (as the Soviets have learned in Afghanistan) that people's minds are the most critical objective. It's time we gave our values our full confidence.

If there is one Soviet interest and two competing American interests in the Third World, there are as many Third World interests as there are governments. You can have benign leaders (Nyerere of Tanzania) next door to brutal despots (Amin of Uganda), collective leadership (Nicaragua) close to one-man rule (Panama), mixed economies (Kenya) neighboring heavily Socialist economies (Ethiopia), chaos (Cambodia) near stability (Malaysia).

Despite the obvious differences, there are some underlying factors that serve as common, if not universal, denominators.

Emotional Background. Many Third World countries have only recently achieved independence from colonialism. In some cases the transition was reasonably peaceful (French-colonized West Africa); in some instances it was violent (French-colonized Vietnam). Leaders who fought for their freedom were often left with a certain toughness and bitterness toward Western nations, their former colonial ruler, or its allies. For example, Mozambican President Samora Machel's feelings toward the Portuguese colonizers and their NATO friends—who supplied Portugal with arms—were so intense that it took years before he could manage to communicate civilly with an American ambassador. The resentment also reflects a lack of confidence in being treated as an equal by Western powers. (The passage of the Panama Canal Treaties did much to contain this attitude in parts of Latin America.)

Such anti-Western emotions are countered by a clear pull toward Western practices. Many Third World leaders were educated in the West, and most retain an attraction for Western culture. Former President Leopold Senghor of Senegal, for example, is a world-renowned philosopher with deep roots in the French intellectual tradition. Others have developed strong personal ties with Westerners that transcend politics. In January of 1980, when I met with President Machel in Mozambique, he spoke at length about his respect and deep affection for Robert Kennedy.

This love-hate—or, to be more correct chronologically, hate-love —relationship is on constant display at the United Nations. For years most Third World countries lambasted the West in that arena as if it were a rite of passage. It was obvious that beneath the three-piece suits and diplomatic charm were some very bruised psyches. I have often witnessed a Third World acquaintance spill out his bitterness in a public forum. Such conduct may or may not be rational, but it is a force that must be dealt with.

Soldiers Who Become Administrators. The strong emotional rejection of colonialism was accompanied by a strong emotional rejection of capitalism. The Third World countries were going to be models of socialism. With philosophical leaders like Nyerere, the search for economic equity became the guiding beacon. Country after country searched out its own variant on that theme; there would be no more exploitation of the poor by the rich.

By the end of the 1970s, however, the memory of their colonial past had begun to fade, and the realities of running a nation had begun to dominate Third World thinking. It was one thing to be a skilled guerrilla fighter; it was quite another to deal with balance-of-payments problems and austerity plans caused by the skyrocketing costs of oil.

As the years wore on, the advantages of an "incentive" economy became more obvious. The purely Socialist societies were beset by bureaucratic inertia and a lack of innovation. In overcompensating for the desire for economic equity, they have ignored incentives. There were conspicuous examples of economic progress in "mixed-economy" countries like Taiwan, the Ivory Coast, Singapore, Kenya, and Brazil. But it was hard to find Socialist nations to hold up as viable role models.

More and more leaders began to explore, at least intellectually, a move toward a mixed economy. It became clear that the need for trade, investment, and technology transfer could be adequately satisfied only in the West.

A classic example of this kind of thinking is the Prime Minister of Zimbabwe, Robert Mugabe, who must be as complex a man as any leader in the world. As an individual, he is a psychohistorian's delight. He is a crack guerrilla leader with the mind of an intellectual. His quiet, often morose personal style belies a toughness that enabled him to rise to the top of his tumultuous, often violent political party, ZANU.

I first met Mugabe in early 1980 in Mozambique, where he had been exiled for several years while conducting guerrilla warfare against Ian Smith's white regime in Rhodesia. His ZANU forces had battled with the Smith army in the East, while Joshua Nkomo's ZAPU guerrillas had fought in the West, operating out of Zambia.

In March 1978, Ian Smith tired of the struggle and attempted to achieve an internal settlement by agreeing to share power with three black leaders, led by Bishop Abel Muzorewa. In April of 1979, elections were held, which the ZANU and ZAPU people boycotted, and Muzorewa was chosen Prime Minister.

Mugabe and Nkomo continued to wage their guerrilla war. Conservatives in Great Britain and the United States began a move to lift the existing economic sanctions against Rhodesia, and that effort was given a boost when the Conservative leader, Margaret Thatcher, became Prime Minister of Britain. If the United States and Great Britain were to raise sanctions, it would give great credibility to the Muzorewa-Smith regime, which was being shunned by almost every country in the world with the notable exception of South Africa.

Led by Jesse Helms of North Carolina, the U.S. Senate voted to lift sanctions. In the House of Representatives the effort failed, owing to the leadership of Congressman Stephen Solarz. The Carter administration also opposed Helms. For her part, Mrs. Thatcher did not lift sanctions despite an explicit campaign promise to do so: the stern reaction of the rest of black Africa made her consider consequences as a Prime Minister that were not her concern as a candidate.

The focus thus returned to the competing personalities in the Rhodesian struggle. A marathon negotiating session between the parties commenced at Lancaster House in London, moderated by British Foreign Secretary Lord Carrington. The resulting agreement called for a British-supervised election in February 1980. British, South African, and some American money flooded into the Muzorewa campaign coffers. Soviet money was supplied to Nkomo. Mugabe ran on his war record—and won going away.

His overwhelming victory clearly surprised most observers. But it was the only election I predicted correctly in all of 1980. I had known he would win ever since an incident in Rhodesia while I was there in January 1980, when I encountered his grassroots followers face to face.

Chris Chamberlin, my foreign policy staffer, Frank Ferrari of the African American Institute, Jeff Davidow of the U.S. Embassy in Rhodesia, and I went to a Mugabe campaign headquarters in a Salisbury suburb after dark. The suggestion was mine, and Davidow was not pleased by the venture. The reactions to us in the black township ranged from markedly suspicious to openly hostile. The area had been the scene of recent violence and the Mugabe people blamed the white Rhodesian police.

They clearly took us for police. They surrounded us and made us sit in front of a table in the headquarters. One particularly feverish young Mugabe supporter began crowding people into the room and led them into shouting chants and slogans at ever-increasing decibel levels. Having lived two years in an African village, I was quite comfortable in Rhodesia, but I soon realized that this situation was getting out of hand. One look at Davidow's face and I knew he had been right. Our black Rhodesian driver was even more distressed, and tried to explain who we were. He and Davidow took it upon themselves to attempt to defuse the crisis by extolling the fellowship that I as a United States senator felt for the Zimbabwean people. One of the men behind the table looked at my Senate I.D. card and realized that if Davidow was telling the truth, he had better get us the hell out of there.

He smoothly and firmly escorted us through the door to our car while the others looked on grimly. When I tried to engage him in conversation in the street, he looked at me incredulously. He told us to drive away without hesitation. We did. As we took off, I asked Davidow whether he always enjoyed escorting visiting members of Congress. He might have killed me if he hadn't been so relieved.

The ferocity of that event made it clear to me that, irrespective of what was being said in the press, the raw emotions of the blacks of Zimbabwe/Rhodesia had been tapped by Mugabe. He won 57 of the 80 contested seats, a clear majority. Perceived as the more extreme Marxist of the two guerrilla leaders, his election was viewed with great alarm by whites in Zimbabwe/Rhodesia, South Africa, and in the West generally. A diehard Marxist had won— and in an election, no less. This coming to power by the ballot box stuck in the craw of American conservatives.

Seven months later, I again met Mugabe at a quiet luncheon arranged by Secretary of State Edmund Muskie at the State Department. Mugabe was wearing a pin-striped three-piece suit, striped shirt, and dark tie. He had spoken to the banking and financial community in New York the day before and won them over. He talked in quiet and reasoned tones about the practicalities of running a country and about his economic development plans. Listening to him, it was easy to understand why he had started his rule by asking white Rhodesians to remain in the country and by keeping his arch-enemy, General Peter Walls, as interim commander of the armed forces. (He even retained for some months the same Washington lobbyist who had labored for Ian Smith. Of all of Mugabe's actions, that one surprised me the most. The lobbyist, needless to say, made the transition smoothly.)

Mugabe the guerrilla leader was not Mugabe the administrator. He knew he could not feed his people with rhetoric. Zimbabwe had enormous economic potential and he wanted to develop it. And as a trained economist, he knew where he had to go to do it—the West.

All this recalled a remark attributed to Mugabe while he was in exile in Mozambique. He supposedly turned to an American who questioned him on his Marxism and, pointing to the economic problems of Socialist Mozambique, remarked: "I'm not going to make the same mistake."

The "real" Robert Mugabe is of course a matter of debate, but his first year in office was embarrassing to American conservatives. They predicted catastrophe. He made overtures to them. They foresaw Soviet dominance. He waited a year before allowing the Soviets to open an embassy. They forecast violence in southern Africa. He gave assurances of trying negotiations first. Still, the conservatives chafed. In February 1981, the Reverend Jerry Falwell would still be calling Mugabe a "Communist" on television, as if the events of the preceding year had not occurred. The lack of hard-core Marxism on Mugabe's part was clearly threatening to American reactionaries. They wanted him to be a real Marxist, and he wasn't delivering.

The Third World has been identified as the fifth reality in this book. It is the area that lends itself most acutely to American misjudgment. This is especially a problem for the Reagan administration, whose decisionmakers lack broad personal experience in the Third World. And in Washington today there is a clique of emboldened Cold Warriors who want to make up for Vietnam by resurrecting the dogma of John Foster Dulles.

The lack of Third World experience in the Reagan administration is symbolized by its top four foreign policy advisers. Secretary of State Alexander Haig, his Deputy William Clark, National Security Adviser Richard Allen, and U.N. Ambassador Jeane Kirkpatrick have little personal experience with the Third World. And on Capitol Hill, too, exposure to Third World problems is limited. In the Senate, Christopher Dodd of Connecticut was a Peace Corps volunteer in the Dominican Republic and Daniel P. Moynihan of New York was the American ambassador to India. In the House of Representatives, there only are a handful of members who have serious Third World experience.

The want of personal experience is bad enough--that would be a manageable situation if there were a dispassionate frame of reference. However, most Washington decisionmakers regard the Third World from an East-West point of view. They vividly remember the Cold War, and that is the prism through which many judge Third World happenings. I do not say this with total disdain. Most of these men and women are of the generation that experienced the Cold War and its crushing implications. It was their formative experience and they perhaps cannot be blamed for this perspective. But the fact that it is understandable does not make it less wrong. Only when official Washington changes its attitudes will American policy toward the Third World reflect clear vision and true statesmanship. Even more important, only then will it reflect the reality, and only by reflecting reality, will it work. Here are some practical proposals:

Discard the East-West Mentality. We cannot think of Third World peoples in East-West terms for one basic reason: they don't think of themselves in those terms. The leader of a Third World country, having experienced a colonial history, is very sensitive to outside white domination, whether American, western European, or Russian. He is faced with great economic and social problems, currently made all the more acute by the huge balance-of-payments deficit caused by oil imports. The country's economic development is the top priority on his agenda. He understands that running a country requires the skills of a trained economist, not a political theoretician. His needs are trade and investment and technology. The struggle between the United States and the Soviet Union is important to us, but not crucial to him. Rather, being non-aligned is a badge of honor. He may have been once attracted to the anti-colonialist rhetoric of the Soviets, but the invasion of Afghanistan showed their true colors. Besides, he knows that the Soviets can't help his economy except in limited ways and then only with unacceptable strings of influence. As a result, Third World leaders today are far more pragmatic than they are given credit for. They demonstrate a remarkable talent for the sort of situational decision-making that can only exist where there are open minds.

I'll refer to one recent example—Algeria. Algeria fought the French for their independence, and the fight was bitter. We supported the French until the war was nearly over, and predictably they lost. Algeria became independent; under President Ahmed Ben Bella, the Algerians harbored serious anti-Western and anti-American sentiments. Now, should we have isolated them? The Cold Warrior would say Yes. Yet it was Algerians who would later help to resolve the Iranian hostage issue. Despite differences, they put themselves on the line to aid America. This lesson should not be quickly forgotten.

Develop Economic Ties. The trump card of the West is our economy. Third World nations need access to our markets, just as we must have access to their raw materials. The marriage is a natural.

In June of 1980, I co-sponsored, with the African-American Institute, a conference in Boston between American corporations and the former Portuguese-speaking colonies of Africa—Angola, Mozambique, Guinea-Bissau, Sâo Tome, Principe, and Cape Verde. The mere fact that such a conference could be held suggests that reality holds sway, even in the Third World. The exchange between the American corporate representatives and some of the Marxist Africans could not have been more cordial. The Americans were excited about the investment potential of these countries, and the Africans were eager for the investment. The relationships and business arrangements that resulted were beneficial to both sides.

The more trade and commerce there is, the better off we will all be. Since most Third World nations know how to bargain effectively by now, the era of exploitation that has concerned many observers is pretty much over. In addition, many American corporations are becoming sensitive to the need for their representatives to be skilled in the language and customs of the country in question.

Regard Foreign Aid as a Crucial Investment. If there is a single easy target in the budget, it's foreign aid. No one writes to a senator or congressman demanding more foreign aid. Even in a progressive state like Massachusetts, polls invariably show a large plurality in favor of less foreign aid. Amendments to cut appropriations are as certain as death and taxes, and they invariably succeed. The fact that any foreign aid bill passes is a remarkable achievement.

Consequently, foreign aid as a percentage of GNP has dropped from 0.49 percent in 1965 to 0.27 percent in 1980. We now rank twelfth in the world, behind Sweden, Norway, the Netherlands, Denmark, France, Belgium, the United Kingdom, Australia, Canada, West Germany, and Japan.

This development is undesirable for two reasons. In the first place, the human needs in most Third World countries are desperate. Simply as a matter of humanitarian concern, spending 27¢ out of every $100 of our national income to help less developed (often starving) people is not excessive by any sensitive person's definition. The specter of starving children in Somalia and Uganda cannot be irrelevant to a nation of people that believes in its own traditional generosity. Second, it is counterproductive to our own interests.

Beyond humanitarian reasons, national self-interest should be determinative. When Budget Director David Stockman proposed to decimate the foreign aid budget in January 1981, he was partially countered by Secretary of State Haig, who knew that the full cut would negatively affect our international capabilities. Faced with fierce international concern—especially from our allies—the administration restored some of the cuts, perhaps realizing the difference between campaign rhetoric and official responsibility. Reality scored again. As Haig well knew, the single greatest foreign aid program in history was the Marshall Plan. It reconstructed Europe, strengthened their people against the appeal of communism, and made them a lucrative market for our goods. It was a remarkably successful plan—for them *and* for us. The more we tie countries to the West, the less attractive will ties to the East appear.

The same principles are applied to the Third World by West Germany, Italy, Japan, and France, where in recent years, foreign aid to the developing nations has increased. These countries know that commercial market opportunities follow foreign aid programs. If West Germany wants to gain a trade foothold in a particular country, the most effective way is to maintain an aid mission to open the necessary doors. As the United States reduces its presence in those countries that have great economic potential, our European and Japanese competitors will take up the slack and reap the economic benefits. This negative attitude toward foreign aid must be reversed, and only the corporations and unions of our country can accomplish it. Corporate and union officials with both investment and jobs at stake must join with the traditional humanitarian groups and make a concerted effort to educate the country, the White House, and the Congress as to the worth of foreign aid.

Stop Giving Up Nations to the Soviets. At some point we decided that the way to topple a government was to withhold our diplomatic recognition. It has never worked. We refused to recognize the Soviets for fifteen years, to no avail. It took us thirty years to recognize the People's Republic of China. Despite our diplomatic stance, these nations did not vanish. Eventually, reality prevailed over dogma. The Nixon overture to open up China in 1972 was a brilliant and paradoxical diplomatic coup by a tried and true red-baiter.

The shift in our relations with China has forced a fascinating restructuring of our attitudes. For years the Chinese were the enemy. When I arrived in Ethiopia in 1962, I was warned by other Peace Corps volunteers not to say anything of consequence in the Peking restaurant in Addis Ababa, since it was supposedly owned by Red Chinese, and therefore had to be bugged. I faithfully adhered to this admonition, and our discussions there were the essence of mindless pap. (In later years, I often wondered what a Peace Corps volunteer could possibly say that would interest the Chinese.) I never knew whether the restaurant actually was wired, but the fact that we all took the idea seriously suggests the prevailing attitude.

The recognition of China and its role as a wedge against the Soviets has wrought a startling change. Many Americans have found it hard to adjust. I was listening to a Boston talk show in 1980 in which a caller was going on about the "commies" and our need to stand up to all of them. He said we had to be strong like the Chinese and join hands with them. When the host delicately pointed out that the Chinese were also "commies," the caller muttered something about their being different and quickly hung up. Still, our readjustments must be less difficult than those of the Soviet and Chinese people, who had to learn to hate each other after years of solidarity.

Almost no one now argues that we would be better off with an isolated China. The pejorative terms "CHI-COM" and "Red Chinese" have disappeared from the common vocabulary. Even President Reagan, who made a career of calling for the "unleashing" of Chiang Kai-shek, the Nationalist Chinese leader, against the Peking regime, now accepts the change. To the dismay of some of his more right-wing supporters, he has not reversed the policy. Indeed, he has proposed arms sales to China. So, with recognition, the Chinese are better off, we are better off, and the Soviets are worse off.

Diplomatic recognition should not be applied for emotional or domestic political reasons. That's true in the Third World as well. We didn't recognize Angola because it turned "Marxist" after its struggle for independence. The bitterness of the Angolans toward the Portuguese for removing everything of value after independence is intense, as is the resentment about the American arms used by NATO ally Portugal in the war. However, these feelings do not cloud the Angolans' realism. They have invited Cuban troops to help put down the UNITA insurrectionist faction, and to offset South African military incursions into their country. But they have also granted major oil concessions to Gulf and Texaco. The relationship between capitalist Gulf and Texaco (not to mention Arthur D. Little, Chase Manhattan Bank, Boeing, and General Tire) and the Angolans is pragmatic and satisfactory. The Angolan presence at the Boston conference referred to earlier reiterated their desire for more trade. Private-sector Americans dealing with Angola have all privately urged our recognition of that country. When I visited Angola in 1980, I asked the nation's leaders, as a gesture of goodwill, to release an American accused of being a mercenary during the struggle for independence. (George McGovern had also made such a request.) I suggested that it would be a positive step toward working out better relations with the United States. The American was later freed.

The Carter administration decided to recognize Angola, but for a number of reasons was reluctant to do so in 1979 for fear of antagonizing Senate conservatives during the SALT debate, or in 1980 for fear of giving Ronald Reagan an issue. This hesitation was to prove substantively erroneous and politically meaningless, since both SALT II and President Carter were victims of events in 1980. After Cyrus Vance resigned as Secretary of State, he called for the recognition of Angola in his first public speech. Vance's view was publicly shared by the president of Gulf, Melvin Hill, by our European allies (who themselves recognize Angola), and by our friends in black Africa.

By not recognizing Angola, we strengthen the forces in that country who are ill disposed toward the United States. One European diplomat told me: "For God's sake, get yourselves in here and fight for influence. Don't forfeit the game." He was right.

The same sentiment was expressed vis-à-vis the Vietnamese when Secretary Haig visited New Zealand in June of 1981. New Zealand, our staunch ally in the Pacific, sharply criticized the American policy of trying to "isolate" Hanoi, which the New Zealanders felt was pure folly—and self-defeating.

The same rationale applies to Cuba. For over twenty years, we have tried to make Castro evaporate, and instead he has become a hero of the Third World. Like former Egyptian President Gamal Abdel Nasser, who used his attacks on the Israelis to unite his people, Castro needs only to rant and rave against the United States to accomplish the same purpose. We should deny him this easy avenue.

By avoiding the field of battle, we will not effectively offset Soviet influence. We give the Soviets a free ride. They would be deeply concerned if we abandoned this forfeiture of influence and sent emissaries to Havana, Luanda, and Hanoi. Doing so, however, would not in the least represent approval of those governments or their activities, any more than the presence of the American ambassador in Moscow indicates approval of Soviet policies. It is ironic that we should refuse to recognize nations because of Soviet influence on them while we recognize the nation most subject to Soviet influence—the Soviet Union itself. Yet even the most conservative theoreticians no longer argue that U.S. interests would be served by the non-recognition of Russia. Recognition of these Third World countries, as Senator Zorinsky put it in talking of Nicaragua, would symbolize a decision not to "cut and run" anymore.

We should believe in ourselves for a change. I am convinced that all three countries, given encouragement, would begin to loosen their ties with the Soviets and move in the direction of non-alignment. This evolution is inevitable. Any nation that has experienced the heavy, arrogant, self-serving embrace of the Russians prefers neutrality. One has only to ask Egyptians, Somalis, Sudanese, Ghanaians, or Guineans. We should not repeat the mistake of China. Who "lost" Cuba and Angola and Vietnam can be decided by historians. The urgent task ahead is to "find" them and show them a way out of the Soviet orbit. However we look at it, one thing is clear. In terms of our influence over events in those countries, we could not be any worse off than we are today.

Continue to Be Identified with Human Rights. In an era of tension around the world, the United States should stake out the moral high ground. We must continue to fly the banner of human rights. President Reagan's ill-fated attempt to appoint Ernest Lefever— an outspoken foe of human rights considerations in U.S. foreign policy—as Assistant Secretary of State for Human Rights speaks volumes as to the reversal of the staunch policy of Jimmy Carter.

Where does this leave America? One American involved with the human rights issue in Argentina related a story to me after the Lefever nomination. A prisoner in that country, after being beaten, staggered into the common toilet. There on the wall was scribbled a remarkable variant on the most common graffito in Latin America. The scrawled message read: "Yanqui, take me home." The prisoner later told the story to the American to symbolize the impact of Carter's human rights campaign. America had stood for something that Latin Americans could identify with—something the Soviets had tried to preempt.

Jacobo Timerman, the Argentinian publisher who wrote about his torture by the anti-Semitic government of Argentina, told me that human rights was more than just a policy; it was an ideology. And as an ideology it would devastate the appeal of Marxism. He referred to human rights as a uniquely powerful and uniquely Western mechanism. The decision to abandon it in pursuit of Lefever style "quiet diplomacy" was, to Timerman, a forfeiture of American morality and American self-interest. The Senate Foreign Relations Committee, for a number of reasons, agreed—and rejected Lefever by a 13–4 vote, with a majority of the Republicans joining all the Democrats to reject the Reagan nominee.

Turning our backs on human rights would be a retreat to "good old days" that were not so good for thousands of beaten, tortured, and murdered innocents around the world.

But even before the arrival of Reagan, the congressional performance on this issue had been somewhat inconsistent. Whether violations of human rights are condemned or ignored often has nothing to do with the issue. Conservatives tend to focus on the outrageous actions of leftist governments while ignoring those in countries like Argentina, the Philippines, Chile, South Korea, and Iran under the Shah. Liberals are eloquent about the horrors of rightist governments while overlooking those of Afghanistan, Libya, Ethiopia, and

Cuba. Human rights are human rights; they should be consistently defended.

Given the Soviets' atrocious record on domestic human rights, the world needs a credible exponent of these basic values. They are rooted in our culture and history, and we should champion them. Third World people need to have us honor this principle because if we don't, no one effectively will. And ultimately it is the moral and economic strength of America that will count, not just our military might.

I have participated in enough athletic (and political) contests to feel very strongly that if I am going to lose, I want it to be because the other side was better. I don't believe in allowing an opponent to win because I made mistakes or didn't try hard enough.

In the realm of U.S. policy toward the Third World, we have often made mistakes—Vietnam being the worst example—and we have often not tried hard enough (forfeiting American influence at the first sign of a Marxist). It's about time we smartened up and began showing courage and self-confidence. In doing so, we would further our national interests, both political and economic. We would also contribute to the economic, political, and social interests of the Third World. With tens of millions of people on this planet dying of starvation, facing abject poverty, or living under political turmoil, we have a deep and abiding moral obligation to stop being so doctrinaire.

Haile Wolde, a student of mine in Wolisso, was a small, very bright, and intensely earnest young man who struggled to overcome a stuttering habit. He was the kind of person who gives of himself and becomes part of you. After I left Ethiopia, I often wondered what became of him. In 1977, I found out that he had been executed in the violence of Ethiopia's revolution. Like two other Ethiopian students of mine who were also executed (as I later found out), Haile Wolde was just one more person. But he is still a part of me. And I feel deeply about people like Haile in the Third World, who need the stability, gentleness, and courage of an effective American foreign policy.

Paradoxically, we are faced with a rather happy situation. The reality of the Third World dictates a particular American policy in order to be effective—and that policy happens to coincide with the best of our moral principles. Rather than having to choose between expediency and principle, as conservatives who lack confidence in these principles would have us believe, the reality is that we can either choose both or we choose neither.

Clearly, then, given this unique linkage, if we opt for the dogma of the reactionaries, we will deserve our misfortune. If we opt for reality, we'll just have to learn to live with the grousing of the far right, who are never happy when things are going well. I, for one, can live with that.

7/International Trade: The Sixth Reality

For several years we have been spending more dollars on imports (especially for oil) than we were earning in return sales. In the last five years of the decade, our balance-of-trade deficit totaled $105.4 billion. As a result of this hemorrhaging of U.S. capital, the dollar weakened in overseas markets. This made imports all the more costly in America. The fact is that if we don't increase our exports dramatically to offset our imports, this deficit will eventually overwhelm us. If the United States hopes to sustain a viable economy, it must take international trade very seriously. The West Germans and Japanese long ago faced up to this reality. Although both are far more dependent upon imported oil than we are, they make export trade a top priority, and in the same five years they enjoyed balance-of-trade surpluses of $88.8 billion and $55.6 billion, respectively.

When the Ford Motor Company in 1980 introduced its fuel-efficient automobile, the Escort, it was identified as a "world car." Ford was not just aiming at the American market but at the global market as well. The Escort would be both manufactured and sold at home and abroad. It marked an awareness of the need to expand corporate horizons and was a very visible effort by an American firm to consider foreign markets.

Why are we so slow to wake up to this reality? Mostly, it's a result of our past experience. During the greater part of the twentieth century, the United States produced goods primarily for the United States. The home market was so huge that our production could be absorbed domestically. There was no need to concentrate on the far more complex international market. Even as late as 1970, 93.6 percent of our GNP went into domestic sales. The economy was robust and relatively self-contained. As with energy, productivity, and the environment, if the short term was satisfactory, why worry about the long term?

Four developments almost simultaneously unraveled this neat package. First, the quadrupling of oil prices in 1973 and 1974, followed by another doubling in 1979, sent the cost of energy imports from $4.3 billion in 1972 to a staggering $80 billion in 1980. This body blow to the American economy resulted in serious, continuing trade deficits in our international trade account.

Second, imports began to secure a substantial percentage of the domestic market. In textiles, cameras, shoes, steel, television sets, and automobiles, among other things, overseas competition made serious inroads, and tens of thousands of American workers became unemployed. The consumer was buying cheaper, better-made products from abroad.

Third, more and more of our high-technology products were being manufactured by companies whose cash flow and production schedules depended in significant part upon foreign markets. For these companies, foreign sales were a vital factor in their economic well-being. As these markets became increasingly attractive to other foreign competitors, concern grew about the future prospects for America's fastest growing sector of the economy.

Fourth, as our economy and that of other Western nations matured, growth markets were to be found in the developing nations. That was where we would have to be in order to have our industries prosper. It is a fact of history that success comes to those who follow the markets. From the Phoenicians of antiquity, to the English of the eighteenth century, to the Americans after World War II, to the Japanese of today, the linkage has been constant. Equally predictable has been the fate of those who don't pursue the markets, but instead hang on to the status quo.

We had entered a brave new world without realizing it.

The past was your neighborhood Chevrolet dealer selling you an Impala. The present is your English-speaking sales colleague for IBM trying to market a computer in Kenya, while competing with a Swahili-speaking Japanese sales representative who can offer better financing terms.

Every segment of the American economy—business, labor, and

government—must realize that we face a new, highly competitive situation and had better get prepared for it right away. The first thing we have to do is think in specific, disciplined terms about the competition.

But before dealing with particular policy recommendations, let me address two arguments that debunk the need for an aggressive export policy.

There are some who argue that the balance-of-trade deficit is not a matter of great concern because "current accounts" are in balance. The current account includes services, like insurance, and return on foreign investment to the trade account, to arrive at the "overall" picture. This school of thought is half-right, half-wrong. They are absolutely correct that the current account is in balance. They are absolutely incorrect, in my opinion, that there is cause for great comfort, for several reasons.

Any rapid growth in foreign investment here would rapidly offset the return on our investment abroad, so our strength is a reflection of what they have not yet accomplished, but are increasingly pursuing. Our advantage, then, is illusory.

Also, the recent jump in recorded return on foreign investment is caused to some degree by companies bringing funds back to America to take advantage of high interest rates. This, of course, is a temporary and artificial source of strength.

Finally, living off returns from foreign investment is just coupon-clipping writ large. It is a static benefit derived from past competitiveness. To have the edge that enables you to invest abroad successfully requires a lead in technology, production, and management know-how. No return of foreign investment can continue if there is not movement up the product scale and a retention of the competitive edge.

As a former member of the House Banking Committee, I used to observe the dollar's ups and downs with ambivalence. If the dollar appreciated in value in the foreign currency markets, that was good, an American dollar would go further overseas. If the dollar depreciated, that was also good, because it meant our products would be cheaper relative to the products of those currencies. I couldn't figure out what to cheer for—appreciation or depreciation. Much of the same confusion reigns today.

Yet, upon analysis, the benefit of the doubt should be with appreciation. Depreciation makes imports more costly and exacerbates the problem of inflation. Thus, inflation, in turn, influences the cost of American goods, offsetting in part the selling advantage of cheaper dollars. Although one clearly would not wish to have the dollar appreciate to the point of pricing itself out of the market, nor to contrive to force up the dollar artificially, the fact is that countries with strong currencies (Switzerland, West Germany, and Japan) have managed to maintain both that currency and an effective capacity to sell abroad. The view that we should not worry about the balance-of-trade deficit, since it produces a cheaper dollar, is not supported by the experience of this country or of our major trading competitors.

American Business

The typical American entrepreneur who ventures overseas is equipped with limited skills, considering the challenges he faces. As a people, we lack the long history of international transactions to educate our eager executive. So he wanders around Abidjan, Karachi, Helsinki, Quito, and Manila like Alice in Wonderland.

American companies must learn to "think international." That's not as easy as it sounds. Anyone who has learned a foreign language knows the difference between speaking in another tongue and thinking in that tongue. The former is a process of afterthought; the latter is a natural part of one's perspective. The businessman must examine his current product lines and instinctively ask himself, "Can I sell these abroad?" and "Where can I sell them abroad?" He must know about exchange rates and currency devaluations, and international insurance programs, and who's the key person to see in Malaysia and Paraguay, Taiwan and Hungary. He must think not only about the American housewife in Dayton, Ohio, but also about the housewife in Caracas and Oslo and Nairobi. Most of all, he's got to foresee what his Japanese, West German, Swiss, and Brazilian counterparts are planning and try to be first with the best product.

This sense of what will sell well abroad is not part of our business tradition. An American company marketing electrical appliances in foreign countries, for example, is inconvenienced by the fact that the Japanese, among others, have different electrical standards. A Japanese company assumes that there will be different standards in various countries and as a matter of course designs its product to meet local specifications and tastes. The contrast in attitude is substantial and it shows on the bottom line. The U.S. coolness to the metric system is one more manifestation of the unwillingness to think international. Adopting this standard would greatly facilitate the adaptability of American products to world markets, and yet there is sharp resistance to the change. Eventually, the metric system will be accepted, but in the meantime much international business will have been lost.

The businessman must learn what the first Peace Corps volunteers discovered in the early 1960s: he has to speak the language and know the culture if he hopes to be effective. The purchase and sale of international commodities hinge on more than the quality of the product. Goodwill is just as powerful abroad as it is in the United States. In America, companies spend millions on their clients, taking them to sporting events, keeping tabs on their favorite brand of Scotch, remembering the birthdays of directors and sending them gifts at Christmas. International markets require the same kind of approach—to an extent it means *baksheesh* (as opposed to bribes). But in many countries, the most important advantage is to be able to speak to the potential client in his native tongue and to talk knowledgeably with him about his history and culture. There is an increasing resentment in many parts of the world about always having to do business in English or French. More and more, especially in the Third World, the attitude is becoming one of "If you want my money, you'd better be able to negotiate the terms of the sale in my tongue, not yours." This emerging national pride puts Americans at a particular disadvantage: When we meet foreigners here, we expect to converse in English. When we visit their country, we still expect to talk in English. This desire to have it both ways does not characterize our competitors, and their linguistic capabilities are enormously useful abroad.

American businessmen must work at rationalizing our often doctrinaire foreign policy. They will have to persuade members of Congress (and Budget Director David Stockman) to understand the critical importance of foreign aid. They must educate the public, the White House, and the Congress about international economic and political realities. Economic ties to the growing markets in the Third World should be aggressively pursued. Gulf Oil should deploy its brigade of lobbyists to convince the White House and the State Department that the refusal to recognize Angola is counterproductive. There has been some effort in this respect by U.S. companies involved in Angola, but it's been hesitant. GM and Ford must attempt to urge the government of South Africa, as well as our government, to push for a peaceful evolution to majority rule. The companies have to understand the importance of stability in opening up viable long-term markets in Africa. Many corporate leaders did help shepherd the Panama Canal Treaties through the Senate. This exercise of realpolitik should not remain an asterisk in political history. The powers-that-be in corporate America own a stake in a rational U.S. foreign policy. They need access to foreign markets, and they should become more aggressive in saying so.

American Labor

American labor must make adjustments as well. Trade union leaders should think of their corporate counterparts as part of the same team, not as opponents. The competition is the Japanese or the West Germans or the French.

There is a natural coming together of interests here, and such a liaison should be taken seriously. Labor should be asked how it can help management to be competitive internationally. The traditional response has been to push for trade barriers to protect domestic industry, but protectionist policies do not solve long-term problems; such policies simply invite retaliation by other countries, and reduce the benefits from trade. Worse still, an import quota suggests that the problem has been solved and puts off the inevitable decisions necessary to be competitive in the future. History shows that protectionism is a last ditch effort, not a rehabilitation program.

More American union officials should visit Japan and experience the incredible sense of sharing that marks corporate-worker relations. I am not arguing that we should follow the Japanese example slavishly. But I do know that they are thriving whereas we are not, and we should try to see what we could learn from them.

At a minimum, a priority on the union agenda for collective bargaining sessions should be a simple question: "What is management doing to keep us competitive internationally?" If the answer to that question is unsatisfactory, union officials should make the appropriate demands. In the early 1950s, Walter Reuther of the UAW was urging the auto makers to produce small cars for both American and foreign markets. He met with little success.

This reorientation won't be easy. There are inherent disadvantages in the American union structure today as it relates to foreign trade. Growth corporations tend not to be unionized to the same extent as traditional, sometimes declining companies. Since the growth businesses are both more innovative and more competitive internationally, their people do "think international." That sort of thinking is not reflected in the labor movement in any reasonable proportion.

A second problem is that labor unions represent men and women currently working in a factory. Once a worker has been laid off, he is no longer represented in the same way, nor, in many cases, can he vote in union elections. The focus tends to be not on keeping the greatest number of people employed, but rather on keeping those who are employed happy. Consequently, a union official who "gives in" on issues like quality control that can make his industry competitive internationally may make his members unhappy if he hasn't persuaded them to "think international." It's easier not to cooperate on such issues, and keep the constituents in line by arguing for tariffs and other Band-Aids. Those who get laid off because the company is no longer competitive can't vote against him. Thus there is a built-in bias against policies that are essential in the long term, but cause disruptions here and now. Only a concerted effort to educate union workers as to where their true interests lie can turn the situation around.

American Government

For years, promoting exports has been low in the Washington hierarchy of important issues. Americans want to increase exports the way they want to have the snow removed after a winter's storm: it would be helpful, and we hire people to do it, but it's not the kind of question likely to be highlighted in the State of the Union Address.

The government's attitude is expressed exquisitely in the tradition that governs the policies of the Export-Import Bank, the key international financing institution. The *de facto* mandate of the Bank is twofold: one, promote exports; and two, don't lose any money in the process. It's as if to say, remove the snow but don't pay to get it done. The guidelines inherently conflict, given the real conditions that prevail in the international trade market.

While there is no sense of urgency and critical need for international trade in the United States, such attitudes do not burden foreign manufacturers and exporters. The government's laid-back policy in the late 1950s, the 1960s, and most of the 1970s set the foundation for our inaction—and our competitors have taken advantage of it.

The gradual awakening of the past two or three years has been encouraging, but mostly rhetorical. The decision by the Reagan administration to view the Export-Import Bank as artificially propping up exports has reversed this trend. International trade must be raised out of its present doldrums and made one of the centerpieces of America's economic strategy. This means a commitment to four general policies·

Competitive Financing. There are virtually no products made in America that do not have a viable foreign counterpart. For the new Boeing 767, there is the French-British Airbus 310. For the General Electric power generators, there is the same product made by Siemens of Germany.

When American products are marketed, their saleability can often be affected by the simple question of terms. The Japanese and Europeans are well aware that financing is sometimes as important as product line, and consequently offer terms that are attractive and concessionary.

We have usually assumed in international trading that the best product will sell itself. It's considered appropriate to offer the American consumer a rebate to buy a Chrysler car, or a toaster to open up a savings account, or a low interest rate to buy into a condominium. The same rationale should apply abroad.

If Country X is interested in purchasing four airplanes for medium-range service, it will choose between the Airbus and the Boeing 727. Assume that the Europeans offer the planes at 8 percent interest over ten years. Under current policy at the Export-Import Bank, we must offer the planes at the market rate cost of government borrowing, or 13 percent at the time of this writing.

Now, assume that the Export-Import Bank were allowed (indeed, encouraged) to be competitive and offered 8 percent over ten years as well. The cost to the taxpayers of such a concessionary term arrangement is $910,000, given the 8 to 13 percent differential.

Those who've controlled American policy for many years, including the Reagan administration, argue that the taxpayer should not be called upon to subsidize Country X to such an amount. On the surface, that argument is compelling. But let's look deeper and analyze what really happens.

The cost of the three planes is $69 million. If we use a multiplier of 2.5, the national economy has increased by $172 million. Consequently, the tax increases payable to America by that $172 million would be $5 million. In addition, the government would have been saved the costs related to unemployment insurance, food stamps, and so on, due to loss of work. (It is estimated that each $1 billion of lost exports results in 40,000 lost jobs.)

Every other industrial country has looked at the ledger and concluded that such subsidies are well worth it.

Recently, the government of Egypt asked for bids from foreign companies to modernize its country's telecommunications network. Egypt's needs in this area are extensive and long term. The first contract will be for six years and pay around $2 billion; subsequent contracts will be awarded for a total of twenty years of work. Four American companies, headed by A.T. & T., presented a proposal to the Egyptians with a price tag of $1.8 billion. The Egyptians found the package first-rate, and were ready to sign, but they needed help on the financing. The U.S. government failed to provide the necessary assistance. A second bid, submitted by CFTH (of France), Siemens Austria, and Siemens Germany, eventually captured the contract, after their governments had worked in concert to provide an attractive financing package.

So six years of work worth close to $2 billion (with the potential for twenty years of work long term) was lost because our government failed to support the American companies to the degree that the competitors were backed by their governments.

This kind of situation is simply not in our interest. Of all the countries in the world, we should be most able to provide financial terms that are competitive with major trading nations. The Export-Import Bank must be mandated to set terms and conditions that are realistic. Its primary function should be to promote exports aggressively, not act as a profitmaking enterprise.

There is an obvious counterargument. Why enter into a bidding war with the French, for example, when only the purchasing country will benefit, and either America or France will subsidize that export? Why not allow the products to compete in the traditional marketplace rather than draining off part of the profit by a subsidy of terms? The argument is not without merit. It certainly would make more sense to live in an atmosphere of free trade without the intervention of other criteria. But that's not the situation that prevails. Our competitors are using terms of sale offered by their government financing institutions as a weapon in the rivalry for exports. To the extent that we refrain from the use of similar concessions, we give our competitors every reason to continue them.

As in the "real" arms race, the only way to reduce concessions is to achieve parity, have each side recognize the senselessness of such ventures, and then enter into de-escalation agreements. It may seem absurd but I think it is the only method, given the willingness of our competitors to pursue their current practices.

Indeed, one of the unfortunate effects of the Reagan administration's debunking of competitive export financing was the impact on the chances for an agreement to end the export subsidy war. This unilateral disarmament on the part of the United States (by an administration fond of "second-to-none" terminology) removes the incentive for an accord. The 1980 negotiations in Paris among Organization for Economic Cooperation and Development countries had resulted in an agreement consented to by all nations except the French. What will happen to that consensus now remains to be seen.

Competitive Structuring. Having the proper product and the proper financing does not automatically result in exports. The private sector must still develop certain skills in order to be viable in the international trade market.

But there is currently a disadvantage for American exports, imposed by law. This liability is rooted in three regulations that have served us well in the domestic economy yet are now obstacles in the international arena. They deal with anti-trust (the Sherman and Clayton Anti-Trust Acts); with precluding banks from commercial activities (the Glass-Steagall Act); and with the taxation of Americans abroad (Section 911 of the Tax Code).

These policies were enacted to deal with obvious abuses taking place in the private sector, and, in the case of Section 911, with the issue of tax equity. (Another example of why laws and regulation inevitably follow abuse.) Today, however, the regulations hamper our capacity to be competitive. Again, the issue is one of perspective. If the focus of attention is domestic, then these policies are arguably worthwhile. If the focus, however, is the future—the international market—then they are obsolete as currently drawn.

The anti-trust laws were devised to prevent collusion, and thereby preclude large companies from destroying competition. They were badly needed and have been beneficial to American companies and consumers; but in their present form, they obstruct our capacity to survive in international markets. Theoretically, the objective of anti-trust laws is to offer the consumer a viable choice. If the consumer has available to him products from a West German company, a Japanese company, and a Swedish company, cooperation between American companies seems less important.

Given current law, General Motors, Ford, Chrysler, and American Motors do not cooperate in the various sectors of their operation. They do not pool their resources for basic automotive research. They must, independently, invent the wheel or power steering. This is a very efficient way to squander the resources of major companies. In earlier times, the law ensured competition.

Now, Datsun, Toyota, Honda, Renault, Volkswagen, Volvo, Saab, Mazda, Fiat, BMW, Mercedes, and other models provide the competitive market the consumer requires. The Japanese in the 1960s, faced with an industry in disarray and needing to be world competitive, promoted mergers of their auto companies and helped finance two such combinations. With competition ensured for the American consumer, the anti-trust laws provide no real protection. GM and Ford cannot conspire to raise prices unduly because the consumer can always buy a Honda.

The issue, however, goes beyond the question of benefit. Today, such anti-trust laws are no help to the consumer and a serious disadvantage to the producer. The four American auto companies are in a fight for survival with enormous consequences to our economy, not to mention the many thousands of workers whose jobs are at stake. The threat to that survival comes from overseas —the same provider of the consumer's choice. What do we gain if we continue our anti-trust practices and diminish the chances that GM, Ford, Chrysler, and American Motors will all survive? And if they don't survive, the repercussions will be felt by more than our GNP. For threatened industries, like automobiles, where international competition ensures consumer choice, we should provide anti-trust exemptions to allow cooperation between firms and, where necessary, mergers. Otherwise, there will ironically be fewer products on the market and less competition available for the consumer.

The anti-trust doctrine also dissuades many smaller firms from joining forces to compete internationally. The Webb-Pomerene Act of 1918 attempted to give trading associations a limited exemption from anti-trust, yet the exemption is so vague that firms just don't want to run the risk of Justice Department prosecution. This situation would be changed by the Export Trading Company Act, which would allow the Commerce Department to certify or reject requests for trading association status in light of export potential and domestic trade efforts. Firms would know where they stood and could divert their energies away from the Justice Department toward the international markets.

Laws designed to promote competition in other circumstances serve to diminish competition under present-day conditions. It is a classic example of refusing to reexamine assumptions, of dogma prevailing over reality. Raising the question of restructuring the anti-trust laws produces an immediate outcry about protecting the consumer, not the companies. In our brave new world, the best way to protect the consumer is to keep American companies competitive. It's about time we started to confront this reality.

After the Great Depression, Congress passed the Glass-Steagall Act in order to prevent American banks from investing in commercial enterprises. Such investments had resulted in large asset losses for hundreds of financial institutions when the stock market crashed in 1929; before the dust settled, over 9,000 banks had failed. So the law then made sense.

In the international trade market of today, however, the law makes less and less sense. Let's take the case of a small company located say, in South Bend, Indiana. It has two hundred employees, and manufactures a component part for electric switches. Chances are that company has always sold its product domestically. Even though the product may have export potential and the owner of the company knows it, the complexities of setting up an international marketing operation are too overwhelming for a small operation.

In Japan, an entrepreneur in the same situation would join forces with a bank with branches overseas and an exporter with trade experience. An export trading company would sell the product in Stockholm and Lagos and Kuala Laumpur.

The South Bend businessman needs to have the laws adjusted so that such a consortium arrangement is possible for him. As it turns out, the people most skilled in providing such outreach services are banks. Liberals who formed many of their policies during the Depression have always sought to contain the power of banks for several reasons, some related to past historical abuses, others to the fact that they are the core of the Republican financial structure.

Giving banks the right to combine with companies for export trading purposes is indeed a risky business. It is, however, a risk that must be taken and that can be minimized. Bank exposure can be limited and regulators can have final approval. I think we have been well served by keeping the banks out of commercial enterprises, but that doesn't mean such a policy is unamendable and will work forever. How do you explain to an unemployed South Bend worker the theoretical value of keeping Glass-Steagall intact? I am not arguing that the government's role of watchdog over the banks should be abandoned, but we must develop policies for the 1980s that are congruent with the realities of the 1980s.

Finally, the Tax Code should be adjusted so as not to penalize Americans who work abroad. Under current law, Americans pay taxes to the host country—and then, after deducting that sum, remit taxes to the U.S. Treasury. At first, this seems most appropriate. However, the citizens of our international competitors do not pay domestic taxes when they work in a foreign country. This results in two genuine problems.

One, American companies bidding for contracts must adjust their figures to compensate for this tax differential of their employees, thus losing a competitive edge. And two, if they hire non-Americans, there will be fewer jobs for our own workers and poorer acquaintance with the product line.

So the American presence abroad is diminished, with a resultant loss of trade. Nations in competition with us do not impose such a tax policy, and we should revise ours to deal with the international economic reality, not the domestic political situation.

The Department of Commerce should educate the American businessman about opportunities in foreign trade—through trade journals, seminars, outreach sessions, and the other myriad ways available to it. No exportable American product should remain at home because a manufacturer lacks information about the export market.

Many nations—not just in the Third World but also industrialized countries, with Japan being the most wily—have erected barriers to prevent American firms from penetrating their markets. The United States should engage in a reciprocal policy. Access to our markets ought to be a function of access to theirs. Too many countries have taken advantage of our goodwill for too long. Given our trade deficit, we can no longer afford such inequality.

Thoughtful liberals could well conclude that I am advocating a variant of situational ethics, arguing for policies that violate long-standing traditions because such traditions have become inconvenient in today's world. Indeed, there is some truth in this.

Others would protest that this aspect of a new liberalism, of compassionate realism, is really just old-fashioned conservatism. Big corporations have been trying to undo the anti-trust laws for years, big banks have wanted to abolish Glass-Steagall, and the multi-nationals are lobbying for the repeal of Section 911.

I don't dispute the contention that the dilution of these principles is a threat to our system; I would much rather see them continue. But what is the cost of an absolute adherence? If international trade is necessary for the sustenance of our economy, as I believe it is, then the cost is quite high and also a threat to our system. And we must weigh these threats against each other. If we want the anti-trust and the Glass-Steagall laws to remain untouched, let us at least acknowledge the price we are paying. But I think the economy must be preserved for the sake of those who leave the working force when the economy falters. It is quite possible to retain the regulations in a modified form to relate to domestic matters and to re-structure them to meet the realities of international trade. That way we can both meet the reality and maintain the principles.

8/ The Environment: The Seventh Reality

The next two decades and the next century will bring home one largely ignored reality: that the biosphere we inhabit is becoming overloaded. We are treating Mother Earth like a giant garbage can, and somehow we expect her to absorb the refuse without comment or retribution. It is an attitude that reflects our disposable society.

Every Sunday evening I haul out the trash, and every Monday morning it is taken away. I never give it another thought: it's gone. But it doesn't disappear. The fact that it's no longer on the sidewalk outside my back gate does not mean that it has vanished. It may have disappeared from my sight and thoughts, but it has not left the earth. Last week's trash is still around, somewhere, in some form, as is the trash of the week before that, and the week before that.

This is a mundane example of a serious reality. The earth is a self-contained unit. Its resources are limited, and exhaustion or abuse of those resources accumulates bills that must eventually be paid.

Love Canal is one of those bills. The people who will starve to death while this book is being read are paying for the incapacity of food to equal population. The biosphere is overloading, and will become a threat to its inhabitants. This chapter deals with four of the more serious threats: population, hazardous wastes, energy residuals, and water depletion.

Population

When the founding fathers were writing the Declaration of Independence, there were approximately 840 million people on earth, all

of whom were able to partake of the earth's resources without
straining them. By the turn of this century, those same resources,
or what was left of them, were being shared by 1.6 billion people.
By the mid-point of this century, the remaining resources were
available to 2.5 billion people. By the 1980s, the population was 4.4
billion. By the end of the century, the figure will be 6.2 billion. This
means that for each person living at the conception of our republic,
there will be 7.4 people in the year 2000.

This growth has taken place on a planet that has not enlarged,
so that the competition for the earth's resources is 7.4 times what
it was in 1776, and the social strain is much greater. In addition, the
amount of biosphere pollution that affects each individual is many
times greater as well.

Mexico City is an example of the potential for overload. At the
end of World War II, there were 3 million people living in Mexico
City. By 1980, there were 15 million. The projection for the year
2000 is 31 million. How can 31 million people inhabit Mexico City
without enormous upheaval? Where will the water to drink come
from? The food to eat? The jobs to employ people? The energy to
keep it all going? How in God's name can it possibly work? I don't
think it can. Such a situation will be a breeding ground for violence,
dissension, and revolution. And yet no revolution will solve the
basic problem of limited resources.

The United States thinks of itself as a crowded nation. The traffic
is bad in our urban areas. Cities that once adjoined rural areas now
border on suburban sprawl. The beaches are body-to-body all summer long as quiet coves give way to the onslaught of an ever-
increasing population. But we are not alone in this dilemma.

Imagine a United States with a population density 8.3 times as
great: California with 188.8 million people; 190,000 cars trying to
cross the George Washington Bridge every morning; 15.6 million
people trooping through Yellowstone Park every year. Unthinkable? That is the current population density of India—and it's still
growing.

It is estimated that in 1981 some 150 million people face starvation
and malnutrition in Africa alone. In 1980, tens of thousands succumbed to the ravages of malnutrition. Tens of thousands of people,

one by one, dropping lifeless onto the dusty, barren lands that have been over-farmed and under-restored. Men, women, and children, with glazed eyes and parched throats, and hearts of despair.

How does the average American who worries about his waistline expect his private world to be immune from the harvest of bitterness and agony of people starving on our earth? What of the ethical questions involved? In America, the right-to-lifers and those for freedom of choice argue over the unborn. In many countries around the world, the born are already dying slow, agonizing, dehumanizing deaths because there is not enough food for them. Does the despair of a starving child not exist because we don't feel it? Does the tragedy of a mother's grief not exist because we don't see it?

In 1965, I sat in the library of the Yale Law School and tried to read my textbooks on contracts, torts, procedure, and criminal law. I read about Mrs. Jones, whose toe was hit by a clock falling from a railroad station wall when the train roared through; I was supposed to figure out who was responsible for her injured limb. My mind easily wandered to the people of Wolisso, Ethiopia, whom I had left a few months earlier with all their problems, and I wondered why the hell I was reading about Mrs. Jones. I found it hard to care about who was to pay for the injured toe.

Sometimes, I sat through classes and remembered the beggars and the deformed of Addis Ababa. It was all so strange, and I wondered which was the real world. The truth was that both were. Both worlds existed at the same time, and on the same earth. What America would soon learn was that all such worlds were connected.

It's not just the emotion of a former Peace Corps volunteer with a bleeding heart. The misery visited upon an overpopulated world sows seeds whose harvest will eventually affect us all. It creates situations of despair, where normal behavior is rendered valueless and only thrashing violence appears to be of use. We have seen the terrorism of groups who felt they had nothing to lose and lashed out at the world in mindless rage, killing innocents with impunity. Often we do not connect such violence to the ravaging human conditions that breed the savagery.

The world's population must be controlled. The specter of increasing billions of people vying for declining supplies of energy, and scrambling for food produced from fewer acres of agricultural lands, is ominous. In addition to the physical needs, the political consequences are devastating. In those many countries where population growth exceeds GNP expansion, there is a lowered standard of living, leading to inevitable social and political unrest. And we must understand the relevance of this reality to us.

The have-nations will be secure only if the have-not-nations are able to bring population expansion below economic expansion. The United States must move with serious conviction to help the world control its population. Countries like Taiwan, China, Korea, and Singapore have managed to accomplish this successfully. Others, like Bangladesh, Nigeria, Kenya, the Ivory Coast, and Honduras, have been totally unable to overcome the problem.

There must be a broad-based international program strongly urged upon all nations. It should be both multi-national, calling on the resources of such organizations as the World Bank, the United Nations, and the Inter-American Bank, and bilateral, with direct country-to-country aid. It should involve the education of the people of each country about the need for smaller families, as well as providing the traditional population control mechanisms. It should be a regular item on the agenda at all general international gatherings, as well as at the summit meetings of the superpowers and of the Western powers.

This approach is not without controversy. There is historic opposition to population control by some religious sects, as well as the residual charge of racism that is sometimes leveled by leaders of black nations.

But the reality of overpopulation won't go away. In time, faced with the horrors of too many people struggling over too few resources, the only available solution will be for the strongest to obliterate the weak—a monument to Charles Darwin. And the violence of that alternative will diminish all the survivors, including those on Main Street, U.S.A.

We still have the time to deal with this dilemma. Should world population be stabilized, we will then be able to concentrate on an improved standard of living for all inhabitants, and so effect a decrease in human misery and its attendant violence. This situation will clearly benefit the developing nations, but the have-nations will reap the benefits of a more stabilized world as well.

Hazardous Wastes

In the 1940s, and 1950s, excess chemical wastes were dumped into an area near Niagara Falls known as Love Canal. For years those chemicals remained there, and started to seep inexorably into the nearby environment. Hundreds of families went about their daily lives oblivious to the danger lurking below them. Eventually, this silent hazard began exacting its toll in cancer and birth defects.

The words "Love Canal," with their ironic overtones, would take their place alongside *Silent Spring* and thalidomide in the lexicon of man-made horrors. Citizens across the country would begin to realize that their peace was jeopardized by the byproducts of their lifestyle. Increasingly, Americans would wonder about the air they breathed, the water they drank, and the food they ate. Were the nitrates in bacon, the color in red dye, the saccharin in a Diet Cola, and BHT in bread, modern-day hemlocks? The dangers of lead paint were matched by the hazards of mercury levels in fish. One could deal with a concern about the effects of cigarette smoking by quitting. But how does one stop breathing, eating, and drinking?

Many Americans viewed these dangers as absurd. Skeptics made much of the saccharin ban: an additive that was helpful for diabetics was going to be banned because some rats were fed the equivalent of eight hundred cans of diet soda per day. The excessiveness of that particular example gave people a sense of comfort. It is cold comfort, however, because the amount of hazardous waste being dumped into the environment in the latter part of the twentieth century is truly awesome.

At present, we generate about *57 million metric tons* of hazardous wastes per year. The annual output of this waste grows at the rate of 3 percent a year.

In 1980, the Environmental Protection Agency (EPA) estimated that the handling of only 10 percent of these wastes complied with the new 1981 standards. The EPA also estimated that 50 percent of the waste is disposed of in unlined surface impoundments, 30 percent in non-secure landfills, and about 10 percent by incineration under uncontrolled conditions, dumping into sewers, spreading on roads, and injection into deep wells.

This dumping imposes a severe strain upon a society because the hazardous wastes are simply moved to another place. They are intact, for the most part, and can eventually reenter the ground water or air or other conduits to human consumption.

There are and will be victims from this dumping. Some will be immediately identified; some will realize their plight a few years later, as did the parents at Love Canal; others will die within a twenty- to thirty-year time frame, like the workers at shipbuilding facilities during World War II who are perishing today because of problems related to the inhalation of asbestos fibers.

This last example can serve to outline the dimensions of the potential danger.

In the United States, the insurance industry estimates that there are some 8 to 11 million people who are potential victims of asbestosis and other asbestos-related diseases. Of these, about 60,000 to 70,000 people a year will require medical assistance. Perhaps 20,000 people a year will die. We are totally unprepared to meet this crisis, both medically and financially. Insurance companies today are concerned that their exposure to liability in asbestos-related disability far exceeds their capacity to pay, with potential claims estimated as ten times greater than all the liquid assets of the insurance industry combined.

The same looming dilemma awaits us as the nation begins to understand the effects of the defoliant Agent Orange, used in Vietnam. There are some 100,000 potential victims, who must concern themselves with the possibility of both cancer and birth defects. Then there are the controversies surrounding the pill and DES, the use of formaldehyde in mobile homes, and other risks.

The situation is explosive for two reasons. The number of people affected by the hazardous waste invasion of our biosphere is limitless. In Massachusetts alone, there are an estimated nine hundred dumping sites that offer potential health hazards. This is true of virtually every state in the nation. The number of hazardous sites in the United States may be as high as 50,000, according to estimates of a study prepared for the EPA.

And there is no refuge from the danger. Since people must eat, drink, and breathe, and since people consume products from the marketplace, they are all potential victims. Rich or poor, it makes little difference.

This menace is similar to the Soviet threat in that it triggers society's survival mechanism. It introduces the element of deep-rooted, all-pervasive fear, one that will dominate the thinking process. Any person who has attended a citizens' meeting on hazardous wastes knows what I am talking about. The threat to the physical well-being of a person and his loved ones will not be assuaged.

Since the dumping of wastes continues, and since the effects are generally mid- and long term, the uproar over the issue will increase over time. Congress has enacted a Superfund bill to help in the cleanup of current hazardous wastes. It is not enough, because the dumping will continue. As more and more victims are "discovered" and more and more hazardous sites are found, the issue will cry out for a comprehensive solution.

That solution will eventually require the recycling of hazardous materials so that they need not be dumped, at least not in the same quantity. The various processes now being developed to reduce the volume and toxicity of wastes will have to be mandated. Greater penalties will be enacted to punish both the producer of the wastes and the actual dumper. The average American must begin to calculate his lifestyle in order to accommodate the abused environment. For example, more and more consumers will seek to purchase "homegrown" food, or grow food themselves, in order to be free of contaminants and additives which they perceive to be a threat. Property owners will demand from their city and town halls a program to ensure that the water they drink is clean. Citizens will demonstrate in front of factories that are despoiling the air.

In time, the issue will become more pervasive and emotional than the consumer movement ever was. It's one thing to be overcharged for car repairs or utility bills; it's quite another to feel physically invaded by threats to your personal health. And it doesn't matter whether the person is a liberal or a conservative, Democrat or Republican. It is said that a conservative is a liberal who just got mugged—an activist is a conservative who just found out his drinking water is contaminated.

Energy Residuals

Present energy consumption patterns in America and throughout the world raise all sorts of questions, as detailed in Chapter 2. There are the primary issues of concern, such as supply interruption, effect on the economy, national security implications, and so on. There is also an entire range of additional concerns, which relate to the byproducts of energy consumption that do violence to the biosphere.

I will focus on three examples: carbon dioxide buildup, acid rain, and nuclear wastes. Like unchecked population growth, these represent silent waterfalls. They are distant in terms of obvious widespread effect, but of immediate importance in terms of the decisions needed to obviate their impact.

Carbon Dioxide Buildup (the "Greenhouse Effect"). One of the more chronically insidious devices ever invented is the car exhaust system. It serves a real and necessary function, but it also insulates man from understanding the implications of the automobile age.

Remember the last time you saw a car with a defective exhaust system? Chances are your reaction was one of dismay at the foul clouds being emitted and outrage toward the offending motorist. The effect of that emission was obvious and the reaction to it was bound to be strong.

Now, if that same motorist had his exhaust system fixed, and passed you the next day, you would never have noticed him. And yet that car is still spewing forth emissions, only you can't see the pollution. Out of sight is out of mind.

The same is true with all the processes that burn fossil fuels— electric power generators, factory boilers, apartment heating complexes. These enterprises consume a product, produce heat or steam, and then discharge the byproduct. The byproduct in the burning of fossil fuels is mainly carbon dioxide (CO_2), along with water vapor, trace minerals, ash, sulfur oxides, nitrogen oxides.

This carbon dioxide generation has, of course, increased as we continue to burn more fossil fuels, and as the capacity to absorb the carbon dioxide and turn it into oxygen is diminished with the depletion of the earth's forests.

In 1980, I chaired a hearing of the Senate Energy Committee on the effects of carbon dioxide buildup in the atmosphere. The witnesses represented a cross section of scientists whose credentials were not open to question, including Dr. George Woodwell of the Woods Hole Marine Biological Laboratory, Dr. David J. Rose of M.I.T., Dr. William W. Kellogg of the National Center for Atmospheric Research, Gus Speth, chairman of the Council on Environmental Quality, William Hayne of the State Department, Ruth Clusen of the Department of Energy, Dr. Gordon McDonald of Mitre Corporation, David Burns of the American Association for the Advancement of Science, and Dr. Wallace Broecker of Columbia University.

The hearing enabled us to witness the technical evolution of an issue. The testimony traced the gradual shift from confused scientific evidence to a perceptible coalescing of consensus as to what was happening, if not as to what it all means.

Over the last thirty years, fuel-generated CO_2 emissions have been increasing at an almost constant rate of 4.3 percent per year. If this current emission rate continues, the quantity of CO_2 in the atmosphere may rise by 50 percent in about thirty-five years, and double in about fifty years. (The uncertain rate of CO_2 assimilation by the biosphere accounts for the range of estimates.) The data showed that the rate of CO_2 growth is accelerating as the world use of fossil fuels increases.

In addition to the burning of fossil fuels, current land clearing and deforestation practices have contributed to the CO_2 buildup through the subsequent oxidation of cut-down plant material and the removal of plants that use CO_2 during photosynthesis. Human activity thus appears to have increased CO_2 levels at a greater rate than can be naturally absorbed by the natural recycling mechanisms available on earth (vegetation, oceans, etc.).

The physical characteristics of CO_2 are the crucial issue. Despite the fact that CO_2 comprises a relatively small part of the earth's atmosphere, it exerts a significant impact on the thermal structure of that atmosphere; CO_2 molecules reflect the infrared radiation (heat) that is emitted from the earth's surface that would otherwise escape into space. Because glass in a greenhouse also serves to trap the sun's heat, this phenomenon has come to be known as the "greenhouse effect."

The effect is not the kind of phenomenon that can be ignored. Like the hazardous waste issue, it will eventually trigger the human survival response mechanism.

At a minimum, most scientists agree that a doubling of CO_2 content in the atmosphere will cause a critical rise in global temperatures and that such a warming will be conspicuous by the beginning of the next century. They estimate that average temperatures could increase about 3° C (about 5.5° F), with substantially higher increases at the poles.

This global warming could bring about a number of serious climatic and geographic changes with attendant environmental and societal consequences. Some glaciologists foresee a rapid melting of the West Antarctic ice sheet that could raise sea levels as much as 25 feet in a matter of decades, causing major disruptions of coastal regions. Under a seriously discussed "worst-case scenario," heavily populated low-lying areas of Florida, Louisiana, Texas, Georgia, South Carolina, Delaware, New Jersey, New York, Massachusetts, and California could be submerged.

If the sea level of the earth were to rise 15 feet—a more modest amount than the 25 foot increase some have predicted—the following areas would, according to one study, be inundated: 24 percent of Florida; Washington National Airport; 51 percent of Louisiana's property values, including all of New Orleans; Corpus Christi, Texas; much of Boston, Harvard, and M.I.T.; $22 billion worth of New York real estate; Sacramento and the Sacramento River flood plain; much of Charleston, South Carolina; Savannah, Georgia, and Norfolk, Virginia. In all, some eleven million people would be displaced.

This is just a representative list. It does not begin to suggest what a 25 foot rise would mean, nor does it speak to the catastrophic possibilities for other nations, such as the Low Countries of Belgium and the Netherlands.

In addition, a warming climate could cause significant shifts of the agriculturally productive regions of the world. While a warmer climate might lengthen the growing season in higher latitudes, it might also produce prolonged drought in grain belts such as the Midwestern United States. Water availability could be threatened as a result of altered precipitation patterns and enhanced evaporation via soils and plants. Ground water reserves would be reduced by decreases in soil moisture. Fish populations could be displaced northward by a warming of the surface water layers of the ocean.

Why isn't something being done about this potential calamity? In truth, there is no certainty about the possible results. The buildup of carbon dioxide is certain, but there is disagreement about the severity of its effect. Many studies and investigations are being conducted to confirm or disprove the fears expressed by the scientists; these will probably not be available before the United States decides to embark on a massive long-term commitment to fossil fuel burning. Thus, in making this energy policy decision today, we are handicapped by the absence of sufficient information as to what the full ramifications will be. Having made a decision, however, it will be too late to reverse it once the effects are being felt.

The situation is not uncommon for policy makers. Many scientists fear that, in another twenty years, CO_2 accumulation in the atmosphere may be producing effects that are irreversible.

Another reason nothing is being done is because it is a long-term issue *politically*. People do not worry about long-term issues; they may understand a danger intellectually, but they don't feel it emotionally. The concerned constituency is restricted to a handful of scientists, academics, and environmentalists. No political leader need feel the pressure to do anything, and since to prevent long-term effects of carbon dioxide buildup would inflict short- and mid-term inconveniences, the issue is a classic loser.

Furthermore, resolution requires international cooperation. The response to this issue would involve a worldwide commitment to four programs: energy conservation, renewable energy resource development, land use policy, and reforestation. These measures represent the tools necessary to meet the issue head on. But what happens if we adopt these policies and other countries do not? Or what happens if a more Machiavellian situation occurs, whereby some nations will actually benefit by a CO_2-induced shift of rain patterns (the Canadians and Soviets, say) while others are hurt by it (the United States and China)? Clearly, the CO_2 issue must be raised in international forums and be a priority item of both scientific research and intergovernmental cooperation.

Acid Rain. In 1980, I also chaired hearings of the Energy Committee on the matter of acid rain. Again, we called on a distinguished panel. The scholars and scientists took one position, while the energy industry representatives took another.

"Acid rain" is actually a catch-all term for the broader phenomenon of atmospheric acid deposition by rain, snow, dew, and so on. It is created when water vapor in the atmosphere combines with oxides of sulfur and nitrogen, produced in large measure by fossil fuel–burning power plants, to form strong sulfuric and nitric acids. These pollutants are carried by prevailing winds and fall back to earth, often great distances away, as acid precipitation.

The acidity of precipitation is measured on the so-called pH scale, where pure water has a pH of 7.0. Because normal rainfall has a pH of 5.6, rainfall with a pH level below 5.6 is known as "acid rain." The lower the number, the more acidic the substance.

In the Eastern United States, the average pH of rainfall is now between 4.0 and 4.5, a quantum increase in acidity in the last twenty-five years. Some rainfall has been reported at pH levels as low as 3.0, almost equivalent to the acidity of lemon juice or vinegar. Acid rain not only appears to be spreading in severity but also in the geography affected. In 1955–56, the area where rainfall was recorded to be below a 4.6 pH level was located in parts of Ohio, Pennsylvania, West Virginia, New York, and New England—precisely where sulfur dioxide emissions were highest. By 1975–76, the area with an average pH below 4.6 had extended as far west as the Mississippi River and as far south as Florida.

The Northeast, particularly New England, has been most heavily impacted by acid rain, largely due to the pattern of prevailing winds that transport pollution from the Midwest. The advent of tall stacks, built to decrease pollution locally, has further contributed to the long-range problem by emitting pollution higher into the air and causing it to be carried farther away. For example, in New England, while roughly 44 percent of the acid rain is self-generated, 30 percent is attributable to pollution from the Midwest and mid-Atlantic states, and 17 percent from Canadian sources.

Acid precipitation can cause a number of serious environmental problems, notably sterility of lakes and fisheries, damage to crops and forests, decreased soil fertility, and corrosion of man-made materials and structures. It also adversely affects human health. This environmental and health damage can, in turn, be translated into billions of dollars in economic loss.

Over one hundred lakes in the Adirondacks and eastern Canada have already become devoid of fish life. The Adirondack lakes have grown several times more acidic (from an average pH of 6.8 in the 1930s to about 4.8 in 1975), thus destroying the balance needed by the fish to survive and reproduce. In addition, increased acidity mobilizes certain metals such as aluminum, mercury, cadmium, and lead in the water, and elevated concentrations of these metals can be toxic to fish.

Acid rain threatens to reduce agricultural crop yields because it can cause nutrients to leach from soils. It also accelerates the deterioration of cement and marble buildings and monuments. Architectural treasures such as the Acropolis and Parthenon in Greece and Cleopatra's Needle in New York City have decayed more in the last 50 years than in the preceding 2,000 years.

In addition to the primary effects on human health attributable to acid rain (inhalation of acid mist may result in lung problems), evidence of secondary effects is also cause for grave concern. Acidity in water can increase the intake of mercury and other toxic heavy metals by aquatic organisms, including fish. These toxins can "bioaccumulate," or increase in concentration as they move up the food chain to human consumption. Acid rain can also heighten the bioaccumulation of toxic metals from the soil to grain and other crops, and to cattle. Drinking water supplies, too, are threatened by the leaching of toxic metals either from the watershed or from pipes that corrode from contact with the acidic water. Ultimately, human exposure to these higher levels of pollutants can cause damage to the nervous system, kidneys, liver, and heart, as well as other disorders.

As with the carbon dioxide problem, the solution requires energy policies that either minimize or control the emission of sulfur and nitrogen oxide—with coal burning being the most prolific polluter. Again, the answer involves energy conservation and the development of renewable energy resources, as well as emission controls on fossil fuel burning.

As with the carbon dioxide problem, again, the reasons for inaction are several. The scientific data are not complete. The matter is not felt by the electorate. The victims are not easily identified. And, most important, there are powerful interests that are served by the matter remaining a dead issue.

The danger of acid rain represents another example of man's unwillingness to think through the ramifications of his present actions. Those ramifications do not diminish because they are currently overlooked. What we did yesterday, what we are doing today, and what we will do tomorrow are seeds whose harvest inevitably awaits us.

Nuclear Wastes. Unlike CO_2 buildup and acid rain, the issue of nuclear waste is broadly recognized. As a component of the nuclear argument, it invariably is mentioned at my town meetings as a perceived threat.

In some respects, the contrast is ironic. While CO_2 buildup, acid rain, and nuclear waste all represent byproducts of benefits to our society and costs levied on future generations, the problem of nuclear wastes may be the least intractable to deal with.

The issue should be set in its technical context. Nuclear waste involves primarily four categories: commercial spent fuel, which contains highly radioactive fission products and long-lived transuranic wastes; military high-level liquid and solid wastes; commercial and military low-level wastes (discarded clothing, rags, discarded equipment); and uranium mill tailings.

Nuclear waste is not solely a function of electrical generating nuclear power plants. Much of the waste (particularly the highly radioactive liquid wastes stored in tanks) is the byproduct of military uses—research and production of weapons, as well as nuclear-powered aircraft carriers and submarines. Thus the issue will be with us irrespective of the resolution of the no-nuke/pro-nuke debate.

The health hazards stem from the carcinogenic and mutagenic effects of the wastes. In the terms used above, they are powerful violators of our biosphere because they are powerful violators of ourselves.

Historically, the reaction to this issue has been one of neglect. Industry and government placed liquid wastes in carbon steel tanks to solve the immediate problems of the 1950s, and by the 1970s those tanks were beginning to leak. This should not be surprising. It is cheaper for the nuclear industry to avoid dealing with this issue on a permanently resolved basis, and it is politically difficult for government to do any better.

And yet, if the issue remains unresolved, it will eventually endanger the populace and undermine the viability of nuclear power itself. Public confidence in the integrity and credibility of industry and government will be reduced to a point where even technologically appropriate solutions (some people obviously will argue that there is no such thing) are not accepted.

But addressing this problem now is critical, not only for itself, but to fashion a model of concern about the impact on the environment of our energy practices, and so enhance the chances of a serious look at the CO_2 buildup and acid rain while there is still time.

What is a possible solution? The goal is permanent disposal of these wastes in some stable geological formation (granite formations and salt domes are the most frequently mentioned). Both isolation from the environment and the avoidance of possible ground water intrusion must be assured. Many approaches, such as glassification of the wastes, exist, although none has yet been adequately demonstrated. But even some nuclear skeptics acknowledge that the technological difficulties can be overcome by careful and scientific selections of site, geological function, disposal media, repository design, waste packaging, and so on.

As with CO_2 buildup and acid rain, it is the social and political problems that are the most nettlesome. The utter seriousness of the issue for our own and future generations has caused great social concern at a time when the mishandling of waste disposal in the past is undermining public confidence in government and industry's ability to address it. Siting a disposal facility is that much more difficult when the public hears about the radioactive leaks from the last round of quick fixes. Yet even now, there is a push for an intermediate surface storage facility. This reduces the pressure for a permanent solution and so also reduces the chances for one.

The focus is short-term. The problem is not.

It is time for all parties in the nuclear debate to realize that a resolution of this issue is in the interest of everyone. Industry must accept the economic costs; government must recognize the oversight and regulatory burden; and the anti-nuclear constituency must admit that there exist enormous quantities of waste, here and now, which have to be dealt with.

At this writing, such responses remain elusive. Meanwhile, every day, the wastes build up. Every day, public confidence erodes just a bit more. And every day, the reality still refuses to go away.

Water Depletion

"Water, water, everywhere/Nor any drop to drink." The familiar cry of the Ancient Mariner contains the seeds of truth for those on land as well.

America has entered on a brave new world where water, once the most plentiful resource, is becoming one of the most endangered. The very characteristics of water—its omnipresence and its function as solvent—make it the logical conduit of pollutants. More and more, people are picking up their local newspapers to read that their water supplies are being threatened.

The contamination is caused by three sources: industrial discharges, municipal sewage systems, and so-called non-point sources (run-off from fertilizers, urban streets, livestock waste, salts, etc.). The first two are controllable only by money and regulation—the classic interventionist (non–free enterprise) solutions. The last, by its sheer diffuseness, is more difficult to control.

Despite the Clean Water Act and other legislation, the task is formidable. In 1980, 10 percent of community water supply systems (most are small) were violating EPA microbiological standards and 20 percent were violating EPA chemical and radiological standards.

These problems are related to the issues raised earlier (regarding hazardous wastes) in their effects on human health and their difficulty of resolution. They will not be belabored here, because a further dimension has reared its troublesome head: we are now using water in volumes that exceed the earth's capacity for restoration.

It's interesting how obscure place names can spring up and overnight turn into symbols of larger events. These names become shorthand for history—Waterloo, Pearl Harbor, the 38th Parallel, Selma, Watergate, Love Canal, Three Mile Island. One currently obscure name that will become a familiar term by the end of this century is the Ogallala Aquifer. Few outside the plains states have heard of this underground water reserve covering an enormous area in the south-central United States. What will give it prominence is not its sheer size, but rather its depletion. The Ogallala Aquifer is the source of irrigation for thousands of productive farms in states like Nebraska. But the water currently being pumped out of it and other aquifers in America exceeds the water returning back, with estimates ranging up to a staggering imbalance of 21 billion gallons each day.

As with the oil crisis, this depletion cannot continue forever. Instead of a finite diminishing resource like oil, water looms as an infinite diminishing resource. Its use is growing geometrically in those areas where it is most scarce (the Southwest), and its major sources are those that are the most difficult to replenish (ground water reserves) or are already over-committed (the Colorado River).

Part of the problem comes from federally financed water projects, which distort the true replacement cost of the water (the reader will recall here the argument for decontrol of oil), and also lead to the development of arid areas, which further increases demand. Part of the problem stems from traditional laws governing the rights to consume surface water, which both emphasize continuous use and provide disincentives for transfer of rights for better use. And part of it involves the relentlessly selfish procedures for ground water use, where there is no limit on pumping for any "beneficial use." In times of depletion, the wise consumer will pump water out as fast as he can before others pump it out first.

Thus our national water policy has been left for resolution to a mixture of marketplace (no limits on pumping) and government subsidy (water projects). Neither option is providing a coordinated plan that accommodates the legitimate needs of the various claimants. Land use planning is today considered heresy. When the Ogallala Aquifer can no longer irrigate Nebraska wheatfields, it will be seriously discussed. But not in time for the Nebraska farmers.

The great task ahead is to protect our earth and its atmosphere. But how do you prevail upon society to appreciate the fact that the biosphere is a self-contained unit? How do you persuade mankind to stop fouling his own nest?

Unfortunately, it appears that very little will be done unless there is a crisis. Before people begin to address the hard fact of the rape of the earth, they will have to be confronted by their own neglect.

I have thought about the issues contained in this section for some time. I care about them the way I care about a lot of things— peripherally and intellectually. What brought the issue home to me emotionally was what occurred at a site several hundred yards from where I grew up in Lowell.

A company named Silresim undertook to recycle chemical wastes. The owners were engineers of considerable talent, who were taking the chemical byproducts of several eastern Massachusetts industries and reprocessing them into reusable chemicals.

It was a marvelous idea, but one whose time had not yet come. The dumping of hazardous wastes was then infinitely cheaper than recycling them. In time, the company could struggle no more, and it closed. Superficially, this bankruptcy was a typical example of our free enterprise system—thousands of firms go out of business every year.

But what does not happen every day is that a company goes belly up with thousands of barrels of hazardous wastes stored within its closed gates. While the financial and legal entanglements were endlessly discussed by lawyers and accountants, the barrels sat there rusting. Exposed to the elements, they eventually began to discharge their contents into the ground. Near the site was Hales Brook, which I used to frequent as a child looking for tadpoles. The wastes were seeping through the ground water into Hales Brook, and then into the Merrimack River, which downriver communities relied upon for their drinking water.

Under the classic "get government off our backs" and "unleash the private sector" theories now in vogue, the matter would be resolved by the free enterprise system. But "resolution" here would mean doing nothing, since it was in no one's economic interest to do anything. The abuse creates a vacuum, into which government is drawn.

The government could not ignore the health and safety implications of this disaster and accepted the responsibility. At meetings with relevant state and federal agencies, we studied aerial photographs of the area. Invariably my eye would wander to the northeast corner of the photographs, to the house where I grew up. It had been my home and now it was threatened by events and forces that were totally alien to it. I experienced a direct, personal sense of invasion. (The cleanup of the site would drag on for years, and at this writing remains incomplete.)

Several months later, I held a town meeting in Woburn and learned from its citizens of the chemical wastes discovered there. The people spoke of their rising fears about cancer and birth defects, fears that were not going to fade away and were later to be confirmed by statistical evidence. They would forever understand what man was doing to his biosphere. Having just experienced the Silresim issue, I was able to "feel" their concern. Weeks later, I watched the issue of Love Canal unfold on television. These homeowners of New York were demanding that the state buy their homes so they could escape from the horrors that had marred their lives. One young mother in particular sticks in my memory. She was on the verge of hysteria, suggesting a deep-rooted, almost animalistic fear.

All over America, thousands of young mothers are living next to sites identified as containing hazardous wastes; in addition, there are countless thousands more who are just as threatened but don't yet know it. They are drinking impure water and breathing impure air, but they are unaware of it. When they learn, someday, they too will feel invaded, wronged, abused. And the obscure subject of biosphere degradation will be *the* issue in their lives.

These thousands can only multiply as time goes on. The violence done to our biosphere is a legacy that won't evaporate. What happens when the raw sewage sludge constantly dumped into the ocean south of Long Island by the jurisdictions in the New York area returns someday and washes up on the beaches of Long Island?

What happens when the drive to produce synthetic fuels expropriates and contaminates water resources that have traditionally been needed by farmers and ranchers in the Western part of the United States?

What happens when the people of southeastern Canada realize that the acid rain originating in the Ohio Valley industrial belt falls on their farmlands and is destroying the productivity of those lands?

What happens if the kepone discharged into Virginia's James River in recent years starts to show its effects upon the people of the Chesapeake Bay area?

What happens when all the abuses of the biosphere exact their gruesome human toll—as they inexorably will?

There will be an outcry, and suddenly there will be an environmental movement that will encompass every corner of society. It will be a movement rooted in the anger and the militancy of those who have been innocent victims of our practices. But it will be a movement that can not avoid the waterfall.

It's too late to start worrying about the carbon dioxide build up when the waters of Massachusetts Bay ebb around the chic doorsteps of the Faneuil Hall/Quincy Market section of Boston. It's too late to start worrying when New Orleans begins to submerge.

Yet, we can't seem to show concern about these environmental time bombs before the bombs go off. I learned that lesson vividly in 1975.

The House of Representatives Interior Committee was considering a bill to provide monies to states to help them deal with the issue of land use. Participation by the states was voluntary. Testimony had shown that an estimated one million acres a year of prime agricultural land was being converted into housing tracts, shopping centers, strip mines, highways, and other such uses. Urban and suburban sprawl was getting out of hand, and the bill tried to encourage states to take the problem seriously.

There was a firestorm of opposition. This was "central planning," the way "the Soviets run their country." It was "federal intrusion upon local affairs." Various interest groups rallied to oppose the measure.

When the committee met to vote on the issue, I told one of my colleagues that the opposition was both astonishing and ludicrous, but we had better be ready to do battle when the bill was debated on the House floor. A few minutes later, it died in committee.

The defeat jolted me—and I have never forgotten the lesson learned that day. If a government seeks to act to curb an abuse, and if that action is going to have a negative impact upon powerful interests, the abuse sure as hell better be felt, now.

This political reality is unhappily applicable all over our planet.

The countries that border the Mediterranean have turned that marvelous sea into a virtual open sewer. The forests of tropical regions like Brazil, Sub-Sahara Africa, and Indochina are being depleted. Half of these forests have been cut down in this century, and half of what is left may be demolished by the end of the century. It will mean serious soil erosion, loss of food-producing lands, and a decreased capacity to absorb and reprocess carbon dioxide.

Fishing stocks around the world are gradually being depleted.

Whales, a critical part of the oceanic food chain, are declining in population, and hundreds of other less conspicuous species of plant and animal life are being consumed or destroyed. Wilderness areas, greenspace, and other natural values are falling victim to the drive for energy and mineral resource development, characterized by the so-called sagebrush rebellion, and personified by Secretary of the Interior James Watt.

The filling-in of flood plains, the construction of homes on shifting barrier island beaches, the dumping of oil by seagoing tankers, the widespread use of DDT in underdeveloped countries, the disregard of toxic tailings of mining operations on every continent, the disposal of tons of chemical additives into our bodies—all of these practices are a reality. A very serious reality. Each and every one of these realities springs from an economic interest dictating policy. And each and every one sows the seeds of chaos and political extremism in future victims who will bear the costs. These victims will increase in numbers as time goes on and will become a force in American politics.

Any society that chooses to ignore the implications is deluding itself.

What is needed is courageous and collective leadership to make the abuse known *before* it is felt, and known in such a way as to create a constituency for change. It won't be easy. But in any case the reality won't change. All the current ideas about less government intervention cannot obviate the fact that abuse creates its own dynamic. In this regard, the traditional liberal belief in government righting wrongs caused by lapses in the free enterprise system will stand us in greater stead as the overloading of the biosphere continues unchecked.

9/Inflation –
Effect, Not Cause:
The Eighth Reality

President Ronald Reagan said it. President Jimmy Carter said it before him. And President Gerald Ford said it before him. *Inflation is the number one issue in America today.* In political terms, all of them were absolutely correct.

Inflation has an enormous capacity to erode public confidence in any government. Left unchecked, it eats away at the foundations of any economic system and will eventually bring about its collapse. (The two examples used by Milton and Rose Friedman in their book, *Free to Choose,* are the downfall of the Weimar Republic in Germany leading to Nazism, and the collapse of the Allende government in Chile in 1973.) History has shown that no society has been willing quietly to endure rampant inflation. That is not surprising, because next to physical security, the citizen needs a sense of economic stability. Threats to that stability are unacceptable, and cannot be allowed to persist. The housewife who sees the price of basic foods at the supermarket rise beyond her budget; the salesman spending an ever-increasing percentage of his income for gasoline; the young couple priced out of the housing market owing to high mortgage rates; the automobile dealer whose sales have slumped because loan interest rates have frightened people away; the blue-collar worker whose income won't keep pace with his bills; the senior citizen who can't survive on her life's savings; and so on.

Increasing numbers of people have a sense of falling further and further behind, a feeling that their economic foundation is now built on quicksand. Thus squeezed, the voter looks for solutions. He will be quick to spot those who he thinks are bleeding the system ("welfare cheats," oil companies) and as quick to believe in any easy solution ("The government is the cause of all inflation"). Any politician who can tap this powerful reservoir of resentment will do very well. In the early 1980s, it is *the* political force.

Well, if that's so, why am I addressing it in the next-to-last chapter of this book? Why does inflation follow issues like energy and international trade? If it is *the* political force, why isn't it dealt with in the beginning where it belongs? Very simple—it doesn't belong there.

I want to make it absolutely clear that it is not possible to deal with inflation if one has not dealt wisely, thoroughly, and effectively with the seven realities described earlier. Indeed, confronting the reality of inflation began in Chapter 2 and has continued ever since. In particular, the chapter on resource allocation should be kept in mind.

Historically, the path is littered with errors of both commission and omission. Lyndon Johnson tried to give us guns and butter, the war in Vietnam and the war on poverty. We got both, and an underlying momentum of inflation. OPEC quadrupled oil prices after the embargo and sent inflationary shocks through an unprepared America. Productivity gains slowed in the late 1960s and then came grinding to a halt by the end of the 1970s, adding to the inflationary pressures. These were the big-tent events that produced large leaps in inflation. There were many other sideshows, of course. But the point is that inflation is the effect of failure in other areas, not their cause. Thus, dealing with inflation demands having dealt with the seven realities discussed earlier.

In March 1981, I held a town meeting in Weymouth, Massachusetts. Toward the end of the two-hour exchange of views, one distinguished-looking middle-aged man said: "Inflation is caused by the deficit spending of politicians." This view is widely held throughout the country, as the polls indicate, and is strenuously promoted by many politicians, including President Ronald Reagan. The seven realities get lost in the claim that inflation is caused by governmental largesse. Thus, we put off the need to cope with the seven realities that are major causes of inflation.

This example of "bumper sticker economics" is the most effective piece of political group-think of our time. Search through the textbooks and congressional testimony and you'll find few, if any, economists who attribute our complex inflationary dilemma solely to budget deficits. It's a chapter in the story, but it's not the whole story. No matter—in a democracy, it's what the people believe that counts.

The second clever piece of political group-think is the notion that somehow defense outlays are not government spending. Thus, it is not only possible but indeed politically rewarding to demand lower government costs and more defense expenditures in the same breath.

The capacity to mold reality to dogma so successfully is something any practitioner of politics must grudgingly admire. There's only one hitch. Getting elected on this plank is one thing; running a country on it is quite another. It's when you gain power that reality begins to assert itself, not when you're on the lecture circuit.

Back to my Weymouth constituent. While right-wing ideologues often attend my town meetings, this man clearly was not one of them. It was obvious that he was a thoughtful, concerned Republican, who had bought Reagan economics hook, line, and sinker. If I told him the President of the United States was wrong, I would have accomplished nothing, given Ronald Reagan's extraordinary gift for public communication.

Instead, I resorted to my standard response. I asked the audience to name two countries which they felt had a handle on inflation and were enjoying thriving economies. The response came back as anticipated: Japan and West Germany. If these two countries were firmly in control of inflation, and if government spending and budget deficits were the cause of inflation, then a comparison of these countries and the United States should conclusively prove the Reagan economic theory. I proceeded to write on a blackboard the percentage of U.S. government spending as a percentage of GNP: 30 percent. I then chalked up the corresponding Japanese statistic: 22 percent. Finally, I put the West German figure on the blackboard: 38 percent. It was more. The audience was surprised.

Next, I drew a second column showing budget deficits as a percentage of GNP. The U.S. deficit was 3.0 percent of GNP. The West German figure was 2.0 percent, which reassured the questioner. Then I put the Japanese figure on the blackboard: 5.0 percent. Even the questioner was surprised. (Indeed, when you con-

sider total government deficits and take into account state government surpluses, our deficit is lower than that of West Germany as
well as of Japan.)

If you went by the figures, it was just as valid (and equally
erroneous) to conclude that the path to controlling inflation was
more government spending and *bigger* budget deficits.

Now the audience was open to persuasion. I then added three
more columns. Personal savings as a percentage of income: Japan
20 percent, West Germany 14 percent, United States 5 percent.
Private-sector investment and reinvestment as a percentage of
GNP: Japan 23.1 percent, West Germany 18.4 percent, and the
United States 14.4 percent. Public-sector investment in infrastructure as a percentage of GNP: Japan 9.3 percent, West Germany 3.8
percent, and the United States 2.9 percent. (I should also have
added the balance-of-trade figures for 1976 through 1980: Japan,
plus $55.6 billion, West Germany plus $88.8 billion, and the United
States minus $105.4 billion.)

There was no way any reasonable person would ponder those five
columns and not conclude that the inflation issue was a bit more
complicated than many politicians were saying. I didn't have to
argue any more; the facts on the blackboard were convincing
enough. Eighty citizens of one town in one state pondered the
matter of inflation in a more thoughtful mood.

This is not to argue for excessive government spending or budget deficits. They are clearly part of the problem for several reasons: The wrong kind of spending absorbs capital that could be
used elsewhere more efficiently. Every dollar wasted by a government agency is a dollar that could have been spent in the pursuit
of greater industrial productivity or greater energy self-sufficiency.
Every dollar of federal deficit must be borrowed in the money
markets. Public borrowing competes with private capital needs
and consequently drives up the cost of borrowing for both. Finally, deficits put off the inevitability of having to make choices in
government spending—and that reality has been avoided for far
too long.

We live in an era when pragmatism is vital, when a commitment
to whatever policy has the best chance of working is essential,
regardless of ideology. Yet the ideological approaches are not with-

out their adherents. Traditional liberals are still wedded to Keynes, despite the recent lack of Keynesian success.

Many people today debate whether John Maynard Keynes failed liberals or liberals failed Keynes. Keynes said we should prime the pump for recession and deflate the economy during booms. But stagflation—inflation with unemployment—makes such a policy ambiguous at best. Wage and price controls (a bureaucratic effort to force the economy to conform) promise structural inefficiencies, black markets, and enraged citizens. Moreover, since OPEC oil ministers are unlikely to halt their price rises, large increases in basic input like energy would render any wage and price controls scheme a shambles.

The liberals are not alone; indeed, they are in good non-pragmatic company. Monetarist economists, for example, remind us that inflation is "too much money chasing too few goods." And few economists contest this relationship between money supply and inflation. It is the recommended cure that causes the controversy. The monetarists would clamp down on the money supply. The cure in this case may well be worse than the disease. Relying strictly on recession to eliminate inflation ignores the fact that in today's economy, productivity falls before wages and prices moderate. The process could take ten years of unemployment levels hovering around 15 percent—a devastating price in human terms. In a totalitarian society, such a price may be feasible. In a democratic society, fortunately, it isn't.

Finally, supply-side economists argue that massive tax cuts will allow us to produce our way out of inflation. Nonsense. Personal income tax cuts, whether inspired by Keynesian or supply-side notions, for the most part motivate additional consumption. Massive personal income tax cuts are a sure ticket for more inflation.

Neither wage and price controls nor strict monetary policies nor a giant tax cut can deliver a quick answer to inflation.

A final word about government spending. Liberals got themselves into trouble by supporting programs that were not effective or were being abused, such as the public service component of CETA and excessive unemployment compensation. As liberals, they were ironically but successfully attacked as big spenders by conservatives who believed in and supported tobacco subsidies, cost-ineffective water projects, duplicative military spending, and local pork-barrel projects. The conclusion is inescapable: The only national resource we will never run out of is hypocrisy in Washington politics.

The answer to inflation is many answers. The solution is the sum total of a lot of different policies, all of them geared to the long view. One of them, clearly, is fiscal responsibility in government spending. And that holds true across the board, for programs that conservatives favor as well as those liberals favor.

Beyond that, it's a matter of attacking inflation at its roots. There is no quick route, but there are ten sound steps that must be taken:

1. *Stop the petrodollar hemorrhage.* A body that continually hemorrhages its blood supply should not be surprised to find that it is feeling ever weaker. Petrodollars exported abroad (over $70 billion in 1980) weaken the dollar, worsen inflationary pressures, and deplete our capital resources. In addition, the continually high demand for oil guarantees ever higher prices for it.

Oil imports must be cut, and cut drastically. President Reagan's statement that "Conservation means being colder in the winter and warmer in the summer" is not only foolish from a policy point of view, but also contributes to the cause of inflation. His decision to eviscerate the conservation and renewable resource programs in the Department of Energy is going to haunt him as the unnecessarily continuing dependence on foreign oil makes the inflation battle all the worse.

2. *Provide tax policies to restore productivity.* An economy whose productivity is declining relative to its major trading partners and competitors is in a losing battle with inflation. We need to cut those tax rates that promise the most improvement in productivity. Without markedly better productivity rates, inflation will remain very troublesome.

3. *Reform the tax code to encourage saving over consumption.* We save 5 percent, the West Germans save 12 percent, and the Japanese save 20 percent. American saving must be increased to provide the necessary pool of capital for investment in our future. Liberalization of IRA/Keogh accounts, and increases in tax exemptions for interest income, are necessary moves.

4. *Eliminate statutory drags on our productivity.* There are a number of traditional policies that will have to be reexamined, such as those raised by the anti-trust and Glass-Steagall laws. Government regulators in OSHA, for example, must view their responsibility as balancing productivity with abuse prevention. The same is true throughout the various agencies. Productivity must be taken into account in the regulator's equation.

5. *Restructure the labor market.* Productivity and quality-control issues should receive due consideration in collective bargaining. The American worker's output capacity should be competitive with that of workers of countries such as Japan and West Germany with whom we are in competition and whose pay scales are comparable to our own.

6. *Increase exports.* The balance-of-payments deficit exacerbates the inflationary pressures. It must be reversed by an aggressive export policy.

7. *Reduce incentives to consume.* In an economy mired in stagflation, it makes no sense for consumers to be buying luxury items when basics like housing and autos are beyond their reach. The country needs a growing housing stock to take pressure off home prices, and it needs a turnover of cars to improve the fuel efficiency of our auto fleet. We can no longer afford to subsidize all kinds of consumer spending. To encourage saving, the tax-deductibility of interest paid on consumer loans should be restricted to autos and homes.

8. *Reject the drive for nuclear arms superiority.* The megabucks necessary to pursue this goal would increase inflation and absorb capital needed for other anti-inflationary policies. The idea of spending dollars with abandon makes no sense either in social spending or in defense spending.

9. *Watch resource allocation.* We must understand the fact that capital and technically trained people are finite commodities, which should be made the most of, and not allocated according to ideological bent.

10. *Be responsive to the Third World.* Adopt a rational and effective Third World policy so that we don't throw away men and equipment and money on oppressive and unsupportable governments. Always remember that Vietnam is mainly responsible for

the severe inflationary pressures still being felt today.

Our inflation policy should deal with the long-term *causes* of inflation, not its symptoms. Counterproductive policies should be avoided. For example, we should not blithely cut back, by raising interest rates, on the capacity of business to reinvest in equipment, since that reinvestment is needed to increase productivity. We must spend government funds in ways that meet long-term inflation problems rather than blindly cutting back on all spending in order to meet short-term inflation difficulties. Our courses of action should be extended and steady; to rely on quick fixes that temporarily appease the public is illusory at best.

Spending cuts in times of inflation do nothing to rectify the problems of productivity and energy conservation that help to cause inflation. The same is true for wage and price controls. These devices are useful only after the causes have been dealt with, when the inflation caused by prior momentum and prior expectations can be controlled. Wage and price restraints and/or restrictive monetary policies by themselves cannot be justified without the commitment to a long-term course of action.

The country is going to have to realize that there is no short-term miracle cure. The individual's role—in terms of buying habits, energy consumption, savings patterns, productivity, and expectations—must be made clear.

There are no easy solutions. It will be a long haul, so we'd better get on with it.

10/Limits and Values

I have tried to show that there are certain realities facing America and that they will prevail over dogma, whether of the liberal or conservative variety. To the extent that these realities are not understood or appreciated, the nation and its political stewards risk the "waterfall."

I will now step back from the specific issues discussed in previous chapters, and try to provide a conceptual frame of reference. The need for this was brought home to me as I was explaining the rationale of this book to Kurt Scharfenberg, a Boston *Globe* editorial writer. Scharfenberg listened to me with a mixture of interest and skepticism. When I finished, he said, "Look, granting the merits of your positions for the sake of argument, what is a 'new liberal' supposed to do if he or she is confronted with an issue that has not been raised in the book? Where are your philosophical guidelines?"

Fair enough. But *are* there philosophical guidelines? *Are* there enduring values? Spending a dozen years in politics, from the city council to the United States Senate, can weaken one's belief in constants. The temptation is to observe the process of decisionmaking and conclude that it's all illusory, all no more than situational ethics—or unabashed expediency—cloaked in appropriate rhetoric. I have frequently seen people and parties reverse themselves on an issue or an approach because it was suddenly in their interest to do so.

I have certainly reversed myself. As a freshman member of the House of Representatives, I opposed the seniority system and actively participated in the ousting of several committee chairmen. At the beginning of my second term, I sought the chairmanship of the

International Trade Subcommittee of the Banking Committee. This meant leapfrogging seven members senior to me, but I felt I knew more about the field in question than those who ranked above me. At first, I received considerable support. Eventually, however, committee members realized how unpredictable and brutal the system would become if there was no guiding principle that could be relied on. Second thoughts settled in, and I soon realized my candidacy was hopeless. By the time of the vote, the first person in line claimed the post and was elected without dissent.

Today, as a seven-year veteran of the Congress, I would fight to protect my "prerogative" of seniority if another senator tried to jump over me for a particular committee post.

Expediency, then, will not go away even if we wish it to. Nevertheless, there are values, judgments, and principles that we hold which compel us to feel as if we participate in a larger purpose. And they make political and social issues worth fighting for.

Here I will suggest a framework of five values that can serve as a philosophical underpinning and that reflect the best of the liberal tradition.

Economic Justice. We must reject the economic exploitation of the individual. It is a grotesque fact of history that the "better" classes of society have been mainly responsible for such abuses. The slave trade was conducted by Europeans of learning, affluence, and culture. Slavery was accepted by those who wrote the Constitution and those who led the nation through its first seventy years. Child labor was aggressively employed by fathers who doted on their own children. Inadequate wages were imposed upon the immigrant masses by the great barons of industry. Areas of economic injustice exist today, but they cannot be tolerated. Resistance requires a sense of outrage, an unwillingness to accept exploitation as "the way it is," a capacity to "feel" a basic inequity.

Social Justice. We must deplore the social debasement of the individual. *All men are created equal*—these words may not recognize the reality of women, but they are of enormous consequence. The concept has become an expectation to be claimed and struggled for. It is not acceptable that men and women of any race, color, or religion should be forced to experience less than the full rights of citizenship.

Political Justice. We must repudiate political discrimination against the individual. The idea of the consent of the governed spread from the American Revolution to other countries and became part of people's goals and expectations everywhere. Concepts such as self-determination, freedom of speech and assembly, no taxation without representation, universal suffrage, have for generations comprised the democratic ideal. Although authoritarian regimes exist in many nations, the principle of political justice is an established doctrine in the world community.

Respect for the Environment. We must protest the plunder of our resources in a manner out of harmony with the needs of our planet. The mechanized, urbanized, disposal lifestyle of modern industrial man clashes with the needs of the co-inhabitants of our earth, who have an equal right to survive. As steward of these resources, man must realize that the earth has a rhythm and a balance sheet, and they must be recognized on the earth's terms.

Concern for the Family of Man. We must repudiate the attitude of overlooking our values once we cross our national boundaries. The principles that we embrace at home—such as human rights— should not give way to expediency in our dealings with other nations. There needs to be a strong sense of brotherhood linking the various peoples of our world. The despair of the poor and helpless in other countries cannot be ignored. Only when we understand that there is a commonality linking all of us will we achieve a clear sense of what it means to be a part of the family of man.

These values are commonly held by Americans in varying degrees. Indeed, the conservatives will argue that they also honor these values, but the true test is when and how they are applied.

To be specific, the preceding chapters began by seeking to ascertain the "reality" of any particular issue. That reality provides a frame of reference for action—i.e., the answer to the question of "what works?" Within that framework, however, is room either to employ or to reject the values referred to above.

Let's take one of these values—economic justice—and apply it to a present-day reality—the energy crisis and the need for the decontrol of oil. Within the boundaries of that particular reality there is a great deal of room for policies that reflect this value, but only if we care to implement them.

Both major political parties endorse the idea of economic justice, but from different points of view. The conservative Republican value system instinctively identifies with the well-to-do, those successful achievers or inheritors of the free-enterprise society. The liberal Democratic value system instinctively identifies with the poor and the middle class—those with the least, or a lesser, capacity to adjust.

Decontrol—plus OPEC price increases—has two consequences: enormous oil company profits and higher energy charges to the consumer.

The conservative is not dismayed by these results; his constituency is well served by these profits and well insulated from rising prices. The liberal is troubled by these results because they violate his sense of values, his interpretation of what economic justice means. While he must accept the reality of decontrol, the liberal must argue for shock absorbers to cushion the impact on low- and middle-income citizens.

Government is supposed to act as a mechanism to protect those least able to protect themselves. Thus, the liberal supports a windfall-profits tax on oil-decontrol profits and would direct those funds to an energy assistance plan to ensure that no person freezes to death, to a conservation bank for low-interest loans to homeowners for weatherization, and to schemes to provide both mass transit and alternative sources of energy to reduce dependency on future oil-price hikes. The goal of realism is thus served, but within a framework of economic justice that recognizes the problems of equity.

How different from the Reagan preference for decontrol without a windfall profits tax—and thus no mechanism to provide shock absorbers.

Let's now consider an international reality, and apply to it the principles of political and social justice. The reality is the striving of the Third World for self-determination.

In the Republic of South Africa, the white man controls the country under the system of apartheid. He votes for his member of parliament, while the black lacks the vote and representation. The white can buy land anywhere in the country; the black is limited to acreage in barren, remote areas known as "black homelands." The white can work and live anywhere in Johannesburg or Capetown; the black who works there must leave the cities in the evening to sleep in segregated townships like Soweto. The white can eat anywhere, the black cannot. The white is free to travel, the black must carry a pass. There are laws against interracial marriage and separate public facilities for the races.

Apartheid is institutionalized racism—an anachronistic system with practices long since rejected in the United States. In America we have over the last 120 years attempted to change the racial status quo. It has not been an easy road, and there have been setbacks, but most of us are committed to this cause.

Now, given all this, the reality of Third World nationalism and the values of political and social justice would seem to provide a nice convergence of policy.

Nevertheless, how to deal with South Africa remains in dispute. The conservative sees a friendly regime in power. Ronald Reagan has said we should not turn our backs on those who have been allied with us in previous wars. (The fact that many Afrikaner leaders, including some eventual prime ministers, were openly pro-Nazi is conveniently overlooked.) From the conservative's East-West perspective, the pro-western stance of the South African government is the ruling value.

Thus, while the conservative may embrace the values of political and social justice in theory, in practice they become secondary to his cold-warism, and thus expendable. (The same can be said for our current policy in El Salvador, and the myriad instances where the human rights banner has recently been lowered by the United States.) The liberal sees in South Africa the supremacy of those practices that have haunted America. Support of the South African government amounts to de facto approval of apartheid, which is by definition a rejection of the values of political and social justice. The liberal, therefore, would employ the weight and influence of this nation to facilitate the coming of majority rule to South Africa and Namibia.

Finally, let's take the value of respect for the environment, which is dismissed by very few. The reality here is the need for electricity. The conservative sees and approves plants fueled by nuclear power, coal, and natural gas. The liberal may see the same need, but only after conservation and renewables have been employed to the maximum extent.

The liberal insists upon an energy policy that provides the energy required, but with a minimized impact on the environment. While the conservative may respect the environment, he's not likely to go out of his way to alter energy policy to accommodate that consideration. These three examples reflect the underlying values that affect the lives of all of us. And in all three cases I truly believe that the liberal values are more *consistent with the realities* than the conservative values. Insensitivity to the economic results of oil decontrol will lead to social unrest. Indifference to the impact of apartheid will eventually lead to violence and revolution. Obtuseness about the effect on the environment of fossil fuel consumption will lead to an all-too-rapid depletion of resources.

Liberal values are thus not only important in human terms, they are also functional. Indeed, the great leaps forward in this country have taken place when these values have broken through old norms. Above all, the values have worked.

But today liberalism is viewed as neither functional nor workable, indeed as a liability ("I am not a liberal, I am a progressive"). That sense of irrelevance affects even successful liberal politicians. To take one example, every year the ADA publishes an analysis of the voting records of members of Congress. When I was in the House, I was among several to receive a commendation as a "perfect liberal," a legislator with a rating of 100 percent in agreement with ADA positions. The ADA, however, was asked to refrain from labeling any congressman a "perfect liberal," especially those with seats in Republican or marginal districts, since such an identification could be highly damaging in subsequent elections.

Yet, liberalism has largely molded our present society. The elderly on social security and Medicare may forget that their grandparents had neither. Workers laboring in safe factories at decent wages may lose sight of the fact that their predecessors in the nineteenth century had neither. Young men finally stopped dying in Vietnam when liberal protests helped halt the war. Millions of children have been nurtured physically under the school lunch program and intellectually under Head Start.

But the liberal tradition was rejected in the 1978 and 1980 elections. I think there were two main reasons.

First, many liberals failed to make a distinction between values and programs. A liberal program devised in pursuit of a given value was held to be sacrosanct, even if it was inappropriate, ineffective, or abused; the program itself became the object of loyalty, not the value it was intended to serve. Thus, when CETA was used as a source of patronage by many of the nation's mayors and county officials, the value was not being served. Liberals hurt themselves and ultimately their own values by not being willing to recognize the abuse of CETA and moving rapidly and convincingly to correct it. Instead, CETA was defended pretty much as is, and the electorate rebelled.

The second reason is more complex, involving limits that are imposed by the realities of time or place. These limits must be taken into account if for no other reason than to understand the chances of translating particular values into practice at a specific time. Because such limits are by definition constraining, many liberals have not wanted to acknowledge them.

Refusing to grant the existence of the problem, of course, won't make it go away. Realities and circumstances set limits, and any policy that violates them will run into trouble. But realities and circumstances do not determine where within those limits a society will stand. That is where political leadership rooted in values can make the difference. The three examples used earlier illustrate this point.

How these limits operate is often difficult to determine and difficult to conceptualize. I think we can all agree that one basic function of society is stability and survival, a sense of what is acceptable given the realities and circumstances of the moment. Those realities define what can be done at a given time. Too often, politicians (of both major parties) ignore these limits.

As there are laws of physics, so there are laws of behavior. The parallel is not precise, but it is at least approximate. Phenomena in physics are predictable because it can be determined how natural forces will perform in certain situations. If you put gas in an enclosed container and increase both the temperature and pressure, the molecules of gas will move about faster and more agitatedly.

Similarly, if you raise the temperature and pressure of a calm, middle-class neighborhood (a rapist, rampant inflation, fear of invasion), its citizens will "move" faster and in a more agitated fashion.

In the pursuit of philosophical values and of their implementation, it is critical to understand the immutable laws, the imposed constraints on collective behavior, the boundaries of possible collective action. Such laws, constraints, and boundaries respond to the realities of a given time. Those who brush aside these limits in well-intentioned pursuit of some given value often don't comprehend what they are doing. They may be quick to defend their actions as "principle" or "commitment" or "courage." What they are doing by moving outside these limits, however, is forfeiting the consensus that is needed to translate their values into policy.

In late October 1980 I spoke before the Cambridge, Massachusetts, Democratic City Committee. It is an unusual body, bringing together traditional Democrats from North Cambridge into a partnership with liberal academic Democrats from the environment of Harvard and M.I.T.

I talked to the committee about the prospects of the Democratic Party, and why liberalism needed to be redefined. I tried to show the reasons why we had gone astray, just as I had done before the ADA several months earlier. I emphasized my point by referring to the 1980 Republican and Democratic platforms.

I cited the idea advanced by hardline right-wing Republicans that appointees for federal judgeships should pass a "right-to-life" test on the abortion issue. Even those in the audience opposed to abortion understood that this criterion was inappropriate in terms of the competence, caliber, integrity, and educational requirements of the judiciary. All agreed it was excessive.

I also directed attention to the proposal of some Democratic feminists at the New York convention that any office-seeker who did not support the Equal Rights Amendment was not a true Democrat, and should not be eligible for assistance from the party. Even though I was a strong supporter of the ERA, I felt this litmus test was just as objectionable as the Republican judicial counterpart.

When I finished my speech, I was approached by a very earnest and distraught young woman. She was furious at me and clearly had to express her anger.

"How could you?" she burst out. "We've been fighting for the ERA and women's rights as a human rights issue. Human rights —how could you equate it with the right-to-life movement?"

I told her that advocates of a right-to-life position believe their view is a human rights position as well. But she would have no part of such an approach to the matter, and left totally unmollified. To her, the cause of women's rights (which I supported) was just, and being tough ("courageous") on it at the Democratic Convention was indispensable to any acceptably supportive commitment to it. To do less was to engage in expediency on her issue.

Given the fact that a backer of the right-to-life movement feels exactly the same way, it's understandable why the Democratic and Republican Conventions took the positions that they did. It's also easy to see why each advocate feels that the position of her counterpart is less worthy than hers.

I think both platforms ignored the limits existing in this country at the time of the conventions. Judges should not be appointed because they hold a particular view on a particular social issue. Nor should the Democratic Party abandon those who disagree with it on one issue.

The platforms responded to the values pursued by these interest groups. Should they remain dormant in the platform, then the issues are moot. Should they become the prevailing practice, we will witness a reaction against them by a society that would regard the practices as extreme.

The issues described in this book threaten to overwhelm us; they can trigger a collective response, an oppressive sense of instability. A leader who burdens the country with a sense of irresolution will soon be politically unemployed because the need for stability is so great. The greater the perception of irresolution in a society, the greater will be the political fallout. The elections of 1932 and 1980 are two cases in point.

Many political figures consider this concern over irresolution to be somehow unsavory. They view it as a kind of pandering to the

246   The Road From Here

current winds and tides, or as situational ethics. What kind of
philosophy is it that merely seeks to identify current attitudes, and
tries not to offend them?

Well, I certainly understand the appeal of that argument. There
are times when one may choose to ignore the limits.

But what happens if these limits are felt to be basic to survival?
The common sense of what is necessary to insure stabilty is not to
be dismissed lightly. It has been given to us—the survival response
mechanism—and we should be glad to possess it.

This accommodation to the need for stability and survival is the
single most important determinant of the potential for success of
any political movement. If a particular philosophy serves the perceived collective needs of the moment, it will encounter little resistance. If it violates those needs, the opposite is true. The same
applies to society generally.

Once we have come to grips with the limits imposed by the
realities, the task is then to reflect upon the role of values. The
capacity to be sensitive to limits is not the same as that for imple-
menting values. The limits provide stability and survival, not direction. The need is to furnish a set of informed and culturally derived
values toward which collective behavior and collective action can
be pointed. A political doctrine that is fearfully incapable of reaching out beyond the realities will not be worthy of a constituency.

But it is important to know what is attainable and when. When
can a value be fully implemented, and how long must it wait for the
appropriate moment? The fact that a value is an ideal whose time
has not yet come may be troubling, but it's far from unusual.

The value of economic justice demanded the end of slavery. The
value of social justice necessitated the enactment of civil rights
measures. Both values were served, but only after much agony and
turmoil.

Assuming the reader accepts the above analysis, a student of
politics will be left with a nagging problem.

Is there a role for political courage that seeks to champion a
value, whatever the limits? What happens when a value and the
limits are in conflict? What happens when time is required to implement the value, but the time seems excessive?

In 1956, Nikita Khrushchev made his "secret" speech to the

Soviet party congress, in which he strongly criticized Joseph Stalin and began to dismantle the Stalinist legend. He is said to have shocked the assemblage with his grim narration of Stalin's horrors and his statement that those responsible had to be held accountable.

At one point in the speech, a voice cried out: "And where were you, Comrade Khrushchev, when all these crimes were being committed?" Khrushchev paused, looked out over the hall, and in a thunderous voice demanded, "Who said that?" The hall was silent. Khrushchev then called out, "Whoever said that, stand up." Again, no one moved. Then Khrushchev looked in the general direction the voice had come from, and said, "Comrade, where you are now is where I was then."

We have not experienced Stalinist-like atrocities in this country, but we have lived through days of darkness. The Red scare promoted by the likes of Senator Joseph R. McCarthy is a clear example. In the 1940's and '50's, thousands of Americans were wrongly accused of being Communists. Some finally spoke out against McCarthy—I think of Edward R. Murrow and Senator Margaret Chase Smith. But there were precious few attacks on McCarthy by President Eisenhower or any of the men destined to succeed him, most of whom were also holding national office during McCarthy's heyday.

Yes, there must be men and women willing and bold enough to fight for values, even if the current limits are violated in the process. But the choices are not easy—most politicians, for example, are likely to pick their targets carefully. If J. William Fulbright had always voted his conscience on civil rights matters, he might have lost his Arkansas seat to a single-issue right-winger, and not been available to lead the battle against American involvement in Vietnam.

I feel strongly that a legislator should subscribe to the admonition of Edmund Burke that he owes his constituents his "judgment." There is great satisfaction in voting your judgment, not your political antennae.

And it is striking how quickly public attitudes can change. I have often found that being out front on an issue did not last long, because the mainstream of opinion quickly caught up.

A majority of the electorate was in favor of the war in Vietnam in the early 1960s, opposed the push for racial equality in the 1950s, and resists the gay rights movement today. These kinds of issues present the liberal with a dilemma because he will find himself in political jeopardy if the opposition generated by his values is added to a perception of irrelevance on other matters. In other words, if a liberal has not fashioned a coherent, aggressive, effective position on the realities, then he will be judged only on those divisive issues where the electorate is at odds with his views. A liberal can only be in a position to exercise leadership in promoting his values if he has taken care to fashion workable programs in such areas as energy, the economy, and international trade.

The conservatives in power today face a similar situation. They have largely been absent, reluctant, or in opposition when the great issues of compassion were debated. An ideology linked to the wealthy and the entrepreneurial class (i.e., the 1981 Reagan tax cut) does not lend itself easily to serious concern about the poor or the blue-collar worker, the disadvantaged or the afflicted. It is altogether consistent for candidate Reagan to state that he would cut only "waste, fraud and abuse" from the federal budget and then, once in office, proceed to reduce or dismantle an entire range of human services. For conservatives, programs that provide economic and social assistance are simply not felt needs.

Given middle-class disenchantment in a time of economic strain, the demolition of programs aimed at the disadvantaged may seem good politics. But is it good government in a democratic society? Can you effectively run a system in which compassion is minimized by an administration whose inaugural was highlighted by the greatest coming together of mink coats, expensive jewelry, and private jets in Washington history?

There are too many bright young minds among the disadvantaged that will be wasted because necessary funds have gone to vested congressional interests through programs like tobacco subsidies. There are too many concerned citizens in the older cities who will be protesting the loss of industries because urban investment programs have been gutted while cost-ineffective water projects remain intact. There are too many average, non-ideological Americans who care about the quality of life, about clean air and water, about good education, about arts and culture, and about children whose intellectual progress is held back because of a lack of nutrition.

The conservative politician can't deal with such unfairness because he doesn't feel it. Those who live on the hill tend to wish that those in the valley below would just keep still. They forget that among the first Americans to regard themselves as victims of an unjust, uncaring, and unbending government were Paul Revere, George Washington, Benjamin Franklin, Thomas Jefferson, John Adams, Patrick Henry, and Alexander Hamilton.

In 1980 the country decided to replace liberals with conservatives. The fact that many of the liberals were bright, honorable, and respected members of the Senate and House was interesting to their constituents, but of lesser importance than the understood needs of the moment.

It was a depressing election for me—I lost a lot of good friends. I think America lost some good advocates as well. But the task is to try to understand that voters felt threatened by events and situations, and they voted accordingly. The process is often cold and strange, but it is *the* determinant of political fortunes.

Conservatives believe (and hope) that their recent victory represents a classic political readjustment. In American politics, however, "victory" is an impermanent term. For Ronald Reagan and the conservatives there will be another round, as there will be for whoever succeeds them. What is important for incumbents to understand is why they were victorious and how they will become subject to the scrutiny and judgment of the citizenry whose sense of realities will impose limits on them as well.

Simplistic conservative notions that are insensitive to the realities of the 1980s and 1990s will falter. But if conservatives are capable of offering policies that, however objectionable to liberals, do not flout the realities, then President Reagan will have begun an era of Republican rule that will be compared in history to the New Deal. As a Democrat in the Senate, I will have to resign myself to minority-party status. That will be of some discomfort to me, but I suspect that the nation as a whole could not care less.

I am convinced, however, that if conservatives do stick closely to their vision of our society, they will, inevitably and soon, violate its limits. They will bring about a degree of social instability that the majority will find unacceptable, and will then face either defeat, abandonment of their values, or the need to repress the discontented. None of these is an attractive option.

The circle is thus closed. A nation raised on liberal values rejected their stewards in 1980, because they were unable to fashion programs that met new realities. Conservatives who may not be prepared to honor those values may find it difficult to deal with the expectations aroused by them. The frustration of these expectations can cause instability. Only time will tell whether the conservatives will be able to sense these perils, and act accordingly.

So the road from here is fraught with pitfalls for both liberals and conservatives. Events will require responses and those responses will reflect particular sets of values. The electorate will comprehend whether the limits are recognized or ignored.

If liberal Democrats once again are chosen to exercise power, we should resolve to be relevant to the great issues. We should honor our past but not be mesmerized by it. In a time when the shortcut and the short term seem to be the guiding priorities in business and government, we should remember that our task is to mold the future.

Does it matter? It certainly does. I have tried to describe the realities that constitute a waterfall in America's future. I am convinced that the programs and guidelines contained herein are necessary if America is to avoid the waterfall.

And avoid it we must. This nation, and indeed the world, is passing through a precarious time. The world can survive only if we do. It's about time we confronted the future with confidence by adopting solutions that represent neither the past nor blind dogma.

This book was intended to outline an approach to the future that both recognized realities and pursued liberal values.

Let the debate continue.

Appendix

Address before National Convention of Americans for Democratic Action, June 14, 1980

It is not popular these days to be a liberal. Every narrow, special interest in Washington is building and attacking our caricature. Liberals, supposedly, are the dreamers—idealogues making Rube Goldberg-type contraptions to regulate the citizen.

The facts refute this cartoon. In the last two decades, which shaped my own set of values, liberals have seen this Nation and the world as it was. We have made practical, realistic changes to make it work better.

Look at the civil rights movement, the great moral challenge of the 1960's. To us, equal opportunity is a crucial principle, but it battled inch by inch with other principles. Reactionaries fought a rearguard action, using the principles of States' rights and property rights. With the help of many people here today, it became an unequal contest. There was no way that this country could withstand the demand for equal rights. A house divided -by color—could not stand.

The principle was that we ought not remain divided; the reality was that we could not.

Look at the Great Society, which aimed to share growing U.S. prosperity among all our citizens. Health care, voting rights, job training, early schooling, and other social programs were pushed through the Congress to help make the ideal of equality a reality.

The Great Society displaced the rhetoric of individual initiative with real chances for self-help and security.

Look at the Peace Corps, an international expression of our commitment to human dignity. The Peace Corps is an expression of American principles—but the bottom line is that it works. I spent 3 years in the Peace Corps, and I see other volunteers here today who put their time into this fresh idea. It remains a practical, powerful investment in peace and better lives.

Look at the antiwar movement, a powerful rejection of the traditional cold war view that we would support repressive and corrupt regimes with our guns and our lives if only they would spout the necessary anti-Communist rhetoric. This legacy of John Foster Dulles remains a threat to U.S. foreign policy.

The world of the 1960's was well-suited to the rationale of liberalism. At home, we marched to achieve a just society, then voted to build a great society. Abroad, we volunteered to serve peacefully, then marched against a war. To someone choosing a personal set of values in the 1960's, liberals were raising the important issues and working toward practical solutions.

Most of us here today remember those exciting years. But in a way, it is a shame that there are not more of you who do not—who are too young to have been participants or even observers. Fewer young people are joining the liberal cause in 1980 than in the 1960's. Our case seems less compelling now. We must look at the world with fresh eyes, and understand why.

The fact is that liberalism is at a crossroads. It will either evolve to meet the issues of the 1980's or it will be reduced to an interesting topic for Ph. D.-writing historians.

In part, liberalism's difficulties reflect a natural cycle of resentment and retrenchment against the gains of the 1960's and, yes, there were some in the 1970's, too. There is an antipolitical, anti-Washington element that conservatives are exploiting. Many Americans are discouraged and confused about current problems in the economy and society. Conservative rhetoric is raising their hopes for a 20-mule-team march into the past.

If we are to mobilize a new generation to move forward with liberal leadership, we must understand that the average young American is just that—part of a new generation. A generation that never experienced the abuses and injustices that molded us. A generation that takes for granted the social equities that we had to fight for. In short, they have never known that anger that fed the liberal cause.

For example: They have not grown up reading about hungry poor people; they have grown up reading about abuses in the food stamp program.

They have not grown up reading about U.S. military adventurism in Vietnam; they have grown up reading about Soviet military adventurism in Afghanistan.

They have not grown up reading about the abuse of factory workers by management; they have grown up reading about union rules that place security over productivity.

They have not grown up reading about the ever expanding American economic pie; they have grown up reading about America's balance of payments problem and the demise of the auto industry's capacity to compete internationally.

This is a different generation. And if we do not speak to this generation in its terms, liberalism will decline. And if we do not meet these needs, liberalism should decline.

Energy and the economy are the center stage—they are about survival. They also share a fundamental complexity that contradicts the political wisdom: "Never adopt a program or philosophy that you can't put on a bumper sticker." But I believe that a growing number of citizens are aching to be treated as adults. They are ready for straight talk—a lot of it negative—on energy and the economy. They want liberals and conservatives to get past rhetoric and scapegoats on these basic problems. They want practical, tough decisions to end our drift and deterioration.

I submit that we have not addressed these issues.

For example: The energy crisis involves one basic fact—that oil is a finite and diminishing resource. Many liberals attack this issue by attacking the oil companies. Emotionally satisfying—yes. An answer to the problem—no.

The problem is U.S. consumption. Who led the fight against the 10 cent gasoline tax—the liberals. Why—to protect the consumer.

That's fine for today. In the long term, to protect the consumer from the reality of the energy crisis is to destroy him. John Anderson talks about a 50 cent gasoline tax, and the young flock to his campaign.

For example: The pressing need of our economy is productivity. When was the last time you heard a union demand productivity gains as part of its contract? Look at the auto industry. Wonderful wage settlements—no talk about productivity and fuel-efficient cars. And now what? 300,000 union people out of work.

For example: If it is necessary, to revive our economy, to provide tax credit to industry as opposed to individuals, how will liberals respond? They will probably vote against it. They will vote for short-term relief and not long-term employment viability.

For example: We denounce nuclear power. No nuclear power means one certain result—massive reliance on coal. Any environmentalist who can accept the severe problems caused by massive coal-burning is not an environmentalist by my standards.

For example: Afghanistan is crushed by a raw exercise of Soviet military power. Where is the concern? Where is the outrage? Why should it be left to the conservatives to champion the cause of the Afghan freedom fighters?

The fact is that I believe that liberalism must extricate itself from the 1960's when we had the answers. We must move on to the pressing problems of the 1980's, and we must have the answers that seem relevant and appropriate to the generation of potential liberals.

Some will argue that if we do not, it does not matter. Nonsense.

I believe that there will be a desperate and crying need for the values of liberalism in the 1980's.

This country is eagerly searching for solutions, and many are looking to Ronald Reagan for leadership. And Congress is increasingly sounding like Ronald Reagan.

This potential return to a cold-war mentality is unacceptable. Do we have to learn the lesson of Vietnam all over again?

This potential return to totally unfettered private enterprise is unacceptable. How many Love Canals are enough?

This potential return to racial benign neglect is unacceptable. How many times must a city burn before we reawaken to the needs of our people?

I call upon the people who will be at the convention to work for a new liberalism —rooted in the sound values of the past but relevant to the all-too-real problems of the present and the future.

I think it means an evolution, but so be it.

We must respond. Because if we do not, we will leave the field to the champions of divisiveness. We will relinquish American leadership to those who are comfortable with exclusivity.

In an age of potential nuclear devastation, that prospect is not an academic one.

I, for one, do not wish that this world, this country—indeed, my family—be incinerated in an orgy of conservative, simplistic ideology.

We must provide the leadership if this country is to be man's last great hope.

The Massachusetts Plan:
Through Survival
to Stability

I. Introduction

The single dominant phenomenon during the next 20 years will be energy. Its price
—and more critically, its supply—will set in motion self-sustaining, market dynamics that will reward the foresighted and crush the complacent.

As a nation, we are unprepared.

As a state, we are unprepared.

As communities, we are unprepared.

As individuals, almost all of us are unprepared.

This plan seeks to confront the future and prepare for it. Its simple premise is
that our state can survive the inevitable body blows of the future only if we so
choose. And by choosing, we can craft a position of relative invulnerability that
will serve as our major economic foundation.

The energy situation is, indeed, the equivalent of war. It threatens Massachusetts more gravely than many less energy-dependent states. We are already suffering economic injury without any plan for self protection.

War it is, and it's about time we began the mobilization.

II. The Plan

The plan asks: What resources don't we have? What resources do we have? What
kind of economic base can we compete for and how do we maximize that capacity
to compete?

A. What resources don't we have? The fact is that we don't have fossil fuels
within our borders. This means the following:

1. Every dollar spent on oil, gas, and coal, for heating, transport, and commercial
use is a dollar exported from our state. The greater the use of these fossil fuels,
the greater will be the drain of our capital.

2. Every economic activity dependent upon the supply of these fossil fuels is in
a critical, precarious condition. Any wise decision-maker in a fossil fuel-based,

energy intensive industry will, if possible, locate, relocate, or expand where the supply is.

3. Every personal activity (i.e., driving to work, heating one's home) is subject to wildly escalating prices and interruptions, thus hindering those activities. Businesses dependent on a human resource base that engages in these activities will, if possible, gravitate to where the disruption is minimized.

B. What energy resources do we have? The fact is that we have remarkably diverse alternative energy resources (resource recovery, low-head hydro, wood, solar, wind). We have enormous conservation potential that can drastically cut our per capita fossil fuel consumption.

This means the following:

1. Every dollar spent on indigenous energy sources (i.e., weatherizing one's home) is a dollar multiplying through the system, reinforcing our economy, not draining it.

2. Every economic activity based on an indigenous energy resource (e.g., the RESCO energy supply to General Electric in Lynn) is for all intents and purposes secure from supply and price disruptions—and thus vitally stable. (See Section III.A.5 and Section IV.B.1.)

3. Every human activity based on an indigenous energy resource (e.g., living in passive solar heated homes, bicycling or walking to work) is also secure, and thus makes more attractive to the decision-maker the location in Massachusetts of human resource based industries. (See Section III.6.)

C. What industries can we compete for and how do we increase our capacity to compete? We can compete for energy intensive industries to the extent that we can link those industries to indigenous energy supply. We can compete for energy non-intensive industries (such as those involved with high technology, health, education, service industries, traditional industries with specialized skills) if we provide the milieu that such industries favor: adequate supply of skilled personnel, assured access by workers and management to the workplace, reasonable independence from energy supply shocks for workers and management.

The Massachusetts Plan is a blueprint for action in each of these areas. It outlines proposed federal, state, local, corporate, and individual decisions which, taken as a whole, will protect Massachusetts from imminent danger and potential disaster. It is a framework to hold onto the human and corporate resources that we have, and to secure from other states newcomers who will recognize the reinforced stability and strength of Massachusetts.

I believe there is an urgent need for serious public debate on Massachusetts' response to the energy crisis of the next two decades. This plan is my effort to open that debate. It is provocative and will, no doubt, prove controversial. But, it is offered with the hope and expectation that suggestions and criticism will improve it. It is an invitation to every Massachusetts citizen to join the debate.

III. Energy: The Priority of Renewable Resources and Conservation

Massachusetts must seriously embrace renewable resources and energy conservation. This basic priority will allow us to maximize a dependable energy resource base, and stem the current $6 billion-per-year capital outflow from Massachusetts for energy resources. The report of the Harvard Business School's Energy Project and many other comprehensive scientific analyses are in agreement that conservation and renewables are our energy future.

They are an absolutely urgent priority because the oil market will deteriorate rapidly in the 1980's. Four nations openly hostile to U.S. interests—Iraq, Iran, Libya, and Algeria—produce one-third of OPEC's oil. Many of the more moderate OPEC nations are reaching production peaks. Domestic oil and gas production peaked several years ago despite increased drilling activity. Even with decontrol, domestic production is expected to decline steadily during the 1980's.

Price eruption and supply disruption in energy are inevitable. They will bring sweeping societal change because how and where we live and work have been influenced greatly by the availability of cheap energy and the assumption that it would continue. A fundamental transformation now is taking place, which we must realize, analyze, and direct.

Massachusetts citizens face extreme, disruptive changes in their lives due to the energy crisis:

Exorbitant energy prices and the resultant economic shocks will make home ownership difficult and will cause abandonments of marginal housing to skyrocket.

The cost of commuting will force some workers into unemployment and create labor shortages for firms located far from their employees.

Gasoline prices and shortages will devastate tourism and retail industries dependent on automobiles. (See Section IV.B.2.)

The Massachusetts economy will be drained by the cost of importing energy. Businesses and their highly skilled workers will head for the Sunbelt.

While the tax base shrinks, the need for social services will grow.

The need for fuel supplies will result in waivers of environmental standards. The burning of coal and high sulfur oil without pollution control equipment will result in significant health costs and will greatly reduce environmental quality, especially in cities. (See Section III.B.)

There is no rationale behind our state of unpreparedness. Massachusetts produces only 3 percent of our energy needs, which causes billions of dollars to drain from the state's economy annually. Massachusetts is 80 percent dependent on oil, of which 80 percent is foreign, and yet 80 percent of our homes are underweatherized.

Even if energy planning were adequate nationally—and it is not—it likely would be far short of what the facts demand for Massachusetts. Quite simply, our energy position will be the single most important factor influencing our lives during the next 20 years. Without careful planning and hard choices, our lives will be shaped and Massachusetts misshapen by drastic energy disruptions. Prodded by our extreme energy circumstances, we must begin to lead the nation into the energy future.

A. Conservation and renewable resources The state's only indigenous energy resources are conservation, solar, hydro, wind, wood, and other renewable resources. Their widespread acceptance depends on millions of individual consumer and business decisions. Private citizens, corporations, community groups and government must all work together to make Massachusetts first in the nation in energy conservation and renewable resource development.

During the past several years, I have supported the outstanding efforts of the New England Energy Congress to develop an action energy plan for our region. Many of their recommendations are reflected here in the broad context of Massachusetts' economic future.

1. Federal role:

The federal government must provide programmatic leadership, financial assistance, and regulatory guidelines. Washington must provide financial incentives to individuals and businesses to invest in conservation and renewable resources; funding for state and local governments to develop and implement energy planning and programs; research, development, demonstration, and commercialization activities for new technologies, and regulations to ensure efficiency standards for buildings, vehicles, and appliances. In particular, the federal government must:

a. Enact and fully fund the Conservation and Solar Bank. This legislation, which I authored, would provide interest subsidies on loans used to finance conservation and solar measures in residential and commercial buildings.

b. Enact and fully fund the Community Energy Act. This bill, which I authored, would provide energy block grants to local governments for planning, programs, and projects in energy conservation and renewable resource development.

c. Extend Daylight Savings Time in order to reduce the amount of energy used during the early evening peak.

d. Greatly expand the low-income weatherization program and make program modifications to improve effectiveness.

e. Establish a program to weatherize multi-family homes.

f. Provide aggressive programs for conservation and renewables in federal buildings. Results from the Norris Cotton Federal Building, an energy conservation demonstration project in Manchester, New Hampshire, should be reflected in construction of all new federal buildings.

g. Develop national building energy standards to require all new buildings to conform to strict conservation standards and incorporate passive solar design elements. (See Section V.B.I.)

h. Target all federal funding for housing, industrial, commercial, public and private development to conservation efforts. Include strict energy standards for all new buildings and require siting near mass transit or require development of mass transit capability. Use highway funding to promote efficient traffic patterns and develop bike paths.

i. Provide an aggressive marketing and commercialization program to expedite the development and widespread use of new conservation and renewable technologies.

j. Establish a program to encourage exports of solar technologies, including demonstrations, export financing, tax credits, information sharing, and international training programs. I plan to file such legislation this year.

k. Fund regional vocational training programs in conservation and solar technologies. (See Section IV.C.I.)

l. Greatly expand effort to raise public awareness and disseminate energy curricular material to public school systems.

m. Provide incentives to federal employees to use mass transit, bikes, vanpools, and carpools. (See Section V.B.2.)

n. Purchase fuel efficient vehicles for official use.

o. Expand eligibility for renewable and conservation tax credits.

p. Levy a 5% gas tax to fund increased federal investment in mass transit for both capital and operating assistance.

q. Extend automobile fuel efficiency standards beyond 1985, requiring 40 m.p.g. fleet average by 1995.

2. State role:

The Governor and State Energy Secretary Joseph Fitzpatrick have initiated several major conservation and renewable resource measures. If we enact the Governor's program and expand these efforts, Massachusetts can become a national model, demonstrating the full range of activity that a state without significant indigenous fossil resources can implement.

State government must:

a. Ensure that every residential and commercial building in Massachusetts receives an energy audit. The Governor and Energy Secretary Fitzpatrick have proposed a Residential Conservation Service program to provide audits that expands and improves upon the federally mandated program. State Senator Brennan has proposed legislation to require an energy audit before a home is sold. Both initiatives deserve strong support. We should also consider requiring weatherization or funds for weatherization in escrow at time of transfer.

b. Modify state utility regulation to encourage utilities to expand activities in conservation and the use of renewable resources.

c. Work with utilities and local governments to exploit cogeneration opportunities and convert 100 percent of Massachusetts urban solid waste to energy. (See Section IV. B. 1. a-b.)

d. Streamline state licensing procedures to expedite new renewable resource projects. The Massachusetts Energy Office's program for low-head hydro is regarded as a national model. This should be expanded to all decentralized renewable resources.

e. Adopt a strict building code that significantly reduces energy use and includes passive solar design elements. DOE has already recognized the state's Building Code Commission for its efforts and refers to it as a national model.

f. Encourage conservation and solar energy in public buildings throughout the state. Massachusetts' recently enacted Alternative Energy Property and Conservation Program will provide $25 million in financial assistance to state, local, and public authorities.

g. Give authority to local governments to enact conservation ordinances and utilize zoning and subdivision regulations to conserve energy. The Governor is preparing legislation to do this.

h. Provide subsidies to encourage conservation and renewable resources. The Energy Development Caucus has proposed an Alternate Energy Development Corporation to provide subsidized financing to consumers and small businesses, and the Massachusetts Energy Office has proposed a program similar to the Conservation Bank to provide interest subsidies.

i. Establish a statewide energy extension service and consumer protection service to provide public information and to prevent consumer fraud.

j. Link automobile excise taxes to fuel efficiency and not age.

k. Enforce the 55 m.p.h. speed limit more strictly and increase fines for violations.

l. Levy a 5 percent gas tax to fund increased state investment in mass transit.

m. Provide exclusive rights of way on highways for van and car pooling and buses.

n. Structure tolls on highways and bridges to encourage van and car pooling.

o. Extend the Massachusetts Bay Transit Authority route system.

p. Make the MBTA a more efficient system by providing a stable funding mechanism and increasing the productivity through better labor and management practices.

q. Finance, expand, and integrate, intercity bus transit through regional transportation authorities and private bus companies.

r. Maximize the use of the commuter rail.

3. Local role:

Local governments have many institutional tools to influence energy use. Because conservation and renewable resources involve decentralized activities, they are more effectively managed at the local level than the federal level. (The Community Energy Act, which I authored, would provide the financial resources to communities for energy initiatives.) Comprehensive community energy planning will play the most critical role in our efforts to make Massachusetts more self sufficient.

Local communities must:

a. Start comprehensive energy planning to assess local energy problems and resources, and map strategies to reduce consumption and utilize renewables. The Franklin County Energy Conservation Task Force is one leader, with projects including recycling centers, fuelwood cooperatives, street lighting reductions, and comprehensive inventories of energy use and local supply potential. The Button Up Northampton program is another important community effort, with conservation education through the school system, a model energy audit program, and plans for bulk purchase of insulation for cost economies.

b. Initiate mobilization using community and neighborhood groups to provide public information, technical assistance, and weatherization assistance. Fitchburg's Operation FACE demonstrated how much can be done.

c. Weatherize single and multi-family housing through rehabilitation programs. Cambridge has proposed an innovative program to do this.

d. Adopt zoning and land use plans that protect sun rights and encourage efficient development patterns along transit corridors. (See Section V.B.2 and D.)

e. Initiate public awareness programs and education programs in the schools. (See Section IV.C.1 and VI. D. 3.)

f. Reduce municipal energy use through conservation and solar measures in public buildings and procurement practices that consider energy efficiency.

g. Actively develop low-head hydro, resource recovery, and district heating projects.

h. Encourage neighborhood co-ops to purchase insulation and conduct solar demonstrations.

i. Purchase fuel efficient vehicles for town employees (e.g., police, building inspectors).

j. Use school buses to expand mass transportation capacity for special activities.

k. Encourage bicycle usage by providing bike racks, bike lanes, and bike paths (e.g., the proposed Greenbush Railroad Right of Way Project, which would provide a 7 1/2-mile bike route from Scituate to the Hingham commuter boat).

4. Utilities' role:

Utilities are in an ideal position to promote residential conservation and solar and to use decentralized options for renewable electric generation such as cogeneration, low-head hydro, and wind. A diversity of generation sources will increase reliability, and decentralized options will require lower capital investments.

Massachusetts utilities must:

a. Offer no interest or low interest loans for residential conservation and solar investments. Pacific Gas and Electric in California, one of the largest private utilities, is offering no interest conservation loans to 1 million customers over the next 10 years. Pacific Power and Light in Portland, Oregon offers principal deferred loans for solar.

b. Establish creative programs of public information to promote efficient energy use and to discourage peak use. Hingham's municipal utility has cut its electric demand through such a program.

c. Offer peak load pricing and install time of day meters.

d. Encourage small power producers through favorable purchase rates and nondiscriminatory back-up arrangements. Work with industry to install cogeneration equipment. Work with small producers to resolve interconnection and loan management issues. (E.g., New England Electric developed a creative financing arrangement for low head hydro in Lawrence.)

e. Initiate a load management program by installing load control devices on appliances and installing residential storage systems. New England Electric is initiating a major load management program.

f. Develop district heating or total energy systems where feasible (e.g., in new developments).

g. Actively demonstrate newer technologies such as fuel cells, utility scale wind machines, residential and commercial photovoltaics. Many utilities across the country have been gaining experience with these systems, which are expected to become competitive over the next 2 to 10 years. Southern California Edison is installing a 3Mwe wind machine and is planning hundreds more.

h. Actively initiate low-head hydro, wood fired generation, and municipal solid waste projects. Many utilities in our state have started to do this. Boston Edison is evaluating resource recovery; the Massachusetts Municipal Wholesale Electric Company is investigating 50Mwe worth of low-head hydro.

i. Utilities should work with local governments and developers to encourage energy efficient and renewable resource developments.

5. Corporate role:

Corporations can be a tool for promoting development of conservation and renewables. Corporations can individually utilize energy efficient processes and expand their use of renewables. They can also act as the catalyst for the energy efficient behavior of their employees.

Massachusetts corporations must:

a. Obtain comprehensive energy audit and take steps to reduce energy consumption and use renewable resources in company facilities.

b. Develop cogeneration, total energy systems, more efficient industrial equipment, and solar process heat. (See Section IV. B. 1.)

c. Provide employee incentives to take mass transit, carpool, vanpool, or bicycle (e.g., MBTA pass programs, flexible hours, preferential parking, elimination of free parking, vanpool financing, and shower facilities).

d. Purchase efficient automobiles for company fleets and institute a regular automobile maintenance program.

6. Individual role:

Energy cost and supply interactions most drastically affect the lives of individuals. We have had sufficient warning. In making decisions in our personal lives, we must seek to protect ourselves and our families from the impact of the coming energy crisis.

There are many steps we can each take. Some examples are:

a. Purchase fuel efficient automobiles, and use your automobiles more efficiently.

b. Obtain an energy audit and install weatherization measures.

c. When buying or renting a home, consider energy factors such as availability of mass transit, energy efficiency of the structure, and suitability for solar retrofit.

d. Schedule energy consuming activities (i.e., showers, laundry) during off-peak hours.

e. Live as close to workplace as possible.

f. Turn down the water heater and the thermostat, and purchase only energy efficient appliances.

g. Use public transportation whenever possible. (See Section V. B. 2 and C. 2.)

B. Other options In the long term, renewable resources and fusion could provide most of energy supply, but projections indicate that in 2000, fusion will not yet be commercial and renewables will provide only between 1/4 and 1/3 of our energy demand. Depending on the effectiveness of our efforts at reducing electric demand, load management, industrial cogeneration, and tapping our indigenous resources, we may need to build additional power plants.

We should not build new oil-fired power plants and, when possible, we should reduce our reliance on base-load oil-fired capacity. By the mid to late 1980's, we will be able to evaluate electric demand growth, assess the results of our efforts in renewables and conservation, and determine how large a gap exists in the mid-term. For all practical purposes, after we maximize efforts to bring on-line decentralized renewable resources, the choice is between coal and nuclear. Given what we know about the short and long term environmental impacts of coal, that option should be avoided. While we must develop more effective environmental controls and new coal combustion and conversion technologies, the carbon dioxide problem (greenhouse effect) which threatens massive climate changes should preclude any large scale shift to coal.

If the nuclear option is to remain viable, we must redouble our efforts to make nuclear plants safer, reestablish the credibility of the Nuclear Regulatory Commission, and restore public confidence. The NRC must be reorganized to strengthen the focus on protecting public health and safety. The lessons of Three Mile Island must be incorporated in all existing and new plants. The technical capabilities of utilities must be expanded. Evacuation plans must be put in place. A technical and political solution to waste disposal must be vigorously pursued. The NRC and the nuclear industry must adopt rather than resist fundamental changes in organization, procedures, and attitudes.

To be realistic, these efforts will take several years. But given our state's dependence on oil for electric generation, we must be prepared in the late 1980's to accept additional nuclear plants—if we have resolved the problems with nuclear and have maximized our efforts in conservation and renewable resources. These are absolutely essential prerequisites. Utilities should not be allowed to build new nuclear capacity unless and until they have demonstrated true leadership in the conservation and renewable resource area as TVA has done. Incurring the costs and risks of nuclear power while allowing relatively benign alternatives to remain unused is not in Massachusetts' vital interest.

The present generation of light water reactors should be seen as an interim option only. Long term reliance on plutonium cycle breeder reactors with their nuclear proliferation risks must be avoided. Research and development efforts in fusion offer some optimism with respect to bringing this new energy source on-line early in the next century. Fusion, coupled with conservation and renewables, should provide electric generation for future generations.

During the next 20 years we must take steps to diversify Massachusetts' energy base to minimize supply interruptions. In the short run we must mount an all-out effort to reduce electric demand, manage electric loads better, and tap indigenous, renewable, decentralized sources. In the midterm we may have to add some coal and nuclear capacity but only under stringent environmental, health and safety standards.

IV. Energy Efficiency and Industrial Development

A. Introduction Energy efficiency must be the prime determinant in our Commonwealth's industrial development strategy. The energy facts for business and industry are no different than for individuals. Massachusetts does not have significant supplies of fossil fuels within its borders. Every year Massachusetts suffers a multi-billion dollar capital outflow for imported fuels. Dependence on imported fuels also guarantees constantly escalating prices and the continuous threat of supply interruptions. Although industry can and will pass along fuel price hikes to consumers, the threat of supply interruptions is devastating to any business enterprise.

For the Massachusetts economy to survive the energy crisis and to remain stable and vibrant, industrial energy needs must be met. In particular, energy intensive industries must be closely linked to indigenous energy supplies, and a concerted effort must be made to ensure that our Commonwealth remains a highly competitive environment for industries with low energy use and high labor intensity.

B. *Energy intensive industries*

1. Retain existing energy intensive industries by ensuring operational efficiency and maximizing use of indigenous resources that can provide reliable fuel supplies at relatively stable prices.

a. Resource recovery: expand the use of waste for energy.

(1) Make maximum use of energy from waste recovery.

(E.g., the United States converts 1% of urban waste for energy; Switzerland converts 40% and Denmark converts 60%.)

(2) Expand current efforts in Massachusetts to tie in waste recovery facilities with energy intensive industries (e.g., in Saugus, the RESCO facility's tie-in with General Electric in Lynn; the Braintree Resource Recovery Plant tie-in with Weymouth Art Leather Co.; Norton Company and Monsanto plans for similar ventures in Worcester and Lynn).

(3) Increase federal assistance for resource recovery through tax subsidies, price supports, and loan guarantees.

(4) Develop state and local government capacity for planning and site selection of resource recovery facilities.

b. Cogeneration: exploit energy wasted in industrial process steam. Require users of process steam to cogenerate electricity for their own use and for sale to the grid, and remove institutional and regulatory barriers to this activity.

(1) Estimated energy potential from cogeneration in New England States is an additional 1000 Mwe—the equivalent of a new nuclear plant.

(2) Cogeneration requires a cooperative effort of industry, utilities, state, and federal governments.

c. Solar energy and energy efficiency: aggressively pursue all sources, including:

(1) Heat recovery/reuse of waste streams (e.g., the thermal recovery system in the Bolt Beranek and Newman Inc. building in Cambridge, which cost approximately $100,000, created unexpected space savings, and is saving $70,000–$75,000 per year in energy and maintenance costs).

(2) Use of smaller electric motors and lights.

(3) Insulation.

(4) Computer controlled temperature and lighting (e.g., the Malden Housing Authority's energy monitoring computer for several hundred subsidized housing units).

(5) Solar energy process heat.

2. Develop comprehensive planning to protect the tourist industry, the number

two industry in Massachusetts. The tourist industry is 80 percent dependent on automobile travel, and is therefore especially vulnerable to periods of energy instability and fuel shortage, when tourist related travel is considered non-essential. Federal, state, and local governments must work to increase public transportation access to tourist facilities and to reduce tourist travel by automobile.

a. Federal, state, and local policies:

(1) Financial assistance to promote integration of transportation and lodging facilities with tourist areas.

(2) Financial assistance to expand and improve public and private mass transportation access to tourist areas.

(3) Development of bicycle paths into and within tourist areas (e.g., the 65-mile Boston to Cape Cod Trail).

(4) Expansion of water transportation facilities to tourist areas.

(5) Expansion of Masspool program for tourist ridesharing and expansion of bus service program to tourist areas for low and moderate income families.

b. Private sector policies (hotels, airlines, museums, art galleries, recreation facilities, bus companies, commercial businesses, and restaurants):

(1) Development of package trips and tours based on public and private mass transportation.

(2) Increased development of brochures, maps, guidebooks, and informational materials which provide information on mass transportation access to tourist areas.

(3) Support for federal, state, and local financial assistance to expand and improve public and private mass transportation access to tourist areas.

C. Energy nonintensive industries Even after Massachusetts maximizes its self-sufficiency in energy by coordinating energy intensive industrial development with indigenous energy resources, our state will continue to suffer in competition with oil-rich states for energy intensive industries. Economic development efforts should be aimed at low energy consumption industries. We must increasingly look to industrial sectors where human resources, a Massachusetts strength, are the key input. Service industries such as education, health, and insurance must remain strong elements in our economy.

We must recognize that, to a great degree, our future rests on our ability to attract and accommodate high technology firms. The high technology industry, a relatively low energy consumptive industry, is now and must continue to be the showcase industry in the Massachusetts economy. High technology companies are non-polluting exporters of high value-added products and importers of income. They sell in a world market, which contributes positively to the domestic economy of the U.S. trade balance, and they attract skilled workers. Massachusetts must educate more productive workers for the high technology industries, which currently face a manpower shortage. We must provide these industries with energy efficient transportation facilities and improved export capability. (High technology industries export 34 percent of their production.) We must reform tax policies to permit the necessary investment in these firms to take place. Finally, we must begin to expand our use of Massachusetts based fish and agricultural products.

1. Development of skills availability.

a. We must ensure that school curricula, at all levels of education, train students in marketable skills.

b. The state should encourage high technology firms to establish engineering scholarships for public and private educational institutions such as the University of Massachusetts, the University of Lowell, Massachusetts Institute of Technology, and Northeastern University. The state should increase funding for engineering programs at public institutions and continue to develop and fund community college programs for technical training. (Governor King and Secretary Kariotis should receive full support for their efforts to focus manpower resources on technical training.)

c. The federal school loan program must be improved. The maximum loan limits must be made more realistic. We must reward future engineers with more generous than average loans.

d. Congress must pass the Research Revitalization Act, S. 2355, which I introduced in March as an antidote to economic stagnation and declining productivity. It would award a tax credit to any firm that contributes money to a university for research—thus creating a cost-effective mechanism to encourage research with practical applications in business and industry. It would provide universities with funds to pay students assisting in such research endeavors.

2. Improvement of Massachusetts transportation:

a. Railroads:

(1) Congress is in the process of deregulating the railroad industry in an effort to allow the rate flexibility necessary to provide capital for reinvestment. Railroads constitute an important and valuable infrastructure which we must maintain.

(2) The Northeast Corridor Improvement Project must be completed as soon as possible with federal assistance. This should decrease transit time and make rail more competitive.

(3) Where appropriate, the state or federal government should buy railroad rights-of-way if the private company is incapable of maintaining them.

b. Massport must continue active promotion of Boston as a major transport facility—a gateway to the United States for foreign shippers and to Europe and other foreign markets for American business and industry. Massport must continue to:

(1) Improve cargo facilities to strengthen our economic base (e.g., increase air freight capacity by building the Bird Island Flat facilities at Logan).

(2) Pursue state and federal funding to further develop the Port (e.g., expand the Castle Island facility, fill 38 acres of the finger piers for containerport facilities, and develop the South Boston Naval Annex property).

(3) Promote intermodal linkage between rail and air or ship transport.

c. The Massachusetts Aeronautics Commission must promote the development of air transportation for Massachusetts products (i.e., additional development of Worcester airport for air freight for Massachusetts high technology firms).

d. The trucking industry must pressure vehicle manufacturers to produce the most efficient vehicles possible, and must promote fuel efficient transit practices within the industry (e.g., reduce trips with empty vehicles).

3. Expansion of export capability:

a. The Export Administration Act, passed by Congress in 1979, attempts to give the Commerce Department input into the Defense Department's awarding of high technology export licenses. It cannot be allowed to fail.

b. Federal assistance must be provided to make U.S. exporters competitive:

(1) The Export-Import Bank must be put on equal footing with the export banks of our competitors.

(2) Taxation of U.S. companies' efforts abroad must be commensurate with our competitors' approaches.

4. Financial Incentives for Industrial Development.

a. Congress must enact a tax cut for industry. Tax reform, aimed at promoting reinvestment, is essential.

b. Congress must approve legislation for Incentive Stock Options (S. 2239). These would provide an incentive to workers to increase their productivity, and a source of capital to their company.

c. Support for Governor King's "social contract" with industry is essential. Particularly, the state must target capital gains tax relief and provide additional funding for the Massachusetts Technology Development Corporation. (This Corporation provides equity capital to fledgling firms with high promise.)

5. New Emphasis on Agriculture and the Fishing Industry:

Agriculture and fishing are two traditional industries that could play an important role in our efforts toward energy independence. Massachusetts, 92% dependent at present on imported food supplies, must face the fact that rising costs of transportation (mostly by trucks) will dramatically increase the cost of food. Thus, an aggressive policy to develop these indigenous Massachusetts resources should be pursued. This will also help to preserve the rural character of small communities, protect them from random development, and enhance the quality of the rural Massachusetts landscape.

a. Fishing and farming policies on the federal level must be structured to assist the small farmer and the independent fisherman. (E.g., FmHA financial and technical assistance programs should have set-asides for the small farmer.)

b. National Marine Fisheries must be funded adequately to support the development of the fishing industry.

c. State tax policy must be restructured to encourage farmland preservation.

d. The $10 million Development Rights Program must be continued and expanded.

e. Local zoning must be structured for the protection of farmlands.

V. Energy Efficiency and Urban Revitalization

A. Introduction Suburban sprawl was made possible by inexpensive, abundant energy resources, and encouraged by federal housing and highway policies. Escalating adverse changes in energy supply and price are highlighting the basic energy inefficiencies of suburban sprawl: low-density, energy inefficient residential housing, and automobile dependency for commuting and shopping. The soaring price of new construction in particular will encourage adaptation of existing structures to housing and commercial needs.

Economic reality mandates that new residential and commercial/industrial development be concentrated in cities. The economic opportunities will be in older, denser neighborhoods and in city centers. Government programs and policies must now be focused on encouraging the urban revitalization, and on maximizing the inherent energy efficiency of cities. Public funds must leverage private investment into urban areas.

B. Federal programs and policies Develop federal programs and policies to encourage energy efficient development.

a. Enact the Community Energy Act to provide funding to state and local governments for energy conservation and renewable resource activities.

b. Require Executive Agencies to undertake, where appropriate, an energy impact analysis program, including development of a State and Regional A-95 Clearinghouse review process to include evaluation and comments on the energy impact of grant proposals.

c. Adopt strict conservation, land use, and transportation policy requirements as a condition of federal funding to state and local governments.

d. Direct existing housing, community and economic development program funds to promote urban energy conservation and urban revitalization.

(1) Mandate energy efficiency standards and passive solar on all federally assisted housing.

(2) Provide incentive funding for energy efficient housing and weatherization.

(3) Reauthorize and fully fund the Home Mortgage Disclosure Act and continue Community Reinvestment Act activities aimed at increasing financial institution investments in urban communities.

(4) Reauthorize and fully fund Community Development Block Grant, Urban Development Action Grant and assisted housing programs, and provide set-aside and bonus funding to promote energy conservation.

(5) Provide assistance and incentives for financial institutions to provide mortgage and investment credit for downtown and neighborhood development.

(6) Authorize the National Public Works and Economic Development Act, to provide funding for infrastructure improvements and assistance to businesses expanding or locating in distressed areas.

(7) Enact legislation to permit continued tax exemption of mortgage revenue bonds, with an emphasis on mortgage revenue bond programs which support community and economic development activities in downtowns and neighborhoods.

(8) Fully fund and support historic preservation programs, with increased emphasis on the use of historic preservation funds through revolving loan pools (e.g., the Architectural Conservation Trust for Massachusetts) and adaptive re-use projects involving energy efficient features.

2. Develop transportation strategies to reduce dependence on the automobile.

a. Develop policies and incentive funding to promote and maximize mass transit use.

b. Provide full funding for Urban Mass Transportation Administration and develop a Mass Transit trust fund.

c. Condition federally assisted housing and industrial development funding on accessibility of projects to mass transit.

C. State programs and policies

1. Develop state programs and administer federal assistance to states to promote energy efficient development.

a. Build capacity to undertake comprehensive energy conservation and renewable resource activities funded through the Community Energy Act.

b. Develop energy efficiency evaluations as part of A-95 State and Regional Planning Agency proposal review process.

c. Provide continued support for state programs which finance business and industrial expansion and development and which finance single and multi-family housing (e.g., Massachusetts Industrial Finance Agency, Massachusetts Housing Finance Agency, and long-term energy residential conservation strategy developed by Governor King and Secretary Matthews).

d. Provide bonus funding and give funding priority to state funded and federally funded activities administered by Massachusetts which comply with state and local energy strategies.

e. Provide recreation areas in central cities. (See Section VI.E.)

2. Develop transportation strategies to reduce single-passenger use of the automobile and overall dependence on the automobile.

a. Reduce or eliminate tolls for car and van pools (e.g., the Massachusetts Turnpike Authority's new fare structure).

b. Provide special lanes for car and van pools.

c. Develop links between mass transit and car and van pools.

d. Reduce insurance for car and van pools and mass transit use.

e. Encourage private industrial/commercial development of state-owned land and air rights adjacent to transit facilities (e.g., Star Market/Massachusetts Turnpike Project in Newton, and Southwest Corridor neighborhood development project in Boston.)

f. Use school buses in non-school hours for special public transportation services, including services for the elderly and the handicapped.

g. Expand water commuting facilities and services (e.g., commuter boat from South Shore to downtown Boston).

h. Give funding priority to road projects which provide access for in-town industrial/commercial development projects (e.g., Crosstown Industrial Park in Boston).

i. Develop publicly owned and feasible privately owned sites for commuter parking.

j. Provide bike racks and bike access on commuter rail, intercity buses and at transit terminals.

D. *Local government programs and policies*

1. Create or amend programs and policies to encourage energy efficient development.

a. Build capacity for energy conservation and renewable resources planning and activities (Community Energy Act).

b. Use local powers (water, sewer, zoning, building permits) to reduce industrial and commercial development that is dependent on automobile use, and to promote development in town and city centers.

c. Direct federal, state and local funds to activities which are consistent with the local energy plan.

d. Direct capital expenditures to support energy efficient development (e.g., street lights, roadways and other capital improvements to mass transit accessible commercial areas).

e. Implement energy efficient building and zoning codes.

f. Develop a local housing policy which incorporates the following key elements to maximize energy efficient living patterns:

(1) Rehabilitate existing housing stock and make energy conservation improvements (e.g., conversion to elderly housing of the Bugle Buick dealership in Taun-

ton, the Cuticura Soap Factory in Malden, Tabor Mills in New Bedford, and the Academy Building in Fall River).

(2) Adaptively re-use vacant or underutilized commercial and industrial space for housing and mixed used development.

(3) Minimize demolition of existing housing.

(4) Mandate passive solar and energy efficiency standards for all newly constructed housing.

(5) Encourage high density, energy efficient construction models for newly constructed housing, including row housing.

(6) Mandate access to mass transit for all new housing, and use local powers to reduce residential development which is dependent on automobile use.

(7) Remove legal and administrative barriers to residential renewable resource use (e.g., remove zoning code prohibitions against solar collectors on single family housing).

g. Establish partnerships with the private sector to:

(1) Encourage the retention and expansion of existing industry and commerce and develop community investment strategies through formal mechanisms such as "business cabinets" and local development corporations (e.g., JOBS for Fall River, Inc., an umbrella agency created to coordinate local economic development agencies, including the local development corporation, the industrial commission, the industrial development financing authority, the redevelopment authority, and the economic development department).

(2) Maximize use of private resources for development, including technical assistance from educational institutions, revenue bond and mortgage loan pool financing through financial institutions, private financing of publicly assisted projects and technical assistance to local community groups (e.g., Springfield Central, Worcester Cooperative Council, Pride, Inc. of Fitchburg, local development corporations and Small Business Administration 502 programs).

2. Develop transit strategies to reduce dependence on the automobile.

a. Use federal highway funds for development of car free areas of the city (e.g., Downtown Crossing in Boston) and for development of more efficient traffic patterns.

b. Encourage Regional Transportation Agencies to provide linkages between local bus routes and commuter rail.

c. Develop publicly owned and feasible privately owned sites for commuter parking.

E. Private sector programs and policies

1. Work in partnership with the public sector, particularly local governments, to promote energy efficient development and development patterns. Establish partnerships with the public sector to:

a. Encourage the retention and expansion of existing industry and commerce and develop community investment strategies through formal mechanisms such as "business cabinets" and local development corporations.

b. Maximize use of private resources for development, including technical assistance from educational institutions, revenue bond and mortgage loan pool financing through financial institutions, private financing of publicly assisted projects and technical assistance to local community groups (e.g., Springfield Central, Worcester Cooperative Council, Pride, Inc. of Fitchburg, local development corporations and Small Business Administration 502 programs).

2. Develop business policies that reduce employee and customer dependence on automobiles:

a. Make use of flexible work hours.

b. Establish car and van pool programs (e.g., Digital's 74-van program).

c. Provide shower facilities and bicycle racks to promote bicycle commuting.

d. Encourage the use of public transportation for customers through Board of Trade and Merchant Association promotional campaigns.

VI. Quality of Life

Stabilization of the Massachusetts economy is contingent upon successful competition for energy non-intensive industries and energy intensive industries that use our indigenous energy supplies. In order to attract such industries, we must also provide an environment that is irresistible to workers and businesses alike. Massachusetts cannot compete with Texas and her energy supply, but the quality of life in Massachusetts will help overcome this disadvantage. We must enhance and better communicate this quality.

A. Historic preservation Massachusetts is best known for her historic sites, which serve as a magnet for attracting both Massachusetts residents and tourists. The rich history of Massachusetts should be optimized as an economic resource in the following ways:

1. Greater state and local utilization of historic sites as a central focus of the tourist industry.

2. Upkeep and preservation of historic sites with combined local, state, federal, and private funding (e.g., the Roman Candleworks building in New Bedford and the Howe Building in Lowell).

3. Location of small traditional industries in proximity to historic sites (e.g., the crafts industries and Old Sturbridge Village).

B. Arts and culture As we rely on the quality of life to attract and retain industries and workers, we must begin to reevaluate people's perceptions of art and culture, and the roles that art and culture play in everyday living.

In order to stay ahead of other states, Massachusetts must cultivate an arts and culture movement from the grass roots up. Community arts should become the rule rather than the exception, and can happen in the following ways:

1. Statewide promotion of the arts and of the Commonwealth's rich cultural heritage.

2. Promotion of the arts through local business networks.

3. Art displays in public buildings of the work of local artists.

4. Implementation of the Commonwealth's Arts Lottery, recently signed into law by Governor King.

5. Utilization of local arts councils to coordinate low cost community-based activities such as:

   a. Arts festivals focusing on indigenous art forms and cultures.

   b. County fairs, exhibits, street fairs, tours and art displays in local firms and educational institutions.

   c. Agricultural, industrial, technological or lifestyle-themed events associated with regular community activities.

6. Special recognition by Chambers of Commerce and local arts councils of the efforts of businesses and community-based organizations in promoting the arts.

C. Ethnic diversity As the first port of entry for many immigrants to this country, Massachusetts has benefited from wide ethnic diversity. Each ethnic group brought along a wealth of tradition and culture; each contributes to the quality of life in Massachusetts. In recognizing the contribution of each ethnic group, we will begin to live out the covenant for peace that will ensure genuine celebration of ethnic diversity without divisive competition among individual ethnic groups.

We must strive to protect the rich multi-ethnic heritage of Massachusetts by:

1. Community-based heritage celebrations and ethnic arts festivals.

2. Multi-ethnic history presentations in schools, churches, temples, service clubs, etc.

3. Public library story-time series (directed at children) on the history and traditions of various ethnic groups.

4. Holiday celebrations in the tradition of various ethnic groups.

5. Funding ethnic museums and mobile heritage displays.

D. Education Massachusetts developed the first public education system in the country and remains a leader in academic excellence in higher education. In order to ensure high quality in public elementary and secondary education, and to prepare our children for an increasingly interdependent world, we must insist on:

1. A "back to basics" strategy regarding proficiency in reading, writing, and arthmetic.

2. A second language requirement at the elementary school level in the context of programs to provide global awareness.

3. Courses on energy utilization and conservation beginning at least at the junior high school level.

4. Urban gardening courses to increase food self-sufficiency.

5. Vocational education programs tailored toward training in energy conservation and renewable resource applications.

E. Recreation The 1978 Statewide Comprehensive Outdoor Recreation Plan (SCORP) lays the foundation for utilization of our natural resources to enhance the quality of life in Massachusetts. As stated in the Plan, "open space and outdoor recreation are essential to the health and vitality of both individuals and communities." The need to provide outdoor recreation in an increasingly urban state is obvious. Open space and conservation programs to help control unplanned regional growth are essential. There are very direct roles that local, state, and federal governments must play to plan for outdoor recreation and open space services. In addition, the role of private organizations in helping to coordinate recreation activities is fundamental to a statewide plan for land usage.

1. Federal role:

The basic role of the federal government in recreation activities is to provide maintenance and funding assistance through:

a. The Fish and Wildlife Service and the National Park Service (responsible, for example, for the Boston and Minuteman National Parks, the Cape Cod National Seashore, and the Parker River and Great Meadows National Wildlife Refuges).

b. The Heritage Conservation and Recreation Service provides recreation planning and financial assistance for land acquisition, development and rehabilitation through the Land and Water Conservation Fund, and urban park rehabilitation funding through the Urban Park and Recreation Recovery Act.

c. The Army Corps of Engineers (responsible for flood control, and river and harbor maintenance services which support recreational boating and sport fishing activities).

2. State role:

The Commonwealth is the largest landholder of open space acreage in Massachusetts, and thus plays a vital role in providing outdoor recreation opportunities. The state is responsible for:

a. Continuing to provide state funds to cities and towns for open space acquisition and development programs such as Urban Self-Help (e.g., High Rock in

Malden) and Heritage State Parks (e.g., Fall River's Battleship Cove, Western Gateway's Hoosac Tunnel Museum in North Adams, Lynn's waterfront projects, and Gardner's crafts programs and tours tied to the old furniture mills—all of which combine open space, historic preservation, and business district revitalization).

b. Natural resource protection through such programs as Wetlands Restrictions and Scenic Rivers.

c. Providing an overall framework through the SCORP planning process for land use, policy determination, and market and research services.

d. Providing technical assistance to conservation and recreation organizations.

3. Local government role:

The role of local government is to:

a. Provide neighborhood and community outdoor recreation services.

b. Protect conservation areas through acquisition, zoning, subdivision ordinances, and other means.

4. Private sector role:

Private sector involvement in recreation services is crucial. The Trustees of Massachusetts and the Massachusetts Audubon Society, for instance, operate landscape, cultural and wildlife areas. In addition, private organizations are responsible for:

a. Construction and operation of such capital-intensive facilities as golf courses, ski areas, campgrounds, and tennis courts.

b. Implementation and support of regional plans for recreation and open space services.

F. The environment At the same time that we provide wider outdoor recreational opportunities, we must ensure a healthy environment. One of the liabilities of industrial growth is environmental pollution. Just as we in Massachusetts have exhibited leadership in our use of our natural resources for technology, so must we take the lead in protecting the environment from the waste products of technological development.

1. Hazardous waste management:

a. Massachusetts must develop licensed hazardous waste disposal facilities to ensure location of industry inside the Commonwealth.

b. Careful enforcement of the Resource Conservation and Recovery Act is essential to discourage illegal dumping of hazardous waste.

c. Appropriate resource recovery technology located near industry must be developed to obviate the need for landfilling and dumping. (Such technology is already in place in Europe, and in Texas and other states.)

d. The option of landfill sites must remain a last resort, and then only under carefully regulated and supervised conditions.

e. Congress must pass the Environmental Emergency Response Act (S. 1480) to pay for emergency containment of accidental releases of hazardous substances.

2. Rivers:

Major public investments in water quality improvements justify increased efforts to ensure public access to and use of cleaned rivers. We must maximize the use of rivers as complex resource systems.

a. Watershed greenways (management plans) must be developed statewide, using public and private funds, for river protection (e.g., Nashua, Housatonic and Charles Rivers with private dollars, and the North River projects with public dollars).

b. The Massachusetts Departments of Environmental Affairs, Economic Affairs, and Community Development must reach an interagency agreement to develop a model program for state river protection.

c. Regional demonstration programs must be developed to protect land and water resources.

d. Clean-up projects must be promoted to enhance the use of our rivers for swimming, boating, and fishing (e.g., the Malden River beautification project).

3. Air quality:

a. No expansion of coal should be allowed at the expense of environmental standards. (See Section III.B) We must speed development of second-generation coal technologies (such as fluidized bed combustion) which reduce sulfur and carbon dioxide emissions.

b. Massachusetts must establish vehicle emissions control systems as well as inspection and maintenance programs.

4. Recycling:

a. Encourage local recycling efforts of paper, metals, etc.

b. Pass and implement national bottle bill legislation requiring deposits on returnable beverage containers to eliminate litter and beautify our country-side.

G. Summary The quality of life in Massachusetts will be the foundation for statewide economic stabilization. Land management, wildlife preservation, academic excellence, cultural diversity, and the historic legacy of leadership are dominant forces in Massachusetts. While energy technology, tax policy, and a skilled work force will provide financial incentives for business development in Massachusetts, the high quality of life will provide the grass roots incentive for community revitalization. With all of the ingredients in place, the energy future of Massachusetts will be secure.

VII. Conclusion

This plan, if implemented, should provide a protective barrier against the inevitable future energy shocks that hang over us. That barrier will secure those within our boundaries from all but the most severe disruptions.

This barrier is intended to be interlocking, with each piece valuable in and of itself, but also acting to reinforce all the others. It is a kind of geodesic dome—strengthened by the totality of its components, however small any single component may appear to be.

This barrier, this security, is meant to be more than just comforting and serviceable to our people. It is meant as our chief marketable asset, the very foundation of our long-term economic viability in an increasingly competitive world.

The Massachusetts Plan is my effort to contribute a basis for discussion that will lead to decision-making. The plan obviously is imperfect. It will be modified where modifications are shown to be prudent.

But it remains a challenge to the six million decision-makers in our state: criticize, probe, amend, question.

But do not reject it without offering an alternative.

A Note About the Author

Paul Tsongas is a Democratic senator from Massachusetts. A native of Lowell, Massachusetts, he is a graduate of Dartmouth College and Yale Law School. He worked for the Peace Corps in Ethiopia and the West Indies, and has served as a Lowell City Councillor and Middlesex County Commissioner. In 1974 he was elected to the U.S. House of Representatives, and in 1978 to the Senate.

A Note on the Type

The text of this book was set via computer-driven cathode ray tube in a face called Times Roman, designed by Stanley Morison for *The Times* (London) and first introduced by that newspaper in 1932.

Among typographers and designers of the twentieth century, Stanley Morison has been a strong influence, as typographical adviser to the English Monotype Corporation, as a director of two distinguished English publishing houses, and as a writer of sensibility, erudition, and keen practical sense.

Composed, printed and bound by
The Haddon Craftsmen, Inc., Scranton, Pennsylvania

Designed by Albert Chiang